dropped threads 2

dropped threads 2

MORE OF WHAT WE AREN'T TOLD

EDITED BY

Carol Shields

AND

Marjorie Anderson

WITH THE ASSISTANCE OF

Catherine Shields

VINTAGE CANADA

www.randomhouse.ca

National Library of Canada Cataloguing in Publication

Dropped threads 2 : more of what we aren't told / edited by Carol
Shields and Marjorie Anderson ; with a preface by Adrienne Clarkson.

ISBN 0-679-31206-4

1. Canadian literature (English)—Women authors.
2. Canadian literature (English)—20th century.
3. Women—Literary collections.
I. Shields, Carol, 1935–
II. Anderson, Marjorie May, 1944–

PS8235.W7D762 2003   C810.8'09287   C2002-904398-0
PR9194.5.W6D762 2003

Printed and bound in Canada

10 9 8 7 6 5 4 3 2 1

For all our dear women friends,
whose conversations and caring are sources of
constant renewal and inspiration

CONTENTS

FOREWORD

When I was seventeen, I read that one is not born a woman, one becomes one. The fact that this was written by a great woman, a French writer, who was at least the equal if not the superior of Jean-Paul Sartre, was incredibly invigorating for me. At first, I had no idea what to do with the truth of this statement. Now, many years later, I see that the truth is many layered and even (to the horror of my seventeen-year-old self!) disputable.

When I opened the manuscript of this second collection about what women aren't told, I realized that it was really about how these writers learned about becoming women. I still believe that the evidence weighs more on Simone de Beauvoir's side. How else can we explain the intense pain, the immediate identification, the instant empathy with all the women who have written about loss, love and the fear of failure that are like a Bermuda Triangle of the soul for all women.

Whether these essays deal with illness, broken relationships or the lack of the father figure, there is a female authenticity to them that is deeply moving. The loss of belief in the principle of male privilege is a constant throughout these essays, and the search for something to replace it—usually inadequate—is the weft of many of these women's life experiences.

The dilemma in which women after the second wave of feminism have found themselves is that it is perfectly acceptable now to be a brilliant lawyer, a great novelist or a caring doctor, but those attempting to do these things must make sure that they are in addition nurturing mothers, attentive wives and solicitous caregivers to the elderly. If the two sides of the equation don't match, women are blamed, and the worst of it is that they accept the blame.

Perhaps what we can reap in these accounts is something that will help us all not feel this "either or" situation. All the subjects here help us to understand that we are not alone. If we are fortunate to have a circle of female friends in different kinds and ages of life, we are learning that on a day-to-day basis through constant communication and conversation, which can make men feel either jealous or left out or both. Because it's true that women talk to each other about what most men would consider to be "nothing." They talk about how they feel, how they have reacted, how their bodies betray or support them. They are not afraid to be weak with each other and, on a regular basis, usually tell each other when they have cried.

In these extremely perceptive essays, bright women suffer because they are bright and know that the favour of their peers, especially in adolescence, is not going to be showered on them for their intellectual achievement. Or they know what it is like to suddenly discover a loving relationship becoming an abusive marriage. They feel the longing to make a transformation from working-class to middle-class life and then an equal compulsion to leave it. They have felt the horror of being treated like totally sexual objects and the disappointment of trying unsuccessfully to have a child.

We are dealing with real situations here—chronic disease, personal discovery of sexual orientation and learning how to cope with a life that has been considered secret since birth.

I wondered after I'd finished reading the text why I was so moved by all these different ways of telling what nobody has ever told you. I suppose one of the reasons is that we are expected in a kind of silent sisterhood to "know these things." The fact is, none of us knows anything, and it is what happens to us in life that teaches us everything.

Freud most famously said that he could not understand what a woman wants. This is probably the greatest example of one sex not listening to the other that has been documented. The accounts in this collection highlight for us that women want everything. And there is an unspoken historic and psychological barrier, which means that when women *do* try to be the most that they can be, they are stopped; they are stopped by the flaws that they have developed, by the society that they cannot manage or by the very idea that a woman could want anything.

In all these essays there is a good deal of wisdom, some detachment and frequently humour. It is a distinctly feminine thing that in none of these pieces is there ever the idea that one could simply accept the stereotypes that we all grew up with—male breadwinner, female homemaker, inevitable children. These accounts tell us what life is like from a woman's point of view, even in such small vignettes. Perhaps that is what women's lives are really like—snowflakes with infinitely different patterns, complete in themselves.

Adrienne Clarkson
July 2002

INTRODUCTION

On a generously mild evening in February 2001, I joined nine contributors from the first volume of *Dropped Threads* at a local bookstore to take part in the Winnipeg launch of that anthology. We anticipated having a modest audience, composed mostly of friends and family members, to hear us speak of our involvement in the book and read from our contributions. What we hadn't anticipated was the size of the crowd—over three hundred booklovers scrunched into the store's café and beamed down at us from the second-floor balcony. And we certainly hadn't foreseen the extent of the excitement and energy that would permeate the room.

Variations of our Winnipeg experience were repeated at launches in other cities across Canada, from Victoria with Carol Shields and the West Coast contributors to St. John's with writers from the East. The energy and enthusiasm from readers inspired similar waves of amazement and pleasure in contributors and editors. Our book had obviously tapped into a powerful need to share personal stories about life's defining moments of surprise and silence. It was as if we were hearing a collective sigh of relief.

In the months following that initial immersion, we were part of a country-wide discussion on what had been missing *in* women's conversations—those hidden nooks of pride, blessing, injury or shame that are revealed only when there's safety and a community of understanding. We were pleased to see that the anthology had been part of creating such a community. Whenever we heard from readers, especially at spirited book club gatherings we were invited to attend, they openly revealed why the stories had been particularly meaningful for them: "They offer affirmation"; "I don't feel so alone or so crazy"; or "This could be a story about my life." Readers also felt free to talk about the dropped threads in their own lives. Some would tell of being refreshed by a surprise or muted by a brand of shame similar to those found in the book; others recounted life-altering experiences that weren't included in the anthology, but might have been.

This focus on what was missing inevitably led to questions: what about lesbian experiences, the single life, relationships between mothers and daughters or the less-than-noble aspects of female interactions—where were these stories? Would there be a second volume, and could they send us their stories, just in case. . . ?" Carol and I felt sure we were witnessing the stirrings of a new venture.

That following summer, we started collecting pieces for this volume, and it was an exciting and consuming task. We put the word out through our droppedthreads.com website and also by direct invitation to writers we hoped to include. The submissions poured in, each one moving in some way for its honesty and intimacy. We understood that these were not just stories, but parcels of women's lives that deserved care and attention. The thirty-five that appear here are offered to you in that spirit.

Many of the essays we've included carry on in the tradition of those in the first collection. Readers will again experience the shock of recognition that comes from bumping up against thoughts and feelings that mirror their own. Other writers expose us to unfamiliar terrain, dark patches of brutality or misfortune that many of us may never experience personally. What is common to each of these accounts, though, is a journey to the heart of one woman's private experience that she wants—and needs—to tell others.

In the first section, "End Notes," writers chart their movements through trauma, loss and bewilderment to an understanding of how incidental moments of attention and caring can transform a life. Commonplace things like the sound of a bird singing, the protective embrace of a sibling or a glance at a particular book on a shelf become instruments of survival for these women. And for us they become haunting images or startling insights that linger long after the reading experience.

The essays in "Variations" balance the celebration of women's commonalities with emphasis on the individual shadings of their lives and experiences. More than one writer recounts her version of a familiar female circumstance, such as breast cancer or child rearing. But of course, no two are exactly alike from the inside. Each writer points to different moments of intensity and to individual strategies for coping, all of which draw our attention to the unique particulars of women's lives.

In "Glimpses," women show how they manage to envision themselves beyond either their own limitations or the restrictive expectations of others. For some, this creative leap is achieved simply by imagining bolder versions of themselves. For others, it requires piercing the assumptions that lurk behind familiar decrees on normalcy and politeness—to be "nice," to prefer the love of men over the love of women, or to defer to authority, whatever the cost. By casting aside

4

these restrictions, the writers reject what stifles the spirit and, in turn, demonstrate ways to insist on living authentically.

It's fitting that this anthology of writing by women ends with pieces under the banner of "Nourishment." It is what we offer to and receive from each other. It's what we soak up from our conversations and connections—whether over a pot of popcorn in the kitchen with a child, across language barriers with women of different cultures or when a dear friend is dying. And it's what these writers trust in themselves: the guidance from the nudges and whispers inside— to move, to learn, to release their tips, their wisdom, their secrets and sorrows.

Nourishment is exactly what I have received in abundance over the four years I've worked on the *Dropped Threads* anthologies. It has come from the continued connection with my gracious friend Carol, the model for all nourishers, and from my liaisons with the wise, talented and—glory be— organized women who helped with these projects. And, of course, from all the writers who honoured and trusted us with their stories. I feel safe in the universe we've created together. It's not made up of atoms that can be blown apart; it's made up of stories that connect us and sustain us.

Welcome to this place of sustenance and continued conversation.

Marjorie Anderson
August 2002

End Notes

Losing Paul:
A Memoir

Jane Urquhart

That summer evening, the phone was not working— probably a bad connection, interference from someone operating machinery in the village or perhaps a distant August storm. I remember that the receiver seemed to melt in my hand as he told me the job in Toronto was not working out, that he was going out with some friends for a beer, that he would begin the 150-kilometre drive home in an hour or so. It would be longer than that, I knew, because this had happened before, the beer or two with his friends after a disappointment. Not often, but enough times that I knew what to expect. At best, he wouldn't be home until after midnight. Still, something about the difficulty of hearing his voice, something about the way I had to ask him to repeat what he was saying, caused the anger I might have felt to be replaced by a twitch of fear.

The sense that the phone was melting in my hand— that's what I remember most. That and the fact that I was wearing green shorts and a tank top because it was so hot, and my bare feet were absorbing the relative coolness of my grandmother's linoleum floor.

We had been living in my grandmother's empty house in an Ontario village ever since our return from Nova Scotia a month before because we had no money to live anywhere else. The art college he had attended in the East had arranged this Toronto job that was not working out, a job in a fine arts print studio where he hoped to use his skills as a lithographer. But the studio in question seemed to believe he was there to work free, as an apprentice or an intern. By the time he made the call on that August evening, we were so poor that we had been living for three days on raspberries, which, despite neglect, continued to flourish in my grand-mother's abandoned garden.

I had described to him the profusion of this garden in its prime: snapdragons, hollyhocks, gladioli and sunflowers on the one side, tidy rows of beans, carrots, potatoes and peas on the other. He had been impressed—especially by the news of vegetables—as we were both pretty tired of the raspberries. Fortunately, I had relatives in and around the village who had been feeding us fairly regularly since we'd come back from the East. Also fortunately, we were young, bound to each other in the twin-like, telepathic intimacy that only the young seem able to muster, and not overly frightened about what might come next because we were fairly certain something would. He managed, until that evening, to have a job, and I would likely get one soon.

During the five or six years I had known him, he had acquired a variety of skills, and although we were young when we'd met he already had a repertoire of talents that greatly impressed me. He knew how to cook and how to darn socks, for instance (two activities I had not yet mastered), and he knew how to carry out certain tasks I associated with a far-gone time: how to saddle and bridle a horse, how to bank up a coal furnace, how to dye clothing in bright colours to make them seem new again. He could make a split-rail fence and boil down maple syrup in the woods, roast chestnuts and make Dutch pea soup. We were young, but we'd been married for almost five years, and there had been other periods of scarcity we had emerged from unscathed: the time he had miraculously been taken on as a repair person in a shop full of Swiss violin makers, for example, because he could tell from the shape of a musical instrument how it would sound. Or the time out East when I had miraculously been hired as assistant to the information officer for the Royal Canadian Navy, despite the fact that I had spent the previous three years enthusiastically and publicly objecting to military activities and should not have passed the security test. We had a car and, for the time being, a roof. We had the relatives and the raspberries and a credit card that we were using only for the gas he needed to drive back and forth to Toronto. It was summer, and our life together so far, much of it spent as students, had led us to believe that nothing really begins until September. "Drive carefully," I said before I put down the phone. Those were the last words I ever spoke to him.

My grandmother's house was in many ways a testimonial to absent men. In the active part of her life, my grandmother had risen every morning at five-thirty to make breakfast for six sons, one husband and one hired hand. She had two daughters as well—one of them was my mother—but in the stories I told myself about my grandmother's labours, the daughters were never part of the collective that she cooked for. In my imagination, and very likely in reality, they were often at her side peeling potatoes or stirring the porridge or removing warm, aromatic bread from the oven of the wood stove that still dominated the kitchen, where I had been talking on the phone. They were placing cutlery and dishes on the table and waiting for the men and the boys to come through the door after completing a series of masculine outdoor chores.

The boys grew up eventually, stopped coming through the door, went off to wars or city jobs or farms of their own. Two of them had died. My grandfather and the hired man had died as well, the former from a heart attack while pitching hay in the barn, the latter following an accident involving a horse. My grandmother was not a woman given to cleaning up after death, and as a result the house was crammed with male paraphernalia. Shaving brushes and suspenders and important papers stuffed into cubbyholes of the rolltop desk. Air force and army uniforms in the closets. Marbles and comics and model planes in the drawers of pine dressers. Books about mechanical engineering and animal husbandry on various shelves. Baseball cards. A pile of *Farmer's Almanac*s from the forties and fifties. Election campaign buttons. And lots of practical clothes: workboots, jackets and rain gear. Even the hired man's plaid shirts remained in his trunk in the storeroom. And my grandfather's clothes were still in the room where we had chosen to sleep. It had been startling at first to see my young husband's jeans hanging on a hook beside my dead grandfather's overalls, but after a few days I had become used to the sight.

By eleven o'clock, I was fairly convinced that this was going to be a night when he didn't come home until very late, or very early, as the case might be. I had passed the time since the phone call in a number of ways. I was reading *The Diviners* by Margaret Laurence, and that had distracted me for a while. I was also working on a quilt that my grandmother had left unfinished, adding by hand appliquéd images from her life—the red brick church, the farmhouse, one of her dogs—to what was otherwise a standard Dresden plate design. That night I began to work on an apple tree: a pedestal of dark brown surmounted by a green cloud-like shape decorated with bright red apples. My grandmother had left the quilt unfinished when she moved into a small privately run nursing home, when she could no longer cope with the house. I would be leaving both the quilt and *The Diviners* unfinished for quite another reason. Both the book and the sewing would bring the long summer night, and my waiting through it, back to my memory so vividly that I would simply not be able to face either the apple tree or Morag's tortuous development as a writer.

13

At three o'clock in the morning, I found myself standing by the window in the storeroom, looking out into the dark night toward the end of the village where, from that vantage point, the by-now very intermittent lights of the cars on the main road could be seen. I was playing a game that I had played in the past when I waited for him at night in places where I had a view of the road. The sixth set of lights would be his, I would guess, and then I would begin counting. At this hour, the counting would take a long time, as often thirty minutes would pass before anything at all would appear. Then, quite unexpectedly, two or three vehicles would move by in rapid succession. These were most often trucks making mysterious journeys to towns and villages farther north. In the stillness of the night, I could hear them gearing down as they descended the hill near where some of my relatives lived. Each time I heard the sixth vehicle gear down, I would experience extreme disappointment, as if my young husband knew he was supposed to be the sixth set of lights and had decided deliberately to disappoint me. How could you let me down like this? I remember whispering into the window glass. Then I would remember the phone call, how I hadn't been able to hear what he was saying, and the twitch of fear would return.

The storeroom was filled with fascinating things. As well as the dead hired man's trunk, there were boxes of old Christmas cards, birth and death announcements, letters of condolence, some hatboxes filled with hats my grandmother had worn at one time or another to the same red brick church I had sewn onto her unfinished quilt. There were several other cardboard boxes that held such items as embroidered christening gowns and crocheted baby bonnets and one long, flat box that contained my grandmother's wedding gown, still beautiful but slightly yellowed by time. Often during my childhood, I had dressed up in this gown while the relatives had discussed important, adult things in the kitchen below. There I sat, gorgeously attired, sorting through the many buttons and buckles contained in an old cookie tin, hoping to find a diamond ring nobody else knew about. Of course this never happened, though at the bottom of the tin I once discovered a rhinestone clasp that my grandmother said was used to decorate a shoe.

I thought about these things now and then as I waited for another set of lights. I also thought about the mud pies I made years before in the woodshed with an earthen floor that was directly below the storeroom. Eventually I decided that I should lie down, that if I went to sleep I might be wakened by the sound of his footsteps on the stairs.

I did lie down, but I didn't go to sleep. The only thing that changed was that instead of waiting for car lights I was now waiting for footsteps. The heat was still intense. It was four-thirty in the morning.

It had never occurred to me that I would be a twenty-four-year-old widow, though by the time the policeman arrived at first light I knew exactly what he was going to say to me. The bedroom in which we slept—my grandmother and grandfather's bedroom—was a long, low room under the eaves and had two small windows placed in opposite walls, almost at floor level. Because the house was situated on the bend and was slightly elevated, we could see the road moving off in two directions from these windows. I remember lying on my grandmother's bed, still in my green shorts and tank top, watching with a pounding heart as the police car slowly approached the house. When it passed by the driveway without turning in, I experienced a huge wave of relief. Short-lived, however, because I could see through the opposite window that the police car had stopped and was executing a U-turn halfway down the village street. Then, very slowly, it whispered back toward me, making the approach to my grandmother's front door.

What followed were months during which much of what I said and did would be immediately forgotten by me, never to be retrieved. What I do remember, however, are the dreams, many of which provided me with unwanted explanations concerning where he had gone, why he had vanished from my life. Sometimes in these dreams he would pass me by on the street without acknowledging my presence, often arm in arm with another young woman. Sometimes he would just come home, drive up to my grandmother's door, greet me joyfully, then explain earnestly that he couldn't stay, that if I were unwilling to go with him our relationship would be over. Once I dreamed that everyone but I knew that he had joined a commune in Manitoba, that the funeral, the grief, the mourning had all been a sham, a conspiracy to convince me he was dead when all he wanted to do was escape from me. The other thing I remember is that I had these dreams during a period when I was experiencing both grief and guilt. Each night, alone in bed, I couldn't seem to prevent myself from reliving every single argument we had had, and every unkind, now unforgivable, word I had said in the midst of them. Some of the arguments had taken place on those few occasions when he had come home late after a disappointment. I knew that on that particular summer night he would have been driving a little too fast, that his blood alcohol count would have been too high. He might have stayed in Toronto overnight with a friend. But he would remember those arguments, and he would be trying to get back quickly, to me.

I spent several weeks answering cards and letters of condolence. Many of the people who wrote to me expressed the opinion, in as tactful a way as possible, that I was young and would, as a consequence, soon recover from my loss and go on to live a full and meaningful life. In fact, this would turn out to be true. But at the time I had been horrified by the suggestion; I believed that this abstract concept of an unknown life of joy would require that I forget about him and our life together as soon as possible. In order to prevent this prediction from coming true, I began a series of lengthy projects in a variety of different scrapbooks, one for each place we had lived. I drew the floor plans of our various flats and apartments and my grandmother's house. I listed all his sweaters, jeans, shirts, even the socks that I had come to know so well because of physical closeness and because I was the one who had most often done the laundry. I drew every piece of furniture we had owned. I wrote lengthy descriptions of the views from all the windows (omitting the view from the storeroom). I catalogued favourite songs, books, poems and works of art. I pasted our few photographs onto these pages. I remembered and sketched significant objects from the early days of our relationship: his knapsack, his guitar case and guitar, his Zippo lighter, his cowboy boots. I jealously guarded his artwork, all the prints and paintings and drawings he had done at the Ontario College of Art and in Nova Scotia. One of these in particular can still bring me close to tears: a beautifully rendered realistic pencil drawing—exact size—of his left hand.

It was my grandmother who was able to give me words of comfort. Though she was nearing the end of her own life and was often unfocused, she was always coherent on the subject of loss. She told me that after my grandfather died, she had awakened in the same bedroom where I had seen the police car approach, then withdraw, then turn and make the journey back. She hadn't been quite awake, she said, and before she opened her eyes she became aware of a birdsong. "Charlie," she had whispered, "what kind of bird is that?" Charlie, my grandfather, who had been beside her in the bed for all those decades, had not answered, of course, but the bird went on singing. "The bird went on singing," she told me, "it just went on singing and singing." I believed I knew what she meant.

My Life
as a Shadow

Alison Wearing

It began so innocently. I was working as a waitress and sketching with words in spare hours of the day. One afternoon, in one of those moments that seems suspended from reality, so fated is the feeling, a book fell before my eyes, and I devoured it in one delectable crunch. I had never read anything that had delighted me more, so decided to write to the author and tell him. Except for a large exclamation mark that took up most of the page, I don't remember much of what I wrote. I never expected a response, and when one did arrive, I found it a bit clunky and forgettable.

About a year later, perched at the restaurant's counter, flipping through the newspaper at the end of my shift, I noticed that the author was in town that night to promote his new book. I shimmied my arms out of my shirt, turned it around so all the coffee stains were at the back and jogged twenty-six blocks to the theatre. I had no idea what to expect. But he was captivating, utterly mesmerizing. He did the reading from memory, with the exception of the last line, which he read, slowly, deliberately, gracefully. I rode the streetcar home, his new book in my hands, replaying the evening over and over in my mind.

And wrote another letter.

This time, I waited, painfully, for a response. And the response was painful. He offered standard greetings, thanked me for my letter, twirled a few witty phrases and then dropped the casual news that he was about to fly off to the other side of the world to meet up with a woman he'd known only eight days. It was all terribly romantic. Like something, say, from a book. I was crestfallen, but amused. I sent a rambunctious letter to his contact address and went on with my life.

At the invitation of a friend with a spare room in his belfry, I moved to Tuscany and continued writing. The day I arrived in Italy, I learned that a Canadian literary magazine had accepted one of my stories. My first published story! It was an auspicious beginning.

Several months into my stay, the bulk of the novel I had been bashing out on my friend's manual typewriter blew out the window of my Room-with-a-View on a gust of wind that smelled of rosemary. I raced down three flights of stone steps and began gathering up the fluttering pages from the cobblestones, but I never found them all. It didn't really matter. The novel was unimaginably bad, and I burned every retrieved page that night in the fireplace.

I needed new direction. I decided to leave glorious, hopelessly romantic Italy and travel to war-torn Yugoslavia. I contacted friends in Serbia, gathered visas and supplies, found a magazine interested in my ideas. A few days before my departure, after a day of battling consulate officials in Florence, I trudged wearily up the steps of the belfry to the sight of an airmail envelope waiting on the mat outside my door. I still remember the dazed—fateful— feeling as I read and reread the author's name on the back of the envelope.

The body of the letter was unimportant. Lots of jokey, well-written nonsense. It was the last paragraph, the bit about things not working out with the woman of eight days, that made me dance around the room. I spent most of the evening sitting in a thick, round chair crafting a response. Cheshire cat grin on my face. Chianti within arm's reach on the stone hearth beside me.

The letters continued back and forth over several more months and countries, until eventually we were in the same city at the same time and we arranged to meet. I think I can speak for both of us when I say there was a moment, when we finally sat across the table from each other, of enraptured anticlimax. You could practically hear the thud. He, I believe, was expecting me to be the very image of a Botticelli painting, blond tresses trailing behind me as I leapt, nymph-like, from the Tuscan landscape. Instead, I was haggard and sleep-deprived, having just rolled off a plane from Serbia. I believe I was expecting him to be the narrator of his stories: relaxed, easygoing, open-minded. Instead, he was jittery and judgmental, clearly nervous.

But we managed. And a week later flew off to an island dotted with pastel-coloured houses to begin what felt like our honeymoon.

Terribly, terribly romantic. Like something, say, from a book.

It never occurred to me that this was anything but the purest and most triumphant of love stories. I never imagined that I might have fallen in love with the Author (or the Narrator), not the man; or that he might have become entranced with the Fan (or the Devotion), not the woman. And that this might become a problem. No, the Problem.

Shortly after our "honeymoon," we moved in together. We were both writing (he was in the middle of a novel; I was hoping to write a long tale about my travels in Yugoslavia), but we were also newly in love, and so spent countless days doing what amounted to lying around smiling at each other.

I must be able to find solitude in the midst of all this togetherness. Otherwise I fear I will forget the sound of my own voice, I wrote to myself, prophetically, during those lazy days of bliss.

Within a few months, my money (and the euphoria) began to run out. I managed to cobble together my Yugoslav tale—"the essential difference between us," Michael explained after reading a draft, "is that you write metafiction and I create art"—then I found a job. I planned to write in the evenings and on weekends.

It is eerie to read my journals from that time. I feel as if I am peeking over the shoulder of someone else's life, reading another's words, so foreign is the voice. When I pore over the pages, the hundreds and hundreds of pages, I can see the pieces of myself left at various points along the way. Like a child in a movie theatre, I am often tempted to yell, "Look out!" when I see the dangers approaching.

The summer came and went and I built not one word. When he is writing, I am teaching. When we meet up at the end of our workdays, we simply enjoy each other, and I scarcely notice I'm not writing.

He didn't want me to leave the room tonight while he worked, begged me to "please just sit here with me while I do this." I never thought I would find myself agreeing to such a thing, but I am incapable of letting him down when he makes such a request. He is so appreciative when I provide simple support—and how difficult is it? I found something to read, lay on the bed and held him from across the room as he worked.

Not the least bit coincidentally, but utterly unconsciously, I began reading and rereading *The Journals of Sylvia Plath*. I told myself it was the descriptiveness and complexity of her writing that intrigued me, but this is one of the passages I copied into my own journal: "It is as if I were sucked into a tempting but disastrous whirlpool. . . . We are amazingly compatible. But I must be myself—make myself and not let myself be made by him." I also found myself thumbing through biographies of painters—Picasso, Hopper—and scrutinizing the pages that talked of their wives. Any mention of these women as selfless, endlessly supportive, forever catering to their creative, all-consuming husbands disgusted and angered me.

My descent, and no doubt that of every other shadow artist before me, occurred in gradual, imperceptible steps. I didn't flop to the ground one afternoon; rather, I allowed myself, slowly, insidiously, to become secondary, dependent, hollow.

Last night he asked me to help him with his grant application. We went through his reviews, his files upon files of adoring reviews, and I sat there wondering who in the world I am trying to fool. I do not have that writing style, those ideas, that depth. I am the fool, for believing I could write. I have spent these last months listening to him spin words into majesty. If I sit in silence and concentrate, I can remember a time when my life was built of my own words. Now, most of the time, the only voice I hear is his.

The difficult part was that we had so much damn fun together. Michael had an extraordinary sense of humour and such an infectious laugh that it was impossible not to join him when he started. He'd normally have me laughing the moment I woke up: pretending to be a Polish cleaning woman trying to change the sheets while I attempted to sleep in; making up a song, in French, with vague choreography, about the red suede shoes Stalin used to wear to breakfast. His antics were always surprising and always delightful, and even though my standard response was to groan and beg him to *leave me alone!*, I loved it. We went to films, concerts and plays together, then discussed them animatedly all the way home and into the evening. The discussion would lead to lovemaking and midnight snacks in the kitchen by candle-light. We'd talk and talk and talk; tell wild, unbelievable sto-ries; plan long, exotic journeys until we were both covered in maps. On nice days, we'd take long walks and end up in a gallery somewhere, wandering and staring, touching finger-tips and sharing the silence.

"He is so much fun to live with," I remember telling my mother. "Every day there is some kind of beautiful, sponta-neous adventure."

When Michael was invited to Europe to promote transla-tions of his previous book, it seemed like the perfect opportunity to travel together. But after several weeks of accompanying him to countless readings and receptions in Paris and Rome, I began to tire of it all. I was used to jour-neys of my own making: paddling through rain forests in South America, exploring the deserts of northwestern China disguised as a Uighur peasant. Suddenly, I found myself being ferried about from hotel to restaurant to hotel, intro-duced as Michael's girlfriend, "also a writer." Feeling so out of place among the literati, amid their lofty discussions about the technical devices used by so-and-so, the philosophical underpinnings of such-and-such, I longed to hurl myself out the nearest window. But Michael wanted me there; it was important to him. Who was I to spoil his big moment with a reckless flight through glass?

After the literary tour, we returned to my little belfry in Tuscany. One evening, I curled up in the same thick, wooden chair, but this time, I wrote to myself:

Michael anguishes over his novel, phrase by phrase, letter by letter. His frustration leaks out into the air like pollution and taints everything.

I make dinner. We have a deal, at the moment, that I take care of the necessary banalities of daily life while he gets down to the business of creating. He is so close to finishing, he says. He just has to put his nose down and concentrate. After that, things will level off, equal out. Balance.

So tonight I made dinner. As eggplant sizzled in olive oil, pasta bubbled and garlic roasted, Michael called out that he felt a bit guilty about how much I was doing for him these days. "Don't worry," I said, laughing. "Someday, when I'm finishing my book, you can do all this for me." He didn't look up from the typewriter as he said it, jokingly; always jokingly: "Yes . . . too bad I don't really know how to cook. . . . "

I have the feeling I'm being consumed and don't even realize I'm disappearing.

I am not a writer. I am someone who thinks about writing in the abstract and spends her days doing nothing. Idly watching days die: dreading the morning, celebrating twilight. I count the bells of the clock tower and am disappointed—each time—when I am left with echoes. Michael builds a novel while I read other people's, almost forgetting that I wanted, at one time, to create one of my own, back in the days when I still felt I was capable. Before I began to realize that my words were like jumbles of stiff tin soldiers, abandoned after a child has grown bored.

We walked to Oliveto today. Spectacular views and air that felt like silk. Michael did most of the talking—I have grown relatively silent, I notice. I don't mind, but I notice. I picked bay leaves from hedges and rosemary, sage and oregano from clusters of green that wriggled out of stone walls. Italians sleep among gardens of herbs.

I know I should be happy. That I have so much here, so much to delight in, that Michael is wonderful in so many, many ways. I wish, more than anything, that I could see the form of a book in my head. That I could manage to collect my scattered and cat-eared ideas and arrange them in a way that made sense. Without that, my words are as good as etchings in dust.

Michael sits, carving into bedrock beside me.

After we returned to Canada, I began to get ill. Perpetual colds, sore throats, exhaustion that had me sleeping up to twenty hours a day. One morning, a friend called to ask how I was feeling. "I have this tremendous ache around my eyes," I told her. "It hurts to see." The next moment is forever chiselled into my memory. I was sitting at Michael's desk, looking at a small picture of me taped up on the wall, noticing the way my face was almost entirely hidden behind his piles and piles of manuscript papers. "What is it," my friend asked, "that is so painful for you to see?"

I was diagnosed, in medical terms, with chronic fatigue syndrome; it was either that, I was told, or a parasite. (Uh yes, I almost said to the doctor. He's standing right over there.) My recovery was slow and difficult. Letting go of Michael was, ironically perhaps, the hardest part of all.

Five years later, I was giving a reading in Michael's hometown. He sat in the audience, laughed at all the right moments, was the last one to stop clapping, asked a question at the end. Then he bought his own copy of my book and asked me to sign it.

for michael—

"You're signing on the wrong page," he interrupted.

I shook my head, and laughed.

with love and gratitude . . . Alison

In My
Mother's Arms

Mary Jane Copps

The "ordinary" family is capable of inflicting much pain upon its children. Pain which, by necessity, moves inward, creating adults who must either unravel their secrets or perpetuate a legacy of betrayal.
— *Jan Austin, psychotherapist*

I am startled awake by the quick, cold hands that hoist me to her shoulder. She impatiently pats away my instinctive cry of distress.

At three, sleep was a place I went to, like going to the playground with my sister, or running in the backyard with Prince, our cocker spaniel. Sleep was even a favoured outing, always surprising me with who, or what, would show up to play.

I loved surprises. I believed in them, saw them as a necessary part of life. My days were filled with looking for them. Head down, I would walk along sidewalks, intent on finding a shiny coin or sparkling jewel. Whenever possible, I would turn over rocks and dig in the earth beneath, sure a treasure was awaiting me. And always, I pulled at the pockets of adults, convinced that the clinking I heard was something they were carrying as a gift, just for me.

So on this night, as the sliver of light slashes across my tumbled crib, and her fragile hands wake me to darkness, I can ignore my siblings' sudden silence and fill my sleepy head with thoughts of Santa Claus.

In my house, midnight Mass distorted the reality of Christmas morning. My parents and brothers and sister would return home hungry, ready to get on with the opening of gifts, and I would be wakened to join them. I suspect that my mother, faced with the day's prospects of too many in-laws and the endless details of the holiday meal, simply wanted to get something out of the way and pushed to establish this Christmas-in-the-dark tradition.

But it isn't snowing. Perhaps the Easter bunny, then, or maybe my birthday. I snuggle deeper into her neck, closing my eyes tightly, for it is bad luck to ruin a surprise.

I've inherited my reverence for gift giving from my mother, a devout orchestrator of holidays and celebrations. These hallowed events were staged in one of two places, depending on the occasion. The living room couch, a much-protected piece of furniture, elaborately displayed the wares of Easter, St. Patrick's Day, Valentine's and birthdays. Always, I would build up the moment of surprise by walking down the stairs facing the wall, averting my eyes until the last possible second from the splendours that awaited me.

Sweaty from slumber, I cling to her coolness as she carries me down the stairs. Once in the living room, I push myself away from her shelter and look toward the couch in eager anticipation. It is empty. Unsettled, but not deterred, I close my eyes and once again set my drowsy hopes on Santa Claus.

Christmas was truly fantastic. The den, a large addition at the back of the house, became a holiday shrine. In one corner stood the magnificent tree (Scotch pine was her favourite) with lights, fragile decorations, aged tinsel, a golden angel and, of course, a circle of brightly wrapped gifts. Stockings hung from the top of a built-in bookcase, bulging with candy and the unwanted but necessary tangerine. And beneath them, the unwrapped deliveries from the North Pole. All this was held from view by heavy, brown brocade drapes that shut the den off from the dining room. Opening these drapes required her permission.

I feel the presence of my siblings as we reach the dining room and pop my eyes open in delight. All significantly older than I am, my two brothers and my sister are my playmates, my caregivers, and I love them fiercely. They stand huddled together near the kitchen door, looking not at me but at my mother. They do not make a sound. Behind them I see the open drapes and know for certain this is not about Christmas.

I must have seen their terror. I must have sensed her anger. But I had already chosen my role in this house, to remain hopeful long after it was prudent. My desire for a gift would not be quelled. Perhaps it was what saved us.

Once we are in sight of the other children, her voice rings high and loud above my head. This is her never-ending-flurry-of-words, all racing out of her mouth, bumping into one another, falling together and never making any sense— at least not to me. But the others seem to understand. They turn in unison and enter the kitchen. From behind, she shoves each of them toward the stove.

If I had not been struggling against the mist of sleep, I might have seen her eyes, wide with panic and veiled with the glaze of prescription drugs. If I had been a little older, I might have smelled a day's alcohol on her skin and heard the madness of her demand.

She is asking her children for proof of their loyalty, their unshakeable love. She gathers us around the stove, my brothers on her left, my sister on the right and me still in her arms. She turns the large front element on high, the electricity crackling to life and slowly changing the colour of the black coil.

"If you love me," she says, "you will move your hand toward this element until I say stop."

Her voice booms and bounces in the quiet kitchen. My siblings squirm. I remain mesmerized by the brilliant spiral below me.

"You first," she says, nudging my sister with her elbow.

The shaking hand of my eleven-year-old sister begins a descent from its highest height toward the glowing orange element.

I am annoyed. I know about going first—about opening the first present, being served the first plate, getting the first piece of cake. As the youngest, and very much the baby, going first is my place, my territory in a crowded household. Besides, I have been looking for a surprise and this sun-like object must be it.

With the agility and speed of a three-year-old, I wiggle and lunge, diving toward the burning element.

My sister's hands catch mine. She pushes me back, toward our mother. My oldest brother moves quickly, stepping between us and the stove, clicking off this evening's source of pain.

I giggle and laugh. I think we have invented a new game to play together, a type of dance, perhaps. My sister takes me from my mother's trembling embrace. The speed words have stopped. Tears slide down her face, and she mumbles apologies without pause. My brothers cautiously walk her up the stairs, their footsteps creaking toward her bedroom. I sit with my sister in the kitchen. Held within her tight embrace, I listen to the wild rhythms of her heart.

An Exercise
in Fertility

Lisa Majeau Gordon

"You inject the orange like this," says the nurse, pinching the skin on the orange with one hand and expertly plunging a syringe into it with the other. "Let's try a few more times."

We are at the clinic, Andrew and I. We're learning how to inject me with fertility drugs. It's autumn, and outside the window I see orange and yellow trees.

"These drugs must be administered subcutaneously. Taken orally, your stomach acids will break them down," the nurse said after introducing herself a half-hour ago. "I'll leave you to watch a short video and then we'll practice on oranges."

I cannot watch the video. In it, a smiling woman has just pulled up her shirt and plunged a syringe into her belly at a ninety-degree angle. I feel sick. I have to put my head between my knees.

"I can't do this," I say to Andrew.

"We'll do it together," he says, squeezing my hand. He is trying to be positive for me. Andrew hates needles more than I do.

This is the last step on our medical fertility road. We made our decision last night, over steak and a good bottle of Merlot. Andrew lit candles to mark the solemnity of the occasion. We talked for hours, weighing pros and cons, more like military strategists than a couple desperate for a child, struggling to maintain their sanity. After four years of tests, temperature taking and charting, exploratory surgery, fertility drugs with intrauterine insemination (IUI) and clinically enhanced sperm, a couple of Chinese herbalists and naturopaths on the side and endless counting of days, we're down to this. Our last shot.

We're ordering up some high-test fertility drugs to be injected into me daily. Blood testing and vaginal ultrasounds every other day. The grand finale will be a supercharged sperm IUI. For three menstrual cycles, if need be. Our doctor gave us a fifty-fifty chance over the three months, based on statistics, our history—and the fact that they cannot find a single bloody thing wrong with either one of us.

The nurse shows us how to prepare a clean environment. Then, how to snap open the little glass vials of powder and pure water and draw them up into the syringe. And how to flick the syringe to remove air bubbles. Finally, how to pinch my belly below the naval and stab it, straight in. This last part is done on oranges for practice.

I can't do the injections. I'm unco-ordinated. After several tries, I still cannot hold the orange skin pinched in one hand and stab it with the other. Either I let go of the pinch, or my stab is crooked.

"You have to learn how," Andrew says gently.

"Why?" I ask. "You're going to do the injections. I just have to take them. Even-steven."

"But, Meg, I may not always be there," he says, talking to me as if I'm four. "The nurse just said they must be administered between 6:00 and 8:00 p.m. daily."

"That's right," she says, coming back into the room. "Actually, most women prefer to give themselves the injections.

Once they realize there is a painful burning sensation, they like to do it themselves. Less flinching."

Like hell.

"You'll be there," I say to my husband. "If I have to be there, so do you. We're a team, remember?"

Two days later, Andrew and I have prepared a clean work space in anticipation of our first injection experience. It's 6:00 p.m. He informs me that it's a one-person job. Those little vials and needles break easily. The ones with powder in them are $100 a pop. The fewer cooks the better, as they say. He lines all his materials up in little methodical rows on the island in our kitchen. It feels like a high school science lab. I keep glancing up at the front door, hoping no one rings the doorbell. Anyone happening upon this scene would likely report us to the police.

We move to the living room and I lie down on the floor. Andrew rips open an antiseptic pad and swabs my belly.

"Do you pinch, or do I?" I ask.

"I do," he says. "The person injecting is the pincher too. For maximum control."

I look away, out the big window as he pinches me. I feel the sharp needle poke. But I've taken anti-flinch precautions. I'm holding a leg of the end table in one fist and a leg of the coffee table in the other. It's when he pushes the plunger down that I start to holler. "What are you injecting me with, battery acid?" I shriek.

He finishes plunging and pulls the needle out. It burns. I hug my stomach and roll over on my side. My belly is on fire.

"Meg, I'm sorry. I'm so sorry." He smooths the hair from my forehead with his big hand. I look up at him. His face is twisted in concern. "I don't know about this," he says. "This is not right. It's not natural. What are we doing? Just what in hell are we doing, Meg?"

"Please," I croak. "Please do this for me. Just this one more try. It's not that bad now. See? I'm okay. Really. Please don't quit on me, Andrew."

"I can't hurt you like this every day, Meg," he says, staring at the growing welt on my stomach.

"I'll be better tomorrow," I say.

I see the same blond woman every other morning. She's about my age—twenty-nine. She usually beats me to the Blood Services department of the hospital by five minutes. When I run in at seven forty-five, she is already there waiting for her name to be called.

She usually glances up at me in recognition, then looks down again. We are the only ones there at that time of the morning. We pretend to read the same ragged, year-old magazines that we pretended to read two days ago. I suppose it hasn't occurred to either of us to bring our own.

We don't talk.

On this morning, I swing open the clinic door and, without looking, know she is seated in the second chair from the right. We are wearing our matching elbow bandages. I sit two seats over, as I always do. She usually goes in ahead of me. We're both surprised when the nurse indicates it's me they want first. When I'm finished, I walk slowly back out. My body aches. She's still waiting. The clinic opens early for "career girls like us," as one nurse puts it.

According to my doctor, I should ovulate tomorrow. I won't see the blond woman again this cycle. I take a deep breath, look directly at her and say, "I guess I'll see you in a few weeks." I turn to get my coat from the rack. I don't expect a response. In the time I've been coming here, women in the waiting room look only at their shoes. We are ashamed.

"I hope not," I hear her say behind me.

I look over my shoulder at her. "I know what you mean," I say quietly. "I hope not, too."

December: another Christmas without a baby.

No children in Andrew's immediate family, and none in mine. Another Christmas with our dogs the centre of attention. Another Christmas tap dancing my way through a barrage of baby questions. Another Christmas of feeling barren.

I want to cancel Christmas. I am not interested in playing along this year. I don't want a tree shedding needles all over my house. I don't want to shop.

I want to run away.

But I'm now washing dishes at my parents' house, and the aunts and cousins start in on me. It's Christmas Day. Supper is over and the women have crowded into the kitchen. They're discussing a cousin's new baby.

"Her labour was short, thank God," the new grandma says.

"Lots of babies in the extended family lately," says the cousin nursing her newborn behind a towel, "but only mine in ours. Who'll play with my little Sarah?"

I scrub the roaster pan harder. I know what comes next.

"Meg, why haven't you had a baby yet?" asks an aunt.

"Yeah, Meg. What are you waiting for? You are twenty-nine already!"

They're all looking at me. I'm trapped. "I don't know," I mumble. Then I down a half glass of wine that someone placed by the sink and keep scrubbing.

We have gotten used to our injection routine. It's our last month. I'm trying so hard to stay positive. It's hard to think about anything else.

A couple of times, I've called Andrew on my cellphone as I turn the corner onto our road at six o'clock. He has the syringe ready when I run in the door. All I have to do is throw off my coat and lie down on the floor. It's becoming funny to us.

Today I go home from work at five. I'm thinking about how good I've been, this month especially. Taking care of myself and all that. Little to no alcohol, no caffeine, nine hours of sleep a night, exercise, vitamins. I'm living like a cloistered nun.

5:45. Andrew isn't home yet. We've always done the injections promptly at six. He wants to be very precise. He says it's a process of elimination of factors, and we don't want our inconsistencies to play a part in that. I agree.

I call his cellphone. I get his voice mail and leave him a message. I am not worried. His phone has no service in some areas. He'll be here.

6:01. He's not here. The nurse said between six and eight every night, I tell myself. That would indicate a range of time is acceptable. Calm down.

7:01. No Andrew. I've called his phone eight times. It's turned off, I think, because it goes right to messaging. What's going on? I'm panicking.

7:35. I call his best friend's wife. "Hi, Cheryl," I say. "Is Dave at home?"

"No," she replies wearily. "I'm ready to kill him. The kids have the flu and he's out drinking with his friends."

"Is Andrew with him?"

"I don't know," she says. "He'll get home safe, Meg. Don't worry. It's not like you have kids at home you need help with. Boys will be boys, you know."

"Give me Dave's cellphone number," I say, gritting my teeth.

Dave tells me my husband is on his sixth beer in a little pub in town. He tells me Andrew has been really quiet and depressed lately. That he needs this release.

I am so angry I'm shaking. How dare he. Its not as if I can take a day off from this process whenever I feel like escaping. It's not as if his belly is full of red welts. It's not as if he can't wear short sleeves because the bruising from the ritual bloodletting makes him look like a heroine addict. It's not as if he has body parts he'll never get to use.

It's not as if he's *barren*. Oh! I catch myself. I'm not supposed to use that word. The clinic people forbid it. I'm supposed to say "child-free."

It's dawning on me that I have to give myself the injection. It's ten to eight. Jesus.

I prepare the syringe. I pull down my pants and swab the small portion of my stomach without a hole already in it. And then I stand there. My legs are wide apart. I'm squatting like a sumo wrestler. Syringe in hand, thumb on the plunger. About an inch of belly flesh pinched up with the other hand.

I look at the clock on the stove. 7:55. I can't do it. I have to. I try to decide whether to slide it in slowly, or jam it in from about a foot away. I'm clenching my butt. I'm gripping the syringe too hard. My hand feels like drying concrete.

7:59. I'm still hunched over, staring at my pinched skin. Damn you, Andrew. I breathe in through my nose, out through my mouth like at yoga class. Then I push the syringe that's hovering in front of my midsection. Closer. Closer.

The tip pokes my skin by accident. I wasn't ready yet, but it slides quickly in. I'm surprised. I didn't expect it to go in so fast. I hold my breath as I push the plunger to the bottom and pull the needle out.

Wow. I feel victorious.

"Scoot down," says the nurse. "A little more, please. Scoot. Just a little more."

My naked bum is hanging off the edge of the table, my legs braced in the air. There's a nurse somewhere in the vicinity whom I can't see. She's readying herself to give me my last IUI.

Andrew is standing near my head, shifting his weight back and forth. He's most uncomfortable in this room. We've done this more than a dozen times as we moved from one fertility drug cocktail to another over the past couple of years. But he can't get used to it.

"An excellent sample, Andrew," says the nurse, holding a vial up. "Top-notch."

He blushes. I roll my eyes and grin up at him.

I feel the speculum crank up and my body tighten along with it. An involuntary response. I do my yogic breathing to calm my body.

"All right, now," says a voice somewhere between my legs and under a sheet, "relax."

Easier said than done. She's attempting to poke a long, slender tube full of sperm through my cervix to my uterus. She can't find the opening. Every time she pokes, my back arches and it feels as if someone is pouring ice water into my belly.

Andrew is squeezing my hand too tight. "Ouch," I say, and he lets go.

He paces across the room to the sink but marches back quickly. It's full of bloody speculums from the first five women inseminated here this morning.

"There," the nurse says, emerging from under the sheet. "All done. Stay just as you are for a few minutes, to set it. Then you can go." She smiles and moves to leave, placing my speculum in the sink with the others.

Andrew holds my hand. "Are you okay?"

He looks so concerned, helpless. I feel a surge of love for this man. It's a nice feeling. I smile at him.

We've been fighting so much lately. Probably the stress of this process, I tell myself. A test of our mettle. But more and more often, I think we must be crazy or caught up in a whirlwind we can't get out of. Sometimes I look at him and think, I don't even know this man. Is parenthood with him what I really want? Or maybe I simply hate to fail.

Sometimes I think we should just cut our losses and move on. Alone. There are days when I fantasize about driving purposefully to the airport and jumping on the first plane out of here. To New Zealand. Or Ireland. Maybe the Irish would love my accent. We could discuss Joyce in the pubs over a pint of Guinness. I could get a job as a castle historian. Or something.

Other times I wonder how I was so lucky to find this man, who is willing to love me although I cannot perform this basic wifely requirement.

Andrew rubs my tummy and says encouraging things, kisses my hand. We talk about how this one will work. We can feel it. We did everything right this time. We'll decorate the baby's room with a puppy theme. If it's a boy, we'll name him after my dad. Maybe he'll be a hockey player. Or a doctor. Or both, like Randy Gregg, who played for the Oilers.

We count the months. It will be an October baby. Maybe Halloween! Wouldn't that be our luck, a possessed baby born on Halloween. We laugh.

"Exorcism has a higher success rate than insemination," Andrew deadpans.

Seventeen days later, I'm sitting in a fancy Vancouver boardroom with my boss. We're here for two days to interview candidates for our new B.C. office. We've interviewed three people already today, although I can't remember their names or anything they said. I've been counting hours, minutes, seconds.

I am late.

By my best mathematical calculation, I am forty-three hours late now, give or take. I have never been late before. That is the one thing my body could be relied upon for—regular periods.

Our next interview candidate walks in, shakes hands all around. Her name is Emily. Lovely name for a girl, I think, as I tune out everything she's saying to me. I know that I'm supposed to ask her a question when my boss glares at me. I'm in a fog, going through the motions. There are a million butterflies dancing in my stomach.

Emily leaves after an hour and we take a break. My boss looks at me oddly and asks what I think of our first four candidates. I tell him they all had redeeming qualities and furrow my brow as if I'm really thinking hard about them.

I run to the bathroom. I inspect my white panties closely. Nothing there. Nothing there!

I poke myself in the abdomen. Three times, harder. No cramps. I take off my suit jacket, look under the stall doors to make sure no one else is witness to this, and pull up my blouse in front of the mirror, inspecting my body for signs of bloating. Nope! My pants fit!

I do this several more times during the day. My boss thinks there's something very strange about me today, I can tell, but he's a man and is therefore forbidden to ask questions about why a female staffer keeps sprinting to the bathroom every chance she gets.

The day has been very long; it's now early evening and I'm tired. Perhaps an early sign of pregnancy, I think. Fatigue is common.

I am now officially forty-eight hours late. Two whole days.

My boss wants me to join him for dinner. "We should talk about streamlining our operations," he says, "and discuss today's candidates."

My boss is one of those men who like to drink wine with dinner, and he's quite put out if his dinner companion does not. But I won't have any wine; it would be bad for the baby. I tell him I'm not feeling well, and when it looks as though he's going to object, I play the female card and tell him I have "monthly issues" and must go directly to my room. Humiliating, but completely necessary.

I'm staying at a posh hotel. My twelfth-floor suite is huge and has a breathtaking view of the harbour. I change into my pyjamas and the hotel's white bathrobe. For good measure, I inspect my underwear again, swab my insides, poke myself for cramps and breast soreness and examine my midsection for bloating. I can hardly believe it. No menstrual symptoms whatsoever.

I am having a baby.

I call for room service, requesting the person on the other end of the line bring me the healthiest meal they have, and herbal tea. The handsome young man who arrives with the tray teases me about my healthy choices. I tell him I have a responsibility to take really good care of myself.

Fifty hours late now. I'm sipping tea and watching a parenting show on TV. I don't call my husband, because I know he will ask, and I want to tell him in person, when he picks me up at the airport tomorrow night. I wonder how I'll do it—should I just announce he's going to be a father? Or should I say *Daddy* instead? Maybe I'll buy a baby pacifier and put it in a tiny gift bag and just hand it to him ceremoniously. Or maybe I'll simply run into his arms and cry.

I decide to go to bed. I've made my final menstrual-symptom checks, which were all negative. Fifty-two hours and counting. This is a very fragile time now, I think. I must be careful and get lots of rest.

I slip into the crisp sheets and smile to myself.

Little mean people with pitchforks are poking me. Poke, poke. Ouch. I roll over and realize I'm dreaming. The clock says eleven-thirty. I look around; I'm in the hotel, safe and sound. No pitchforks. What an odd dream.

I feel a little pain in my stomach. What was that? Gas. It must be gas. My salad had green pepper in it. I curl up again and my eyes shut gratefully.

I wake up again with a start and look at the clock. Eleven forty-two. My stomach is aching. I should not have eaten the green pepper.

I'm somewhere between sleep and awake, that hazy place, when the recognition creeps up on me. Maybe these aren't gas pains. I sit up, shake the cobwebs out of my brain. I feel panicky. My heart is beating fast. I hear a cry before I realize it has come out of me.

Please, God. I'll do anything. I'm sorry. Whatever I did, I am sorry. Please let me have a baby. I only need one. Please. I'm suddenly praying to the ceiling, clutching my hands together. Praying as hard as I can to the thirteenth floor.

I kick off the heavy covers and run to the bathroom, pulling my pyjama pants and my panties down as I go. I fall hard on the toilet, take a deep breath and look down.

Oh, no.

No, God. Why me, God? Why me?

I sit for some time like that, clutching my stained underwear in my hand, until my naked bum tingles with numbness.

When I get up, I feel as if I'm in a fog again. But a different kind of one. I'm watching myself from the outside now. I'm throwing things: pillows, the telephone, room service tray. My face is wet. My pyjama pants are streaked with red. I'm wailing, moaning, wandering around the room.

I search for the mini-bar key that I had tossed somewhere upon my arrival here. Aha! I crawl under the coffee table to retrieve it. I concentrate on getting the key into the little lock, wiping my runny nose on my pink sleeve. I pull a little bottle of red wine out of the chest, screw off the lid with force and drink deeply.

I'm squatting on the floor in front of the mini-bar. I rip open a package of chocolates and throw a handful in my mouth, nearly choking on the quantity.

I don't care. I don't care what I do to myself now. It doesn't matter any more. Nothing matters. My husband will leave me anyway. He'll find an emotionally stable, fertile girl and have a whole baseball team of kids.

I will feel empty for the rest of my life. Hopefully, that won't be too long.

The TV is showing late-night child welfare charity shows. Starving African kids look mournfully at the camera. I try to high-kick the TV but wind up on the floor with a thud.

I twist off the cap of another little wine bottle. Then a third.

I'm going to be an old barren alcoholic. Jaded, childless. I'm going to wreck my health. Good health has done me no favours. I want to be mean to someone. I find the telephone and plug it in, closing one eye so the outlet will come into focus. I call room service again. I'm slurring. I don't care.

"Bring me some cigarettes!" I yell.

A knock on the door. I wrestle into the white robe so the person on the other side doesn't see my pyjama pants.

It's the same young man as before. He looks confused. I grab the red pack of du Mauriers from his silver tray.

"Are you all right?" He asks.

"Leave me alone!" I shout, and slam the door.

I have to close one eye again to light the cigarette. It's a non-smoking room, so I use my orange juice glass from dinner as an ashtray. The liquid inside becomes a gray-green sludge. I smoke four cigarettes in a row, between gulps of wine, and when there was none left, of whisky.

"I will become a smoker!" I yell aloud to myself. I will eat junk food, have bad skin and gain thirty pounds. I will drink in the morning. I will look on the outside how I feel on the inside.

Then I scream until I'm hoarse. Long, incoherent wails.

I wake to the loud alarm clock and sunshine streaming in off the glittering harbour.

I'm on the bathroom floor.

My head is enormous. My eyelids are heavy and, when I touch them, springy. I cough several times. I get up slowly, not comprehending at first what brought me to this cold tile floor.

Then it comes back. I am not pregnant. I never will be.

I look in the mirror and am terrified at what I see. Eyelids so puffy that the openings are reduced to slits. Purple face. Grey teeth from red wine consumption and no toothbrush.

I step slowly into the shower. I have to brace my legs wide to remain standing. I feel like a cored apple, fragile outside, nothing inside. My heart hurts.

I manage to apply some makeup and dress in my best suit, ripping holes in two new pairs of pantyhose before I'm successful in getting on a third. My boss is waiting, I know, and I'm late. I nearly vomit on the elevator ride down to the lobby but manage to keep it down.

"You look well," he says to me when I reach the lobby. "You must be feeling better than you were yesterday."

I nod. I wonder if he's being sarcastic. I'm scared to open my mouth in case the wailing comes out again.

"Well, good," he says briskly. "We have a long, important day ahead of us, Meg. Let's not waste another minute."

He begins walking quickly toward the door, into the streams of sunlight. I watch him a moment. Then I pick up my briefcase, square my shoulders and march after him to the waiting taxi.

Cat Bag

Billie Livingston

Just before I started kindergarten, my mother and I moved into a house on Fourth Avenue in Vancouver with her boyfriend, Michael, a Korean War vet with a plate in his head. Michael had a voice like a butcher knife. The same mouth would, one moment, berate my mother for her ape-like behaviour—at four years old, he said, I was too big to be hanging off her neck all day long—and the next, plead with me to call him Daddy. He would kiss and coo in her ear at the kitchen table over beer and, one or two drinks later, backhand her across the mouth for the tone she'd used, a word he didn't like.

I would stare at his back as he left the room, imagining a white dinner plate spinning in the middle of his skull, wondering why they'd put it in there in the first place if it was going to make him behave that way. Mom would sit, silent in her chair. A trickle of blood coming down the corner of her mouth, she'd glance quickly at me and smile, then turn her head in the direction he'd gone and stick her tongue out, look back at me and grin. I'd grin back. It was a sort of pact.

After one of these episodes, there wasn't much to do but follow in the smile-and-act-natural vein, go outside and play. Or better yet, go next door to the hippie house to see Marilyn and Karen.

In 1970, Fourth Avenue was the hippie zone: long wild hair and beards, love beads and drugs, peace and protest. Marilyn and Karen, fresh out of NYU, had closed their eyes, plunked a blind finger down on a map, then hitched their way across the continent and moved in next door. The only constants amid a flophouse of ephemeral roommates, they were my favourite hippie girls in the world. The door was always open. If Marilyn was having a bath, I had an open invitation to leap into the tub with her; if Karen was string-ing necklaces, I got a pile of beads and my own needle and thread. They put on puppet shows, played word games and took me up to the attic to meet the "Gotcha Wizard" (Marilyn's woolly-bearded brother who'd shroud himself in an old sleeping bag). They took me with them to war protests downtown. They took me to the boutique where they sold the clothes and jewellery they made and let me wrap myself in ponchos, beads and hats as though the great-est value their creations had was in their ability to transport and transform me. They were witches, they said, and I believed in their magic like nothing else. I didn't tell them much of anything going on at home. I went to them to play.

Eventually, Black Mike, as Marilyn and Karen had dubbed him, gave my mother one too many black eyes. She told him she was leaving, and he began making threats: "You leave me and I'll kill you. I'll find you and kill you."

She did it anyway, though, waited till he was out one night, packed our bags and we left. Back East, to Toronto.

This wordless slipping-off-in-the-night routine would continue to be our MO. We would leave Toronto two years later and head back to Vancouver in much the same way.

Mom drank on and off, and as a result of one particularly bad bender, I spent my tenth birthday in foster care. From what I could see, this was just one more example of how loose lips could sink ships. My mother had made friends with big-mouthed strangers and somebody had *told*.

Two months later, when I ran away from the foster home back to my mother, she was sober again. I switched schools for the third time that year, and we went back to smiling and patching up any cracks in the veneer. As far as the world was concerned, I'd never been in a foster home. To let that cat out of the bag meant a whole feline gang would follow. Therefore, my mother had no drinking problem, our income came from my father's child support cheque, not welfare, and my parents had most definitely been wed. (Once, at a slumber party, I'd made the mistake of announcing what system buckers my mother and father were, never having been married. The look of horror around the Cheezie bowl changed my story fast). I kept our secrets, in part because it made escape easier. Vagueness allowed for a more seamless shape-shift.

In my teens, I developed a taste for middle- to upper-middle-class families—two-parent, two-garage households, families with boats and summer cottages, swimming pools and electric lawn mowers. I became friends with a born-again Christian at school and joined her church, a place loaded to the rafters with families who were downright rich. Nothing soothed me quite like their yachts and spiral staircases. Around them, I felt clean, well-bred and expensive. I joined the youth choir. I went on camping and boat trips, got crushes on gentle Jesus-loving boys, the antithesis of my mother's taste in men. I never could quite swallow the doctrine, the actual Christianity. And my compulsion to undermine Church authority drove me to tell a few kids I was a witch. Having never forgotten Marilyn and Karen, I invoked their names in times of stress and irreverence and, in the middle of Sunday morning services, drew what could only be considered impious symbols on my wrists.

I couldn't help but like the complexity of my new witchy Christian self. To add yet another layer, I became friends with Bonnie, the baddest good girl in the sanctuary. Using Bonnie's ID, I started heading out with her on Saturday nights to Outlaws, a downtown nightclub. As far as my mother knew, I was just going to Bonnie's for a sleepover. And I did sleep over at Bonnie's. And my body did remain the temple I claimed it was: loath to become remotely like the secret I had at home, I refused to drink alcohol and clung to my virginity like a life raft.

At twenty, Bonnie was four years older than I, perfectly legal and far less interested in discretion: she blabbed all over church about her drunken escapades, all of which happened the nights she was without me. Nonetheless, rumour had it that I frequently got so drunk that I had to be carried from bars. I was considered a "bad apple" by parents now.

One night after Sunday evening service, Bonnie and I were hauled into the pastor's study and interrogated. Bonnie protested that it had been *she* who had to be carried out, that I didn't even *drink*. He said he would have us kicked out of the choir if we didn't apologize before the congregation for our behaviour, adding that my mother would charge Bonnie with contributing to the delinquency of a minor. I shook my head; my mother would *never*. The pastor flattened me, announcing that people from the church were over discussing the matter with her this very instant. I was speechless. He fingered one of his gold rings. "Is your mother an alcoholic?"

No one in this place, *my* place, had ever uttered that word as though it pertained to my family or me. With one question, he had ripped the clean right off me. I started to cry, asking why he would say that. Apparently I'd given his past inquiries about my home life silly and vague answers that were, to his mind, consistent with those that children of alcoholics gave. I looked up at his photograph on the wall shaking hands with the pope, panicked and broke into sobs, nodding.

I didn't realize that he was being a Gotcha Wizard, that he knew nothing but rumours.

When I got home that night, I launched into a tirade against the charges my mother was to file against Bonnie. This was the first she'd heard of my having been in a bar.

But I quit the Church immediately. It was sullied.

Not long afterwards, my mother was drinking again. Deciding to leave, I made arrangements with a school friend who had two parents, a garage and a car and moved in without explanation. It would be two weeks before my friend's mother trapped me in a corner and asked me why I wouldn't go home. I had to come clean. It was the first time. The relief was all but trampled by guilt, but saying it out loud bought me a respite. With financial help from the Children's Aid, my friend's family took care of me for three months. Mom saw my departure as her personal rock bottom. She detoxed that summer, rejoined AA and made a decision that whether I came home or not, she would stop drinking for good.

I did come home, somewhat reluctantly, afraid things would go back to the way they were. As I started Grade 12, though, my mother was going to three AA meetings a week, new AA friends were often over for tea and my mother's former self became known as "that crazy person." Soon, she started counselling other new AA members. One, a former stripper, came by the apartment and saw the photographs of me that Mom had scattered around. She talked her into bringing the pictures to a modelling agency. The word "model" sounded like the shiniest, most expensive-looking thing of all. It spelled "escape." I flew to Tokyo straight out of high school.

Not only did being a model put me in the Thoroughbred category, it published photographs as proof. It didn't matter that I had developed a new and particularly humiliating secret. Food had become my last thought at night and my first in the morning. Most days now involved a ritual of stuffing fresh soft rolls into my mouth in a frenzy, each one smothered in butter and honey, stuffing and stuffing, alternating bites with gulps of hot tea to keep my stomach contents somewhat liquid. I would cram in roll after roll until tears were streaming down my face, my tongue too numb and raw to taste or feel the thrill of the sweet and soft any more. Seconds after I reached this point, I would run to the washroom and ram my finger or a toothbrush down my throat, shaking and crying, determined to get it out of my stomach as fast as possible.

After a couple years of this, I was falling apart—dark circles and broken blood vessels around my eyes. I would bruise if you looked at me wrong, and my throat had become so sensitive that ingesting almost anything could bring on a coughing fit. Ultimately, it was my fear and vanity that stopped the bulimia: if anyone found out, they would think I was a pig, putrid and ugly. Furthermore, I could just as easily get kicked out of my current shiny place for bad skin and bags as I could fat. I took to heavier exercise and vegetarianism instead. I carried envelopes of Sugar Twin in my purse wherever I went.

In my mid to late twenties, a transformation began. I had always written in journals, scribbled poetry in notebooks, scrawled letters home to everyone and to no one in particular, all in the name of keeping my sanity. But somewhere in there, I started writing down snippets of truth in short bursts of narrative verse. It was different from the poetry I'd been writing before. Bits of memory and history—there wasn't much vague about it. I couldn't make up anything, and I couldn't stop slapping it down on the page. Spilling my guts this new way was making me feel muscular. I felt hard and steely as opposed to scrawny and shiny, and I liked it.

I quit modelling and took on three or four part-time jobs—cocktailing in a comedy club, catering weddings, giving out chocolates in department stores. I wrote hundreds of pages, truth until I was sick of it. I began to mix and match, make collages of fiction and fact. Then, using a combo of the two, I started what would be my first novel, determined to be as honest, emotionally, as I knew how. My mother—eighteen years sober and likely figuring I didn't have a hope in hell of getting a book published—gave me her blessing. Other than Mom, I didn't give a damn what anyone thought now.

Then it happened. In the spring of 2000, *Going Down Swinging* was published. The media attention was beyond anything I'd expected, a barrage of television and radio, my picture in national and local newspapers and magazines. And I was afraid again. For me and my mother. No one knew where fact ended and fiction began, but still, I had told. And people would know that I'd lived through at least some of that world or I couldn't have written it.

A woman walks into Chapters one day to browse and sees a novel on the New Fiction shelf. On the cover is a kitten in a martini glass, and she can't help reaching out to it. The author's name pulls her eyebrows together. It can't be. She flips the book over. The child's eyes she remembers look back at her now, thirty years later. She grabs hold of the shelf to keep from falling.

Later, a phone message: "Hi, my name is Karen. You might not remember me, but I used to know you when you were a little girl. Maybe three or four. My friend Marilyn used to call you Billie Badoodle. I was so happy to find you in the phone book. Every couple of years I would look, and this time you were there. . . ."

By the weekend, Marilyn has driven up from Oregon, where she lives now as an artist. When Karen opens her door, the two of them stand and look at me, smiles almost broader than their faces can hold. I don't know who is who any more. All I can remember is the sense of them, the gorgeous warmth I felt being near. They're both in their mid-fifties now, but a wild-haired hippie chick still vibrates through each of them into my bones as I try to hug thirty years' worth in those first few moments.

Soon we're sitting eating cheese and croissants and slurping strong coffee at Karen's heavy oak dining table, surrounded by simple but elegant art in a house bought through twenty years of selling real estate. She scratches the head of Rubio, the lanky Afghan sitting beside her chair, and tells me about the collie she got after I disappeared from their lives and how she named her Billie. I can feel tears coming, but I breathe through them and listen.

They tell me again how surreal this feels, like magic. Thirty years ago, when doctors told my mother she'd be dead by Christmas if she didn't knock off the drinking, Karen and Marilyn had considered kidnapping me, for fear I'd end up rattling around that house on Fourth Avenue alone with Black Mike the same way my child's mind imagined that plate rattled around his head. When I disappeared they called everywhere, social services, Catholic Family Services— no one knew anything, or if they did, they weren't telling.

"I thought of you so often and how much I loved being with you," I tell them, "but I remember being a brat some- times, and I wasn't sure if the feeling was mutual."

"We couldn't get enough of you." And we laugh and hold hands tighter and get weepy, the hair on our arms prickling every so often at the shock of us, here like this again, smiling for real and feeling in love.

✿

There is fabric art hanging from the ceiling of my apartment now, two long strips of silk, dark and light green, dropping separately and doubling back to twist round each other again. It's called *Billie and Me*, a piece from Marilyn's last gallery show.

It's the irony of it that kills me—keeping my secrets all those years for fear of losing people, and it was the telling that found them.

One Step Forward

Shirley A. Serviss

I was surprised and touched when my stepson's mother invited me to pose for a family photograph at his Grade 12 graduation. I joined Greg, his mother and stepfather, his half sister—my daughter—and his father, from whom I was separated. It was a healing end to many years of acrimony.

"Will you step to one side, Shirley? You're in Denise's face," the photographer requested. Greg's mother and I began to laugh. "What else is new?" she quipped. "Let's not even go there," I responded.

I was in my early thirties and wanted desperately to have a child when I became involved with a separated, twice-married man with a two-year-old son. A man who loved his son enough to take on the role as primary caregiver seemed like good father material. I was seduced by his dedication: leaving work on time night after night to pick up his son from daycare and put a home-cooked meal on the table. I was seduced by a small, blond, blue-eyed boy climbing into bed between us in the mornings for "sandwich hugs." I was seduced by an image of a stable family life, like the one I had known as a child, in contrast to my single life following a divorce from a childless open marriage.

Greg was four by the time I moved in with his father, into the house his mother had once lived in and to which she still had a key. Our bedroom was furnished with the suite my partner had given his second wife as a graduation present (as she was to remind us later); our china and crystal was his half of the settings they had chosen when first married. Our chesterfield suite had been chosen by his first wife—a woman I never met, but who contributed more baggage than merely the beige loveseats that managed to outlast all three of his marriages. My partner always claimed these possessions were too expensive to replace; they were costly, indeed.

The symbolism of the house, the furniture, the crystal and china would not strike me until much later. My immediate concern was the preschooler who lived with us more than half the time and whose care had suddenly become my responsibility. When I dropped Greg at his daycare on the way to my office, he would dash in ahead of me and slam the door in my face. Suspecting the problem, I inquired one morning, "What would you say if someone asked you who I am?" He replied without hesitation, "I would say that you are nobody."

When we later explained to him that I was his step-mother, his reaction was one of relief. "Just like Cinderella," he sighed. At least he had a context for me—whether or not it was a positive one.

I had no better an understanding of the role of step-mother; what I did was try to be a mother. I read bedtime stories, made Rice Krispies squares and sewed on buttons. It wasn't long before I was the one making sure Greg was enrolled for swimming and soccer and earning Cub badges.

One of my more misguided efforts was organizing Greg's birthday parties.

I would spend an inordinate amount of time finding prizes for ice fishing down the laundry chute and inventing life-size board games to play in the basement; his mother would breeze in with an ice-cream cake she'd picked up at Dairy Queen. The cake, of course, would be what Greg would mention as the highlight of the party when I tucked him into bed that night.

Greg already had a mother. He would quickly correct anyone who mistook my identity. Mother's Days came and went, usually without recognition for the role I played in my stepson's life. (Although I was both saddened and touched when he showed up at the doorstep on his bicycle one year with some wilted flowers he had evidently been hiding for me.)

Our daughter was born when Greg was five. He was delighted to have a baby sister, his father was thrilled to have a daughter and I was relieved to be a "real mother" at last. My partner and I had still not married. There were too many times when I wanted to jump into my car and drive away from a life over which I seemed to have little control. In addition to his scheduled periods with us, Greg came to spend weekends or stay with us whenever his mother didn't have time to take care of him or had other plans; my time commitments and my plans were largely immaterial.

Once my daughter was born, I abandoned any fantasy I had of raising a child alone. She screamed for most of her first six months of life, and I was extremely grateful for her father's support when he came home from work. I thought that having a child of my own would make me happy; I discovered that as much as I loved her, she was not a solution to my angst. I had, however, waited a long time for this much-wanted child and couldn't imagine having someone else raise her, so chose to maintain my freelance writing business from home. Clients were understanding when I breast-fed her at meetings or changed her diapers on boardroom tables. I found I was adept at typing with one hand. I could work once I got her to sleep at night or while she played at my feet during the day.

Prior to my daughter's second birthday, her father and I decided to marry and buy a house together. I found it discomfiting to have Greg's mother drop in on some pretext or another at any time, or to have her feel free to go through the house looking for something he had left behind. I thought that legitimizing our relationship and having a home in joint title would change the power imbalance. Surely a wife's needs and feelings would matter more than an ex-wife's. Surely a wife would have the right to be considered a bona fide stepparent who could attend parent-teacher meetings. Surely I would have some say over who could and could not enter a house to which I held joint title.

Marriage was not a solution. My home—even with my name on the title—never felt like a safe place for me to be. Not only was it subject to invasion, but it was under constant surveillance. I don't know whether it was simply Greg's nature or whether he was questioned at the other end of the telephone line, but everything we did and said was reported on. Although I attempted to define boundaries over the years, any efforts in this regard were seen as attempts to deny access. For example, not allowing Greg to call his mother until after he had completed a chore I'd asked him to do was denying access rather than eliminating one of his favourite stalling tactics. This goldfish-bowl existence made it difficult for me to relax and be myself.

"All he needs is love," I was told repeatedly by my sisters, who had no experience with, or understanding of, stepfamilies. Love was dangerous territory for Greg and me; it equated with loss and pain. This little boy lived with us only half the time. Each of his departures was like a death. His empty room, his empty chair, his baseball glove by the back door were daily reminders of a missing son. Because of the acrimony between his mother and me, I didn't dare call him when he was there; I could only blow him kisses to the moon and hope he'd know I still cared about him. Loving me was just as dangerous for him. Whenever he betrayed feelings of closeness to me, his mother grew angry.

When he was in Grade 2, Greg started to call me Mom partly out of self-defence. His little sister had begun to say things like "She's my mommy; go back to your own mom," if Greg was sitting on my lap and she wanted me to herself. He told me it hurt him when his sister said I wasn't his mom, because "you're my mom too." His mother read a journal entry he had written addressing his father and me as "Dear Mom and Dad" and made it clear to him that he only had one mom—her. He came back to us a different child. There was no eye contact. He mumbled, walked slowly, didn't answer questions, didn't do what he was told and seemed on the verge of tears. I had to agree in mediation, instigated by his mother, not to allow Greg to call me Mom.

I was not to be a mother to Greg, which left me in the rather thankless position of being an unpaid nanny. Because I worked from home, I was expected to take on much of the responsibility for him when he was living with us. I was expected to do laundry and clothe him, but his real mother had the right to phone and insist he wear the outfit she bought him for his school picture. I was expected to make sure he did his homework and help him with it but not entitled to sign permission slips for field trips or attend school functions.

I began to step back. It seemed safer to keep my distance, lavish my love and attention on my daughter and provide Greg with custodial care. This, however, brought me criticism from my husband and sisters for not "loving" Greg. One complaint was that I used a "frosty" tone of voice when I asked him to do things. I know I did adopt a harsher stance with him so that there could be no question of disobeying—no chance for him to say, "You're not my mother; you can't tell me what to do."

I know I sometimes acted like the classic wicked step-mother, and it's been hard to forgive myself for it. When Greg and I had lunch recently, I apologized for using him as a scapegoat. "It worked both ways," he pointed out with his twenty-year-old insight. "It was easier for me to think every-thing was your fault than to blame my parents."

Surviving in a "blended family" continued to elude me, though not for lack of trying. For years I thought that if I could only be a better person, a more perfect parent or partner, more compassionate toward Greg's mother or find the right rotation schedule, everything would work out. I have a whole shelf of books and a file folder two inches thick with articles on the subject of stepparenting that I'm now contemplating turning into a book-art project—stacking them up and gluing them together in the shape of a zero.

The material I read and the courses I took made it clear that I was supposed to be an "adult friend," not a parent, but how to be the "adult friend" of one child and the parent of his sibling at the same time was something I never figured out. How do you discipline one child but tell the other one he has to wait until one of his real parents is around? How do you cook or do laundry for one child but not the other? Perhaps the adult-friend relationship would have been easier to establish had Greg been older when I came into his life, but this was a child I had taught to print and tie his shoelaces, whose diapers I had changed.

I was not the only one who was having problems with life in the blender, as I tended to think of it. Much of my husband's anger at his former wife was misdirected at me— he would even call me by her name. There were times when the stress in our home was so high that our daughter could be found cutting the hair off her dolls or holes in her favourite dress. Greg referred to "Mom's house" and "you guys' house" never "home," chewed on his hands and was continually in trouble for acting out at school. Once he drew a self-portrait of a small boy being torn in half.

For many years, I was a willing participant in my partner's ongoing power struggle with his former wife. I profoundly regret my role as accomplice. It was safer to see her as the cause of all our problems than to look closely at the man I had married. In fact, for many years she functioned quite well as a smokescreen.

One summer when our daughter was seven, my husband was embroiled in yet another expensive legal battle to have Greg live with us, ignoring my pleas to stop playing a game that was no-win for everyone. Emotionally distant at the best of times, he had become increasingly preoccupied and evasive. When I expressed my desire to leave our marriage, he told me I could go if I wanted to, but he wouldn't let me take our daughter. I knew I didn't have the financial means to fight for custody, and I knew I couldn't give her up. I felt trapped and hopeless. One night, on a family holiday at the lake, there was a meteor shower. She woke up and begged me to take her to the dock, away from the lights, so she could see the falling stars. I was frightened I would drown both her and myself.

I tried desperately to stay in the marriage until our daughter finished school, but I was marking time, not living. When I turned forty-five, I realized I couldn't go on. I decided having a divorced mother would be better for my ten-year-old daughter than having a depressed mother or a dead one. I announced my intention to leave and take her with me. This time my husband didn't stop me.

She sees her father one night a week, alternate weekends and any other time they choose to get together. As I had predicted, he continues to be a caring and involved father. I made many mistakes, but having a child with this man was not one of them. Leaving him was a wise decision too. I am happier than I had imagined it was possible to be. For the first time in my adult life, I feel a sense of hope.

I didn't see much of Greg the first two years after I moved out. He lived with his dad one year and his mother the next. He came for dinner occasionally and I received the occasional phone call: "How do you make macaroni and cheese?" "Do you still have my resumé on your computer?" "Would you write me a reference letter? You know me better than anybody. By the way, I need it tomorrow." During one visit Greg told me, "I know I made things difficult for you at first, Shirley, but look at us now."

I hear from him more often now that he lives on his own. "Shirley, I haven't seen you for ages," he'll say over the phone. "How would you like to get together for supper?" What this usually means is that he would like a home-cooked dinner and has an essay due that could use a proofreader.

I don't have a copy of the family photograph taken at Greg's high school graduation. Neither does he. Perhaps it didn't turn out. I don't know how to view my experience as a stepmother. Was it a success or a failure? At the time I left my marriage, I would have described it as a failure. I'm no longer so sure. The fact that I have a close relationship with my daughter and her brother validates the time and energy I put into trying to create a home and family. It felt like family the other night as I massaged Greg's feet in front of my fireplace while he and his sister visited. He left with the remnants of our Sunday dinner for Monday's lunch and suggestions on how to improve his essay.

"Do you still think of me as your stepmom?" I asked him recently. "Of course. Who else would I say you are?" he replied. "Besides, you didn't divorce me."

Hiding

Pamela Mala Sinha

for Jule

I try to forgive myself for pulling the covers up over my head. Not every day. But in the time before the Blacks—so that maybe I can stop them from coming. The dictionary defines black as the absence of colour. I see it as a colour.

Almost fifteen years ago, I heard a terrible crashing sound. Are they demolishing the building next door? No. It's nighttime. I'm sleeping. So much noise that someone's going to call the police. Another enormous crash. Someone's here. *Inside.* I'm being robbed. What happened next, I've been told, if it had to happen at all, occurred under the best possible circumstances because I had not done, nor could be accused of doing, anything "wrong."

What's incredible is that it almost bores me to write this. I have lived these thoughts so long that everything seems tedious. Redundant. Difficult to imagine as something you would even care to read. I don't want your pity. Everything I need to be here writing this is already mine; otherwise I would be dead. It's that simple. What do I want, then? I must want something from you.

He made me eat his shit. He sat on my face and suffocated me with his ass until I did.

I want it to matter. That's what I want.

I did it. And during that time, I believe there was a moment when I was not *there*. Not passed-out unconscious, but not in my body. It was possible to remain present until that point. I couldn't see with the pillow over my face, but I could think, and I didn't stop thinking. Obeying. Pleading. But when he flipped me onto my stomach I got confused. I didn't know what he was doing pushing my face into the mattress. I was on my stomach. Why my stomach? oh no. That's when I left. I left myself behind to be raped *that way*, left my body there in that bed and walked over—with my nightie *on*—to my little altar that was set up in the corner and asked God to come out of the picture and burn him. I just stood there, in front of God, repeating, "Burn him" over and over, demanding that what was happening in the bed should end in flames NOW. For a long time I left her to that torture while I stood in front of my God. I was busy begging so I left her there.

When I met Jule, my therapist, I saw in her eyes someone who didn't fit in the world the same way I didn't. It wasn't true, but when she looked at me that first day she made me feel not alone, and for a single suspended second . . . I felt like maybe I could live. That maybe we would be able, with that torn fragment of my spirit, to seek out what it was that hated me so much to want to kill me.

During a session of therapy more than a year later, *she* showed herself to us. She called herself Hiding. The parts of that night I couldn't remember, she did. She was left to live what I couldn't and she hated me for it. The Blacks were her way of making me know that if she had to bear it, then I had to pay.

It took Hiding seven years to get my attention.

My parents didn't know the terminology for what he had done to me, just as I didn't know it was humanly possible to do to a body what he had done to mine. My mother went to the rape crisis centre so she could learn what she did not know. She threw up in their garbage can. She and my father went through this without my knowledge and without sharing it with any of their friends or family. Later, some people thought it was shame that kept their secret. But it was love. Love for those daughters of friends and family who might be robbed of their freedom because of their parents' fear; love for me, knowing that pity would have surely killed me, even as he hadn't; and love for their son because they feared that learning of this so far from home would destroy him—that it should wait out the summer until he could see his sister face to face. Wrong or right to those who loved us and deserved to share in our pain at that time, they did it out of love.

And that's good enough for me.

Sometimes during the Blacks, I would go out to bars to find men to rape me. I carried a large knife in my knapsack. I would wait for a would-be attacker to give me reason to use it. Hiding believed that I should have tried to defend myself that night. *There was a window in your bedroom— why didn't you jump out of it? There were hangers in your closet—why didn't you use them? Or at the very least, why didn't you fight him no matter how big or strong or armed or crazy he was because then at least you could SEE the scars of the maiming or at least be dead from FIGHTING rather than lying there like an idiot with the covers over your head, holding your breath, thinking he wouldn't see you, he'd see an empty unmade bed because you were so thin and small and still.*

Stupidstupidstupid girl.

Just before the bars would close, I'd ask the chosen man to drive me out to an abandoned stretch of the lakeshore, park the car and walk with me, miles from any signs of life. He would have *to start*. If he didn't start, it wouldn't count. He would start, I would say no, he would have to try to *force* me and then, only then, could I use the knife. He would have to insist—there wouldn't even have to be a struggle, he just had to insist or it wouldn't count. None of them ever did. They were nice men. They wanted my number.

Doing it "right" means you'll be okay. Not rewarded necessarily, just okay. Sometimes you'll be told how to do something right, and the challenge lies in accomplishing the task. Other times the aim will be to determine what "right" means, then to do it. If you do it right, everything will be okay. And if you don't, everything *won't* be okay. But the problem is the assumption that what happens to you is within your control, that whatever you are doing, your choice determines the outcome.

He orders me to hold the position. On my back, naked, pillow on my face, crowbar on the pillow, arms extended, legs in the air, he's got me by the ankles and he's jerking my legs around—I don't understand what position he wants me to hold. He's yelling at me and laughing at me because I look so stupid and finally he jerks one leg straight up HIGH and the other one bent at the knee. I'M GOING NOW. DON'T MOVE. DON'T MOVE OR I'LL FUCKING KILL YOU. If I don't move if I don't move, he will be gone and I will be okay. I won't move. I hear the bedroom door slam. I hear him walk away in his big boots. I'm not moving. I'm sweating with the effort. My legs are shaking on the inside because I can't let them shake on the outside or it won't be okay. I'm not even breathing. I am still I am superman I can do it I will do it right and it will be okay.

YOU FUCKING MOVED.

He never left.

Pretending to walk away, he walked on the spot. Pretending to leave my room, he slammed the door shut from that spot, all the while standing there quietly watching me, watching. I did not move. He knows it. I know it. We both know I did it right I did it *right*, what he said. But it's not okay. I did it right and it's not okay.

He punishes me for doing it right.

There is not much more I can tell you about that night. Hiding is the only one who could tell you what happened next, but she won't. She still won't even tell me. But I know it was bad and I know he did it again and again and again and again and I know I gave up. He broke me with this one. Because it was clear to me that no matter how right I did anything from now on, it would make no difference to the outcome. *No difference.* He broke my spirit when he robbed me of that belief.

The occurrence of frequent and often violent Blacks seemed to be the only thing I could believe in during those years that followed—going to bars armed with a knife being only one of the horrors of that time. It was the daily rituals that I believe did the most damage. Normal things that terrified me but I *made* myself do. The front door of the theatre school I was studying at was directly opposite the window of the room where it happened. Every day I made myself walk past that window. For three years. I never used the rear entrance. Never. *See, it's no big deal.* After graduating, I moved to Toronto and lived alone. *But I don't want to.* And to bear being touched by the man I loved during those years, I would split off—watching myself "act out" from a corner of the room. It hurts. They were endless, those little tortures. But I think I did them because I needed to live as if life from *before* still belonged to me.

I was invited to perform in a play the role of Artemesia, a visual artist who as a young girl in 1612 was raped by her teacher. For three months, six performances a week, I would tell her story. There would be a rape scene, of course, but I would be *acting it.* People were finally going to listen to her; three hundred people a night were going to listen. And they did.

Until the night the play closed, and they stopped listening. It was as if she didn't matter any more, as if it had never happened, as if she . . . were *garbage*. I wanted to die.

I nearly did.

I woke up one morning to find myself unable to move. Paralyzed. Incontinent. As if my body had simply quit. I had no choice but to be admitted to an in-patient care facility for women who had suffered from the same kind of tortures that I had. There they gave me a name for what was happening to me: Post-Traumatic Stress Disorder. It was a syndrome and it was real. It had a *name*. Even from that half-dead place, I felt grateful. So grateful. I stayed there for a long time. It had taken seven years to get there. A long time I stayed in that place, and finally I went home. That's when we found Jule.

And I found myself in hell.

With Hiding.

And with us in hell was anybody who loved me anybody who loved stupidstupidstupidgirl. They were not allowed any reason to love, have faith in or hope for her. My mother watched me disappear a little more each day: retreating into my childhood bedroom, physically and emotionally becoming increasingly, terrifyingly, dependent. She didn't know if she would ever see me live as an adult again. I resented my father's innocence. I had always loved that about him— protected it. But at his slightest encouragement, I would remind him that I had lost what he could afford to have—not having had it robbed of him. Though I was wrong—so wrong about that—he said nothing. My parents would listen, just listen to me, trying to see and feel the horror, so that at least *this time*, I would not have to be in it alone. I could not bear to see my brother's grief—so I looked away from it. My family of friends I rejected—pushing them away when they wanted to be near. I didn't want proof of their commitment to me. I didn't want them.

They stayed.

What happened to me is a part of who I am. I know this. At the end of my last relationship, what happened feels like *all* that I am—that all I had to offer was pain. Though I now know this isn't true, I still have to work so very hard to hold on to his voice telling me that I was so much more than the pain. That I was Beauty for him too. When I look over at my parents sometimes and feel *yes, I want to live* in answer to a question I didn't even know I was asking, I know it doesn't go away. When I'm in a Black—the kind where I can't get out of bed for days—and my little stepdaughter wants me to sing to her and I can, I know why that is a remarkable thing. I know it when my brother laughs out loud and I feel more grateful than I should.

No, it doesn't go away. But it changes. The Blacks still come, but now I recognize when they're coming and sometimes I even know what to do to stop them. Sometimes I can't stop them, sometimes I *have* to make a cut—a cut that I can *see*, that articulates, that calms the silent screaming. But I haven't had to for a long time.

And when after a day filled with life and love I get into bed and my legs start to shake unstoppably—looking for reassurance that they are not being held at the ankles, that they are *free*—my heart breaks a little at my husband's voice speaking to me ever so quietly, breaks at my need to hear him, so that even as that part of me shakes, the other parts of me fall to sleep to the sound of his voice.

And that's okay.

A woman I call my sister, Tina, still believes in her Creator. She believes that God was raped with me that night; that he couldn't answer. I want to believe that, but I don't. But I *want* to. I still feel Hiding's rage, but I'm almost sure she hates me less. Maybe she's beginning to trust me—trust that I do remember her; that I won't deny her, alone in that bed. I hope she can believe that her voice—though buried under those covers—will continue to be heard and honoured by all of us who know her.

I know why I'm writing this now.

This story no longer belongs only to me. It is yours now, too.

If you'll take it.

A Marriage in
Seven Parts

Dana McNairn

I

On my wedding day, as I entered the banquet hall on the arm of my new husband, I realized with a jolt that the room was clearly divided into two camps. On the left-hand side of the hall, my husband—let's call him Andrew—had guests from all over the globe. His relatives and friends were seemingly cut from the same cloth, striking in their wholesome good looks, pearly white teeth, tuxedos and flowing gowns. Their appearance bore the stamp of stability and easy acceptance of their rightful place in the world. Most had celebrated double-digit wedding anniversaries. They sipped fruit punch or expertly cradled champagne flutes, chatting quietly in well-behaved groups.

On the right—my side—the throng was tattooed, boisterous and roaring drunk. I saw my tiny grandmother reach up and swipe a drink from a huge man in an open-necked shirt with a giant ship tattooed across his chest. Men tugged uncomfortably at unaccustomed ties and ill-fitting dress shirts. Since most of the men's shirts were short-sleeved, rolling up the thin fabric was a cinch and afforded a better view of the snakes, daggers and screaming eagles that coloured their arms. The women on this side of the room preferred jewel-toned pantsuits and took comfort—even in the daunting presence of so many strangers on the other side—in the assumption "the bigger the hair, the closer to God." Most were on second or third marriages. An uncle, affectionately nicknamed "Lurchin' Larry," held court, an unlit cigarette dangling from his mouth as a beer bottle occasionally punctuated the air when he wanted to make a point. His sister—my mother—wobbled beside him, one hand gripping his arm. Her other hand alternated between smacking him and wiping tears of laughter from her eyes, without spilling her drink. Children ran howling and screeching, stabbing one another with chicken wings and carrot sticks.

I looked back to the tranquility of the left-hand side of the room and again to the din of the right. And sighed.

The bride also had a tattoo and was panting for a drink.

II

My husband was tall, dark and handsome. And a virgin. I, ahem, was not. He had just turned twenty, and I, just twenty-two. He married me because, among other things, premarital sex was not an option, given his traditional upbringing and young man's idealized values. We loved each other, so why not make a vow before God and do it up right? Not only did I worship his strength of character and hope some would rub off on me, but I also craved the respectability of a formal union, a partnership.

When we announced our sudden engagement with the marriage date not far behind, Andrew's mother burst into tears and fled the room. She assumed I was pregnant. How little she knew. To show our commitment—or, rather, to be taken seriously because of our age—we paid for everything

and only after much tussling allowed Drew's father to pay for
the liquor. Later, he commented on the prodigious amount
of booze my family and friends had consumed. "See?" he
said. "You should have eloped."

Our wedding night was awkward, clumsy and comical.
In our tender and steamy fumbling, we banged teeth,
cracked heads, blushed profusely and toppled right out of
the giant hotel bed smack onto the carpet. Evidently, we
had both seen too many movies. It was mercifully brief.
Afterwards, we laughed ourselves asleep.

III

We settled quickly into our new life. I took Drew's surname
and practiced writing my new name. For months my signature looked awkward and scrawled—it felt like forging my
mother's on a note for school. When I heard the words "Mrs.
Smith," I never knew who was being addressed—there were a
handful of us—so I tended to ignore the salutation initially
because I kept forgetting that was my name now. "It gets
easier," an aunt commented dryly. "Eventually you'll have a
hard time remembering your old one."

Drew practiced wearing jewellery for the first time in
his life, donning his wedding band with shy pride. We
both worked—Drew in television, me at an ad agency—and
scratched our heads at the piling bills. So we worked longer
hours, sought out increasingly prestigious and better-paying
jobs and fended off the pointed questions about when we were
going to have kids. We moved a couple of times, each place
bigger than the last, until we were in a huge, beautiful house
Drew's parents once lived in. The two mothers-in-law competed for our time, but Drew's mom won hands down. She
was more persistent, and my mother just assumed we'd feel the
love she sent from wherever she was roaming at the time.

Drew cooked and cleaned and folded laundry, accom-
modating my late nights at work. He overlooked my many

failings: a lack of housekeeping skills, an inability to keep my mouth shut at family dinners or to remember anyone's birthday (including his) and, above all, my uncanny talent for disgracing myself in public by using bawdy language and forgetting to wear underwear. I overlooked his abruptness, his sometimes hard-to-live-up-to ambition and those awful pasta-in-a-bag concoctions he was so fond of.

I learned many things during my marriage. Including how to lie.

I lied about liking his grandmother's casserole, about enjoying the semi-annual Smith family reunions and about wanting to have Drew's cousin stay with us. I—the one who had swaggered through high school in square-toed motorcycle boots—had mastered the art of pretense to such an extent that I eventually succumbed to wearing pouffy Laura Ashley dresses and little gold lamé slip-ons while hosting all those damn dinner parties. I did it because I wanted to fit in with this strange, wondrous family who never raised their voices, never swore and never threw things at one another.

I was hungry to be a good wife—albeit with a comforting bottle of Talisker Scotch in the closet and cigarettes outside on the back steps—who regularly shopped with all the tidy Smith womenfolk, made darling apple wreaths and learned how to coo at stuffed animals.

Yet what I really wanted was to pace wolfishly around the house, half-naked in tattered jeans, spouting Dylan Thomas or my own bad poetry. Or go to a séance. Or cover a war for the *New York Times*. Or eat fudge for breakfast. Or have sex on the kitchen table. Or not make the bed every morning. Or, better yet, sell everything in that big beautiful house, pack up some underwear and my bewildered husband and hightail it overseas for a while. I would have settled for an annual two-week car vacation to some dull, dusty town, if it meant I could actually drag Drew away from work. I would have been happy stealing a midday nap with him every once in a while—but enterprising young executives don't permit themselves such indulgences.

Instead, I mastered gift-wrapping for the endless celebrations of family birthdays, anniversaries, retirements, baby showers, graduations and Groundhog Days. Instead, I reluctantly climbed the corporate ladder into an airless office, amassing clients and doing power lunches—and tried to remember to wear underwear. Instead, I attended the mandatory Smith Sunday dinners, quietly chewed my roast beef and nodded sympathetically at conversations I had heard before. I was proud of myself for keeping my mouth shut.

And besides, I had a gold card with no spending limit to anesthetize the empty feelings in my life.

IV

I decided to go back to school to study journalism—and to shake my growing irritability and impatience. If my current career was unsatisfactory, I could hide out in academia and find another one. Even though Drew agreed to this increased financial burden, I wanted to be fair, so I also worked part-time. Juggling jobs, family get-togethers, school assignments, housework, yard work and just trying to get some dinner on the table every night took its toll. Now I was the one never home. And when I was, Drew's abruptness and impatience became harder to ignore. I failed to see what could possibly be bothering him. We had money, a roof over our heads and were pursuing our almighty careers. Yet his biting temper persisted and flourished, so I ignored him. Withdrawing emotionally was the only way I knew to handle the problem. That way, there'd be no shouting—I had had enough of that growing up.

During my last year of school, while I glided on the euphoria of my approaching graduation, Drew admitted he was lonely and had been for a while. He said he had never really experienced loneliness until he got married. I felt sick with guilt and shame. Part of me agreed with him, but part of me wanted to kick over chairs. He was being unfair, unreasonable and unaccommodating! Another layer of love eroded by neglect and selfishness.

v

No one tells you about the arguments and bitter silences that can seep into the marriage bedroom. It was year four, and the wheels were off the wagon. Blinded by our ever-lurking self-pity, we lost sight of fairness and decency. Neither of us was able to shake off the hurts and slights we thought the other intended. Drew became more vocal about wanting kids—he felt it would help us—but I told him I was pretty sure I wasn't ready, pointedly eyeing the limp or dying houseplants, the wine bottles on the counters and the stack of parking tickets on the desk.

He aspired to corporate grandeur—too rigid and structured, I whined. I wanted the freedom of the bohemian—too unstable and unrealistic, he huffed. I responded with increasingly antagonistic and appalling behaviour—staying out late, keeping company with other men and coming home drunk—masking my unhappiness by punishing a man who didn't deserve it.

We both had a decision to make. I had to put as much passion and enthusiasm back into my marriage as I had into my education. Drew had to put as much passion and enthusiasm back into his marriage as he had into his career. We still loved each other—although the intimacy had faltered a bit. Drew, to his everlasting credit, did his best to remain fair and patient. I, on the other hand, did not have the wisdom or emotional maturity to see past my own arrogance.

I went away, far away, to Australia to think. As I was leaving, he whispered in my ear that he would agree to whatever decision I made.

When he picked me up from the airport six weeks later, he knew by the resigned look on my face what the decision was. I managed a weak smile; he bowed his head and exhaled deeply, like a man who had been holding his breath for too long. A couple of weeks later we marched hand in hand, making the rounds to tell the relatives. They listened in stunned disbelief. There had been no fever-pitch battles, no scandal, no abuse, no thrilling financial crash, no plate throwing. They hadn't seen us fighting, nor had either one of us ever spent a night or two on their couches. The families didn't get it; faces crumpled in bewilderment and shock. I had come full circle—my mother-in-law burst into tears and fled the room. Girlfriends wailed I was "throwing away a perfect marriage" and shook their heads. Drew and I soldiered on with our earnest explanations. What mattered was that we could see a future of misery, choking on trying to do the right thing. To our families, the separation was cowardly—pure selfishness on my part and a loss of control on Drew's, for failing to rein in his wife.

A grandfather, who had remained silent during our unexpected visit, finally grunted, "Well, what did you expect, all those bridesmaids dressed in black?"

VI

But it wasn't a control issue—it never was—nor was it titanic ego clashes, religious issues, lack of sex or money, or even nightly wrestling with the toilet seat. Subsumed by being Mrs. Smith, I allowed someone else to define who or what I was, and destroyed a marriage by not being able to discover it for myself. Drew, in moulding himself after his parents, echoed my mistakes: we were both trying to please others rather than ourselves. His family wanted him to succeed and prosper, as they had. I did not want to fail at marriage, as the others in my family had.

He once said, "Truth is love." Now I know what he meant. It is regretful I didn't understand that better in my marriage, but I am honoured that this man was such a big part of my life. He always stood up for truth. I shied away from it because it meant I would probably have to change some aspect of my personality. I wasn't ready to have my weaknesses highlighted—it was arrogance that held my head aloft, not authenticity. The marriage was bittersweet—we were gathering experiences before we knew what to do with them.

VII

A couple of years later, Drew called me one morning in a panic. He had lost his decree nisi and needed my copy—pronto—or he couldn't get married that afternoon. Howling with laughter, I teased him about being a polygamist and blackmailed him for a dinner in exchange. I'm pleased that he finally has what he had wanted all along—a wife who wants what he does and three beautiful children. Probably they all like pasta-in-a-bag, too.

I lead a highly nomadic life now, taking perverse pride in the sheer number of addresses I've accumulated. I eat vegetarian, wear boxer shorts, write really bad poetry and haven't seen the inside of an office in years. I haven't covered any wars yet, but I've been in war zones. While my ex-husband jogs, plays golf and has a platinum credit card, I am perennially broke and worry about lung cancer. But I've never been happier. I'm a writer now, passionate about travel, food and honesty. I still don't have any kids and I haven't picked up another mother-in-law—yet. Drew and I manage to get together once in a while for lunch. We're usually laughing too much to eat anything. The best thing I ever did was marry Drew Smith. The second best thing I ever did was divorce him.

Northern Lights
and Darkness

Lisa Gregoire

The word "dickie" always makes me laugh.

When I was a kid, my mom would buy them for me. She was obsessed with being cozy—it's what happens to people who grow up poor in a family of eleven. They can't understand why you don't take comfort when you can afford it.

A dickie is a knitted bib you wear beneath a sweater so it looks as if you're wearing a full turtleneck when you're not. I always feared schoolmates would mock me if they noticed the bib dangling below my collarbone.

I was twenty-seven and an Iqaluit newspaper reporter of two years when I found myself in the Northern Store thinking about Mom. I no longer cared if people saw my dickie. I bought three in different colours and wore one every day for the next two weeks. It wasn't for the cold, though it was jaw rattling on Baffin Island in February. It was to hide the purple fingerprints on my neck.

I almost died once. Few knew it had gotten that bad with David. One of them was a friend from CBC who agreed to share a bottle of liquor with me the night after it happened. He listened as I dropped parts of the story, like puzzle pieces on the floor, unable to put them together in any sensible order. How it happened where I'd been house-sitting and how, only months before, a teenager had committed suicide in the same bedroom by removing his head with a rifle blast. I know. I saw the gruesome police pictures. David choked me unconscious there. I locked myself in the bathroom after I came to, watching the bruises turn from red to blue. He left in silence at daybreak, and I abandoned my tiled refuge for the couch and a cigarette.

I came to Iqaluit on a lark. I was tired of my weekly newspaper job in Ottawa and eager for real experience. I planned to stay only a year, but I found in Nunavut an enchanting wilderness I could not abandon. The longer I stayed, the more I discovered. I felt tough and privileged among the few living in this barren place.

I collected animal bones. I sat for hours in summer watching the sun dance crimson and orange across the lichen. I was a city girl, for God's sake. I'd never seen a walrus before. Or giant ravens and herds of caribou.

Walking on the land became my favourite pastime. No trees. No people. No power lines. Just crunchy snow and the green shimmy of the northern lights like silent, magic wind.

David chased me from the Legion once, the Legion with the fourth-highest liquor sales in the country. I had decided to leave without him. Booze often stole his beautiful smile, leaving behind hard stares and silent suspicion. Friends knew he was changing his skin and held him back when he tried to follow me. It was part of the usual late-night drama in the North, and they were probably pleased it was me this time and not them.

I started running. He wriggled from his shirt and chased me, bare-chested in the −30° C night. I hid like a rabbit beneath a house propped up on stilts above the permafrost. I halted my panting breath and he ran past seconds later. I heard his footfalls approach and recede. It was the first time I truly feared him. My heart was pumping so fast my ears were ringing. What a rush.

A couple of days later, he wrote an apology of misspelled words on loose-leaf paper and dropped it by my office. He was so sorry. He didn't mean it. He really loved me.

We met for coffee, shoulders stooped and staring at the tabletop. He gave me a pendant, gold letters fused together into "Little Princess." Before he said a word I had already forgiven him. I had seen his family in action before: laughing, crushing hugs of love and seal stew one minute; booze-soaked insults and late-night brawls the next. Like a see-saw between heaven and hell. We hugged with relief and the dizzying ride continued. In us.

Forgiving had a way of returning power and control to me. I was hooked. So this was what it was all about, I thought. This was the story I'd written so many times. Man beats woman. Woman returns to man. Public scorn and confusion ensue. Only now it was me.

I travelled throughout Nunavut as a reporter for the Iqaluit weekly, but few communities were as stunning as Pond Inlet, David's hometown. I covered a conference there in the midst of my madness with him. I had come to know many of Nunavut's leaders. Some were losing the battle with drugs and alcohol; others were worn and wise. They liked to tease the white reporter, and I accepted it as part of my initiation. I was a stranger, and like other transients before me, I would eventually leave. They knew that.

It was a large conference to discuss how the Nunavut

land claim would be settled. Drum dancers and throat singers performed as they would have centuries ago. Men and women cut raw seal and caribou on cardboard on the hall floor and shared news with bloodied lips and hands.

I tried to join in their feast. The caribou and whale blubber were palatable, but I couldn't get near the walrus. In traditional fashion, it had been wrapped in skins and stored for weeks under rocks. The rotting flesh was grey-green and glistening. I retreated to the back of the room to eat vending machine chips with Inuit teenagers.

❧

I tried suicide that year, if you can call it that. Was I trying to fit in? Centuries' worth of Inuit fortitude was fraying among the young, who were killing themselves in alarming numbers. Lost somewhere between raw meat on the land and microwaveable Big Macs at the corner store, they struggled in my world and I in theirs.

It happened a few nights after my neighbours called the RCMP. David was throwing bottles and shouting death threats through thin apartment walls. I spent hours at the cop shop that night in my ripped flowered dress with my shins and forearms raw from his blows. Was this the first time he had attacked me? asked the officer. No. He found me a pack of cigarettes and I wrote out my statements, thinking maybe I should have hidden beneath a house instead.

Days later, I caught a glimpse in the bathroom mirror and did not recognize myself. Someone else's empty eyes. Some poor sucker's flat, grey face. I stared for a long time, wondering how my own flesh could abandon me. My phone calls to old friends and family back home that night left me quietly weeping into the shrill ringing. This final betrayal by my own body felt like an omen.

Then the tears stopped and everything turned slow motion. Calm.

I got a bedsheet from the closet and tied it to the shower-curtain rod for a noose. But when I tested my weight with my arms, the rod gave way and I fell tumbling into the tub. As I sat there with a sore ass and the metal rod on my lap, I started to laugh. My plan was absurd and the result slapstick. I laughed myself straight. Then I went to bed.

I played a lot of hockey that year. It was a welcome distraction and one of the few healthy hobbies I had. Most of my teammates were Inuit, and I made fast friends. For several, it was the only escape from brutal spouses who broke their jaws and hearts. Beneath elbow pads and helmets, they were invincible. They carved deep lines in the ice and barrelled to the net with ferocious intent.

I gathered the courage one night with my female drinking buddies to tell my secret. They nodded and poured more vodka from a bootlegger's bottle. Then they rolled up sleeves and pant legs and we compared scars like old soldiers in a perverted contest to see who was the bravest of the broken. I was unrecognizable even to myself, but here I was normal. It's frightening how fast you fall when the people who love you aren't there to see you slip.

In the end, I dug a firewall to stop the flame from spreading. I told my dad. Oh, not every detail, but enough. "I've pressed charges," I said into the phone. "There will probably be a trial. And then I will come home." I could feel his alarm building by the way he cleared his throat and reached clumsily for something other than "I see," and "Um-hmm." Eventually he found the words. Was I okay? He was sending me a plane ticket. There was no shame in leaving. He wanted me gone. Soon, I told him. Promise.

Mom told me later that he'd spent days alone in the garage after that call, occupying restless hands and quelling the urge to rescue me. I had no choice. My heart was long broken, but telling him meant I was now responsible for his. The rabbit couldn't hide this time. I had set a trap.

David pleaded guilty. Denied nothing. It saved me the publicity of the stand, and I was grateful but not surprised. He never had trouble admitting what was happening. He just had trouble making it stop. Sort of like me.

I didn't have any real therapy afterwards. I tried peer counselling once, but the other woman's story was so horrific that I spent most of my time interviewing her and then left feeling fortunate. She had real problems, I thought. Everything was going to be fine.

Now I stare at these words and wonder how I managed to pull them out without breaking apart. Recalled one by one, the scattered memories had always been manageable. Combined, they felt heavier and more lethal. If nothing else, completing this puzzle has forced me to reveal all the dirty little pieces to my husband, my family and my friends. And there is relief in the telling.

Variations

Like Mother,
Like Daughter

Maggie Dwyer

Our mother leans down to kiss her daughters good-night. Her cheeks are sweet with the scents of powder and rouge. Where are you going? we cry. In our cries she hears a slightly indignant tone. Where is she going without us? It must be a weekend when her father is visiting and watching over the household. She has a date with Dad.

She cherishes the first valentine he gave her. Their courtship was a simple one. He was a close friend of her brother's, and they met at one of the dances that were held in local homes in the final years of the Great Depression. Both families were members of St. Patrick's Church at Kinkora, P.E.I. Their grandparents and great-grandparents, early settlers from Cork and Kerry, were buried side by side in the cemetery and memorialized in stained-glass windows given to the church in their honour. Their marriage banns were read out here, but they didn't hear them. Following the local custom, they had slipped away to attend Mass in a neighbouring parish, avoiding the initial reaction from the crush of well-wishers. It was as if they had eloped. Their friends and neighbours held a wedding shower for them at the church hall and wrote a loving letter of good wishes. They married in September 1940, after the harvest was in and my mother was free to leave her widowed father and brothers.

Their deep and enduring love was the inspiration and foundation for their partnership in marriage and family life. We didn't always have much, she says, but we always shared. Their early married years were spent in northern Ontario at Kirkland Lake, where my father sold magazine subscriptions. Mom contracted a serious illness there and lost her first pregnancy. It would be five years before my older sister was born. Long awaited and happily welcomed.

Their next move was south to Waterloo, where he worked as a machinist during wartime and she as a clerk in a jewellery store. After a few months she gave up this job, which she enjoyed, at Dad's request—women did not work outside the home unless economics required it. She stayed at home from then on.

Several pairs of white high-top leather shoes are lined up in a precise row. It is late in the evening, and Mom has finished polishing them. The thin, chalky smell of the polish hangs in the kitchen air. This is the last on her long list of daily duties. It is after eight in the evening, and her little girls are upstairs in bed. The house is quiet, and she will sit down with her husband now, to read the newspaper and listen to the radio. My mother says she had all of us in these shoes to the age of six, in keeping with the wisdom of her day concerning what was best for young feet.

In those years, homemaking and caring for children were labour-intensive—think of the meals, the laundry and ironing, the cleaning. Six daughters born within ten years and the birth of the youngest celebrated with the gift of a fur coat for their mother. My sisters and I grew up in a house where the linen was fresh, the meals made from scratch, the furniture gleaming, our hair curled in ringlets and our little white shoes polished. There was laughter, music and kindness. We accepted it all in the selfish way of children. She knew the true value of her work. If we forgot to compliment her on yet another delicious meal, we were reminded. She would quietly say, "Well, I guess that tomorrow night, I'll put a bale of hay in the middle of the table. . . ." We'd hurry to make amends and pour her tea.

On a warm afternoon in a long summer season of canning, Mom is efficiently quartering pears. I am breaking a clove into quarters and inhaling its pungent scent while I listen to a story about how she and her mother and sister managed the cooking for a threshing crew of twenty men.

A woman's work on the family farm was essential, respected within the family. The work and roles of men and women were distinct and separate but complementary and accorded equal value. Women looked after the house but were not permitted inside the barn. Mom recalls that her father allowed women to come to the door but no farther. She tells us with pleasure that on days when her mother had to go to town, which meant Stratford, "She wouldn't have the buggy out of the drive before I started to bake." She was ten when she began, and her pastry has always been light. She excelled in the domestic arts, and this excellence was the reason Dad gained forty pounds in their first year together.

Mom has many stories and sayings about women and kitchens, recipes and providing hospitality. One of my favourites, on the occasion of unexpected dinner guests: if you haven't got much to put out, use your best tablecloth. In our house the cloth was white damask and the dishes were her mother's.

On another occasion one of us invited a boyfriend at the last minute. Before grace was said, a whisper went around the kitchen. We took such modest portions that there were unexpected leftovers. "Go easy on the duck" is a remark that still brings a laugh when we are setting an extra plate.

A fifty-seven-year-old woman in her first pantsuit. It is 1970 and my father has been dead for two years. Now, after the early intense mourning has passed, Mom has found a job. The women's revolution is gearing up. She begins working as a clerk at an insurance firm.

Recently, when we were speaking of my elder sister's coming birthday, she commented, "Fifty-seven, that's when my life began again." She got a new look—a work wardrobe—found new friends, travelled and enjoyed her status and her own paycheque.

She has infected us with her love of fashion and good grooming. Her weekly trip to the hairdresser is a must. She delights in having good-looking clothes in her closet: a fashionable black suit, pretty dresses and scarves, sports clothes and "something lovely in the back of my closet so I am ready to accept any invitation." A pretty pair of shoes is a favourite item—she very reluctantly gave up wearing high heels in the middle of her ninth decade. She was delighted to find a stylish coat for this, her eighty-ninth winter and beamed when I told her she looked pretty with the soft fur collar at her neck.

Often when I visit my mother, we take a drive "up home." She points out the handsome red-brick two-storey house and the window of the bedroom where she was born. It pleases us to see that the family name remains on the deed. She is the one who knows the histories of its generations and much about the forty families that made up the membership of the local parish. Each person, the life and the accomplishments, has value as comedy, tragedy or drama. She is the one who remembers. Especially the details of the women's stories. She is the matriarch now, the eldest surviving on both sides of the family tree, and her status is important to her.

My mother provided a model for the role of a wife and mother that was time-honoured, the norm in our Ontario city where few married women worked outside the home. This was the world I knew, and in my youthful ignorance, I imagined that life went on virtually the same way in homes everywhere in Canada. After I left home to attend nursing school, I was shocked to hear other girls trashing their mothers by belittling their lives or claiming to hate them.

And yet in my young adult years, all aspects of a woman's domestic life bored me. I did not really appreciate the worth of my mother's work—until I became a mother myself. This was in the early days of the women's movement, and although *woman* was being transformed into *goddess*, it would not do, politically, to be like the most familiar of women, our mothers. The role of wife and mother was last on the list of choices for my generation.

Although I admired my mother and the way she lived her life, I knew I had choices. I wanted something more. As a teenager and young woman, I did not worry about "turning into my mother." I was determined I would not. I sharply dismissed her life as sweet but dull. I saw her as a lovely, intelligent woman who was lucky to marry the man she loved, someone who appreciated her good fortune in having her own home and in not being relegated to the role of spinster sister who kept house for her father and brothers.

I opted for a conventional career, certain that being a nurse would be a ticket to adventure. Through the sixties and into the seventies, I was studying, then living, *really living*, playing, loving and working as a single woman far away from the dull fog of domesticity that seemed to enshroud my mother.

Until my mid-twenties, I resisted the idea of marriage and motherhood. The idea of a conventional marriage and family life filled me with dread. I imagined it to be the narrowest of existences. I was not so much a feminist as a dedicated contrarian—until I fell in love and married at age twenty-seven. The adjustment to becoming a stay-at-home mother was shocking. I was constantly fighting fatigue and worrying that, yes, I was slipping into the dreaded domestic fog. I hadn't been paying attention; I didn't know how to mother. It did not come naturally, unlike the birth process with its inexorable rhythms. I struggled to keep pace with the world, reading the *New Yorker* while I nursed my daughter. I imagined that my life was taking place off to the side of real life.

It was the shock of the now. The needs of my newborn baby demanded precedence over all else. And from then on, the persistent call of my first duty to my daughters. In this transition from self-indulgent career woman to mother, I looked to my mother and others, sisters and friends, who were there before me. We talked and talked and laughed and cried—and I learned. I saw that there were many ways, many styles and strategies I could adopt.

I found that humour is a mother's very good if not best friend. At parties, when asked that dreaded question, What are you doing these days?, I used to answer that I was working on my doctorate in chemistry—the chemistry of laundry stains—and that my thesis was on the differential extrusion of the banana molecule. I claimed to be attending U. of M. By this, I meant I was keeping sane and current by listening to CBC's *Morningside* program during the LaMarsh, Harron and Gzowski years.

Gradually I came to understand the powerful role of mother and to know that there is pleasure in duty. That the years I spent at home were full of wonder and opportunity. That there was time for me and my interests. That in my mother's life, never so sweet, never so dull *for her*, there were challenges, many and varied, and I learned to appreciate and respect how she managed them.

Over the years, Mom has also revised her views and opinions, especially on topics such as women's rights and marriage. If women's lib had been around in my time, she says, things would have been different. She would not have listened to the doctors who insisted on the science of bottle feedings and gave her a new and improved formula for each of her six daughters. She would not have given up her job at the jewellery store. Now she understands how hard it is for young women who have been living and working on their own to stay at home with small children, even if that is what they want. "My job at the insurance company was good," she says. "I got more out of it than the work." She got a new life. She knew her work for pay was important then. Now we know the value of all her work.

To her daughters and their families, Mom is always encouraging, the giver of sound advice for problems of the heart or head. She delights in all our successes and commiserates in our disappointments. Now at eighty-nine, she is so agreeable a model of how to live as a woman and mother that I try not to avoid turning into her but to keep up as gracefully as she has. Like mother, like daughter. It is a high compliment.

Snapshots

Sandra Martin

Snapshots were always kept in a Black Magic chocolate box when I was a child, waiting for the moment when my mother could find the time to paste them into albums. Of course, that moment never came, and we continued to shuffle through the piles—the way we had once dug through the wrappers seeking out the caramels or the Brazil nuts buried in the second layer.

After my mother died, my youngest sister arranged the pictures and gave them to my father as an act of remembrance. When he could finally bring himself to sit down and go through the books with us, I learned the significance of a snap taken of my parents and some friends in March 1946: six happy young people out for a walk on a spring day. Or so I thought.

Now I know that nothing would ever be as promising again as it was on that sunny St. Patrick's Day in the woods north of Ottawa.

The war was over. My father and his friend Syd were alive. They were both newly married and employed—a feat for two boys raised in the Depression. In the picture, my mother is wearing stockings, spectator pumps and a dress under a wool coat with a Persian lamb collar. She is dressed more elegantly than the other women, who are in baggy trousers and lumpy jackets. Being attractively turned out, especially in public, was like a credential on her resumé. When I was old enough to go to dances, she would often ask me afterwards, "Did they say that you look like your mother?"

Standing in front of my father, she is smiling into the camera, one hand in her pocket, her body slightly angled—the way I pose to make myself look slimmer—the other hand holding her gloves. For years I thought her coat was unbuttoned because she was warm in the spring sunshine. In fact, it wouldn't close over the discreet mound that would become my older sister.

The evening after the hike, Syd banged on the door to tell my father he was wanted on the telephone in the lobby of the quadruplex where both young couples lived. It was the priest. My mother's younger brothers, George and Gerald, had drowned the day before. While she was blissfully walking in the woods, her beloved brothers were dying in the frigid waters of Lake Ontario.

My mother was the eldest daughter of six children from a farming family on Wolfe Island, the largest of the Thousand Islands, about three miles by ferry from Kingston. Her life was hard. When she was seven, the family home burned down, and she was sent to the mainland to live with a childless aunt and uncle until her parents could regroup. In later years, my grandmother was flattened by depression, and my mother often had to forgo her own plans to keep house and take care of the younger children.

In a different age, she might have stayed on the island to run the farm, but of course that went, without question, to her older brother. Instead, she moved to the city in the dregs of the Depression and found a job in a pharmacy on the edge of the Queen's University campus. That's how she met my father.

Although she didn't attend classes, she used to say that she felt like a Queen's grad because she never missed a football game or a formal. When asked, "Did you go to Queen's?" she invariably responded, "Queen's came to me."

The boys, as they were always known, had been out partying. They wanted to get home to see their mother for St. Patrick's Day, but the ice was too thin to drive across, and still too thick for the ferry to navigate the passage. Stymied, they hitched a ride in a small, open motorboat. It capsized, and four of the passengers, including the uncles I would never know, drowned.

How my father conveyed the news to my mother, I cannot imagine. Prompted by the hiking picture, he later recalled that "dreadful night" and talked of how the doctor had come to give my mother a sedative. The next morning, they set out in a borrowed car for Kingston. A day later, they went over to the island on the ferry, the ice having cleared by then. My father can still remember sitting in the smoke-filled cabin and feeling the boat rock as the first hearse drove on, and rock again a few minutes later as the second one was loaded.

I don't think my mother ever recovered from this tragedy; she had mothered her younger brothers, who were only twenty-one and nineteen when they died. Ever afterwards, she made it abundantly clear that at least one of her four daughters should have been a son to make up for the enormity of her loss. This lesson was so ingrained that when I was pregnant with my own children, I refused even to think about the sex of the baby I was carrying.

Illness was as familiar as a radio serial when I was growing up. My mother often had the flu or headaches, and I was frequently expected to make dinner or to come home after school to take care of my little sisters. I don't ever remember my mother making breakfast except at Christmas or before we all embarked on a holiday in the family car. When I was in high school, my youngest sister would carry a cup of coffee and a plate of toast to my mother's bedroom before taking herself off to school.

My mother also underwent a number of serious operations; one was a spinal fusion, when I was two, to correct an old back injury. After the operation, she was encased in a cast from her armpits to her thighs.

I can remember standing in bare feet and nightgown beside my older sister, pressing our backs against the wall, while two men in white uniforms carried a body down the staircase. As they passed, a woman I recognized as my mother rose from the pallet and waved goodbye before slumping back down again. I thought that she had died, and that the husky men were taking her to heaven. Now I realize that the only way her cast could be changed was to put her on a stretcher and cart her back to the hospital by ambulance.

Was that Lazarus-like image the reason I didn't pay much attention when I heard she had found a benign lump in her breast? Was it because I had already confronted her death that the threat of the real thing seemed anticlimactic? More likely I was too wrapped up in my own doings. I was newly married and living in England, where my husband was a graduate student.

From a shy, sickly child with her nose in a book, I had become both rebellious and unpredictable, prone to bringing home unsuitable young men and arguing about politics with guests at the dinner table. My insouciant outbursts about the population explosion or the hypocrisy of organized religion enlivened perfunctory conversations about the weather and the royal family, but they upset my mother's precarious sense of decorum.

Even as a little girl, I had been the odd one. My older sister was cute and boisterous, but I, the unexpected second daughter, was a clinger and a crier. My mother would often look at my glasses and my skinny frame and say, "Ugly in the cradle, beautiful at the table," as though wishing were enough to make it happen.

Most teenagers are deeply embarrassed by their parents, but my disaffection for my mother grew more, not less, rancid as I fled from her nagging and her pretensions about "my father's position." It was the seventies and I hated everything she revered: solid, boring, conventional, suburban respectability. And why wouldn't I? I had never been poor, or homeless, or farmed out to relatives.

My first inkling of trouble was a cryptic remark that she made about the lump being malignant after all as we were walking back from a visit to King's College Chapel when my parents came to see us in Cambridge. Shocked, I said the words "breast" and "cancer" and she told me to be quiet because people—complete strangers living not only in a different country but a different continent—might find out.

That imposed silence became the norm through the years of remission and during the final battle. If she brought up the C-word, we could talk gingerly about her illness, although the prognosis was always off limits. I learned never to raise the subject myself or to discuss it with anybody outside the immediate family.

Monitoring the information flow became her way of exercising some control over her life. Often she would forget she had revealed her secret and then accuse us of disloyalty if her confidants inquired about her treatment. She was always afraid that people were comparing her breasts to see which one was augmented with a prosthesis. To this day, I don't know which breast betrayed her.

As the treatment options narrowed, she retreated into a bitter shell. Not even my father could penetrate her blackness. That was the way I saw it then. Now, thirty years later, as I fearfully check my own breasts in the shower, I envision her face flashing with alarm when she first felt that hard nugget.

Our last trip was to a family reunion in the Maritimes. Nobody was to know about my mother's illness, not even my aunts. My mother was too ill to drive to the cottage we had rented, so my husband and I drove from Toronto to Montreal, where my parents lived. While he continued on in the car, my mother and I flew on a packed plane with my son, who was eleven months old, teething and on the move. Nobody had warned her that the air pressure in the plane could affect her already compromised lungs. As the plane bucked and lurched, and I wrestled with my rambunctious son, I glimpsed the fear in her rolling eyes as she gasped for breath. That moment made me ashamed for all the times I had been irritated and impatient when she snapped and complained. For the first time I realized that she was frightened as much as angry. Rage was her camouflage.

My mother's medical and emotional needs increased, and the dynamics shifted as we all tried to help my father care for her. It was as though children and mother were exchanging roles. By the end of the summer, the cancer had invaded her brain stem and she was admitted to hospital. On my next trip to Montreal, I was terrified to go into her room. Would I recognize her without her wig? And would she even know who I was?

She smiled when she heard my voice and opened her eyes briefly before drifting back into fogginess. As I sat by her bedside, I wept out my frustration and grief for silent, stony years wasted in misunderstanding. What she wanted was a daughter who would win the local beauty pageant, marry well and move up a rung in Montreal society. What I wanted was passionate debates about the pill, the Vietnam War and women's liberation. What we both needed was unequivocal love.

The farewell stretched out for nine weeks. Gradually I found that sitting by her side, ministering to her few needs, gave me an unexpected sense of peace and closeness. She was unconscious sometimes, confused at the best of times, but her lashing out vanished. By finally retracting the portcullis that sealed her from "intrusive" sympathy, she allowed us to soothe her anxiety. Her rage had been replaced with sweetness.

In mothering her, I felt mothered in a way that I hadn't since I was a small child. Even though I never had the cathartic conversation that I longed for, I felt content that everything I had wanted to say and hear was conveyed through touch.

To me, the hiking snapshot is one of two photographs that bridge the great tragedies of my mother's life: her brothers' drowning and her own early death from breast cancer. I saw the other picture for the first time the night my mother died. We were huddled in my father's study, sipping Scotch, after returning from the hospital for the final time. Having made the essential phone calls to family and friends, we were sitting there feeling numb, wondering what to do next, when my father suddenly left the room and returned with a photograph that he handed silently to my sisters and me.

Unlike the snapshots in the Black Magic box, this was a glossy eight-by-ten portrait by a professional photographer. My mother was wearing a white mink derby hat and a rose-coloured wool paisley dress. She had a Mona Lisa smile on her face and a sleeping child in her lap.

Perhaps by showing it to us, my father was trying to erase her shrunken, frozen image from our minds. Perhaps he was reminding himself of her beauty. Nobody looking at that picture could guess that my mother was terminally ill or that the smile and the smashing fur hat were female armour.

My father had taught physics at McGill for decades, and my mother, a faculty wife to the core, was determined that night to attend the installation of the new principal, even though a bone scan had just produced alarming results.

As the festivities wore on, she must have become exhausted and quietly found a chair. There, she was discovered by the youngest of the principal's five children, a sleepy little girl looking for a nest. She crawled into my mother's lap, fell asleep, and a press photographer snapped the picture. The child of a relative stranger, that anonymous little girl, is now an icon in my family's mythology. Each of us has a copy of that photograph prominently displayed. I am looking at mine even now.

That little girl sensed something maternal and comforting about my mother. By crawling, uninvited, into a stranger's lap, she unlocked a warmth and a refuge. And that is what I had also done in my mother's hospital room. I broke through the silence in those hours that I left my own family behind and sat by her bedside, holding her hand, knowing she didn't have the strength or the will to resist.

There is no photograph to record it, but somehow I don't need one.

Inside
Talking

Barbara Defago

May 26, 2000

I am sitting in the dark with a stranger, a man. He seems nice, and for some reason I'm feeling sorry for him. Should we turn on the lights? I ask, even though the subject of our meeting seems better left in the dark. He apologizes, saying he's so used to the dark that he hadn't noticed we were in it. He is an expert, and he has come to give me some news. I know what he's going to say just because he's here. I think about him going home to his family on this Friday night and hope that what he has to say to me won't remain with him when he leaves this windowless room.

There are some cases, he starts out, where we know for sure that there's nothing wrong. This is not my case he's referring to, I think. A cyst is a cyst, he says. If I had a cyst, he wouldn't be here. He's warming up now. Then there are other cases. I am one of the others. The man, this doctor, shifts his position from leaning against the desk, arms folded, to sitting on the edge, a bit like Humpty Dumpty with a firm grip. I uncross my right leg and cross my left leg, adjusting the blue gown to thoroughly obscure any hint of breasts. My position in this little chair with wheels is lower than his. I probably look hunched over, protecting myself. I want to bolt but stay, nodding uh-huh, uh-huh as he continues. Sometimes we're suspicious, and in about 50 percent of those cases it turns out to be okay. This is also not my case. Then there are other cases that are more than suspicious. In those situations we might be 75 percent sure but could still be proven wrong. Uh-huh, uh-huh. I know what's coming. This is when I'm feeling sorry for him. The odd time we're very sure—99 percent sure. Which of those cases am I? A voice has just asked the question I don't want answered. It sounds like my voice, but I haven't felt the words coming out. I want my sweater that isn't here and instead wrap myself in my arms. Very sure, he says. Uh-huh, I say. For a split second the room falls away. No desk. No machines. No chair. His eyes are keeping me from falling. I turn my head away just a little and the room comes back. You have breast cancer, he says.

My life is now divided. The past will become *before* and the present and future will be *after*. The four words from this stranger on this day in May in the year 2000 have formed a black vertical mark on the line that is my life. I can see the length of the line to the left only.

June 30, 2000

Morning. Last night as I cruised the hallways attached to fluid on a pole, my chest felt like a gunshot wound—how I imagine one would feel, that is. But today it's more comfortable underneath all the gauze. I'm up. I'm on my feet. Ready to go. Nothing wrong with me. Bet they've never seen anything like this. I'm a bloody medical marvel, I am. I wait until seven to call home. When are you coming to get me? I ask. Charlene, yesterday's admissions nurse, is just starting her workday. Hi, how are you doing today? What time did you wake up? She has stopped at her office door to converse with me. Her face is one big smile. This hospital is a warm, cozy place. Oh hi, I say. I woke up around six, I think. No, no, I mean yesterday, after your surgery. I don't know the answer and I'm concerned about why she's asking. Did something go wrong with the anaesthetic? Did they give me too much? Did they have to give me a jump-start to get me back to the land of the living? I do recall the anaesthetist accompanying a post-op patient back to the ward late last night. I was on one of my forays down the hall. He hesitated and looked at me a second time, then smiled and waved. I remember noticing. Maybe he was relieved to see me walking around instead of brain-dead after what I'd put them through yesterday. I say none of this to Charlene. Good luck, she says, ending our conversation.

I head back to my one-night room, stopping briefly to help a co-patient manoeuvre herself and her equipment into the bathroom. My roommate sits stiffly on the edge of her bed, gowned, protecting her chest from whatever might be flying around in the air. She is tiny—looks like a child to me—but tells me she's forty-seven. Her mother has come from Hong Kong to look after her. When did you have your surgery? she asks tentatively. Yesterday? Me too. How come you're up and walking around so well? She's crying now.

Afternoon. I am home from the hospital with my drain pinned to the oversize front-buttoned blouse I have borrowed from my mother. I'm a little less bulky. Dr. D., the surgeon, popped in this a.m. to remove some of the bandages. For the long weekend, she said. I wasn't sure what she thought I might be planning. My underarm yells at me if I forget it's wounded and reach out for something. Can't baby myself, though. It's important to exercise to prevent lymphoedema or Big Arm, as some people call it. Dr. D. phones to say the preliminary report on the nodes looks good, in spite of the fact that one had felt suspicious. *We love her.* A nurse will visit every day to check on my drainage. I haven't looked at my left breast yet, or what remains of it.

July 12, 2000

If my breasts were sisters, one would be the good sister, the other the bad. She's out there letting her presence be known, misbehaving. Good sister is diminutive and well mannered, my left breast has rebelled against the surgical assault by becoming larger, in spite of the great hunks of flesh removed—perhaps the bad sister isn't taking this lying down. Today we all troop into the surgeon's office for the first post-op visit. Lift your arm, turn this way, both arms. . . . The surgeon has a student doctor with her, hopes I don't mind. Of course I don't. I'm happy to offer anything in the way of learning experience. This girl is cute, looks about fifteen, as a lot of people do these days. The surgeon leaves momentarily. This woman literally runs around her office in jogging pants and Nikes. Breast cancer is giving her a lot of business. I chit-chat with the student as I'm sitting on the table with my breasts hanging out. I might be imagining some discomfort on her part, but not taking any chances, I ask a few questions about her education, in a motherly sort of way, trying to ignore my own nakedness.

The surgeon returns and aspirates some fluid from the swollen area in my armpit. Doesn't seem to make too much difference. She's pretty happy with her work, smiling as she examines her sewing. And now what I've been waiting for— the pathology report. It will tell me everything I don't know yet: how bad it is; how far it's spread; how long I have to live; if there's any point in further treatment. All that stuff. My fear is that my cancer is like nothing anybody has ever seen before. I imagine the pathologist calling across the lab, *Holy shit, Norm, come and have a look at this. What the hell?*

Apparently, only surgical queries will be addressed here. Every one of the players in my drama has his or her thing. And this player is in a bit of a hurry. I heard the key words in the pathology report. Nodes negative. Good. "Invasive" was there in some context, even though not lymphatic or vascular. Hmm. Narrow margins. Not good, from what I've read in the books on cancer, but the expert tells me she's not concerned about that. But I'm worried about all those bad cells left behind, escaping as we speak. She tells me I have something known as atypical ductal hyperplasia. I think that means breast tissue reproducing itself at an abnormal rate. You'd never know it from the outside. She says they've learned that women with this kind of tissue are more likely to develop breast cancer. Seems to me like a bit of a chicken-and-egg thing. This could or could not be the only cancer I get. I ask for a copy of the report. Later I will attempt to dissect the language.

My husband and daughter are nearly jumping for joy. Hurray. The nodes are negative. A few months ago they didn't know I had nodes. Now we're ecstatic they're negative. Trying not to dampen their enthusiasm, I say, Hang on a second. Yes, this is good, but this alien, which has hopefully left the premises, had me by the throat in no time. It's very sneaky. Complacency on my part could be an invitation for ambush. We can't claim victory yet.

September 2000

This is radiation month. Every day, Monday to Friday. They have a great system here at the cancer clinic. Patients don't have to think about a thing. They schedule all your appointments, including a weekly visit with the radiation oncologist. For now, my life has been taken out of my hands, and that suits me fine.

On arrival each day, I wait with the other patients, usually not for very long, until they call my name. Radiation is like an X-ray, but not really—maybe somewhere between an X-ray and atomic bomb fallout. I'm alone in a sealed room while the treatment takes place. The heavy door shuts with a bang as the technicians hustle out. Outside they turn switches and dials as they scrutinize me on the screen. These few minutes somehow manage to consume my whole day. There is no pain, but for me it's the mental part. I worry that I might move even a millimetre and get radiated in places that shouldn't be. I even worry about breathing too vigorously. I try not to think about what these invisible rays are doing inside my body. Breaking up remnants of bad tissue? What about the healthy stuff near by? Another cancer survivor told me that radiation is a malevolent force that continues to work away inside your body long after the treatments are over. The target area is very close to my heart.

I've gotten to know the technicians pretty well, under the circumstances. I see the same four in combinations of two each day. Three women and one man. They smile and ask me how I am. Good, I say. I bare my breasts to them with the same lack of modesty I felt when I gave birth to my daughter twenty-two years ago. They line me up on the table, matching ink lines on my chest with lines of light emitted from the machine or somewhere. I'm not really sure exactly what is going on since I can only look straight up at the ceiling. They repeat numbers to each other and make adjustments to the table and my body. Don't try to help, just let us move you, they say. There is a TV screen in this room. I see my name on it. There is music in this room. Something by Tina Turner. Who, I wonder, is in charge of selecting the music to accompany a radiation treatment?

My thoughts bump into one another, fall apart and pile up again. I try to focus on the music or count the number of petals on the ornamental cherry trees in the poster on the ceiling; instead, I listen to the discordant chant of my breathing and the erratic rhythm of my heartbeat. Some days I relent and take half a milligram of a sedative on the way here. Usually my daughter Ashley comes with me, even though I've said I'm quite okay to drive myself. It's nice to have the company. She's decided not to go on a trip this summer, doesn't think she'd have a very good time, considering . . . my condition. She wants to be with me, she says. Not that you need to be looked after or anything like that, she adds. She's my child and she would make it all better for me, if she could. My husband, Nick, has taken some time off work. I think they call it compassionate leave. He accompanies me to some appointments, usually asking more questions than I would like. I always talk to him about that later. Sometimes I'm cranky. I say things like, Next time be quiet, or, If you don't mind I'd prefer to do my own talking. Sometimes I remind him that certain questions are to be asked of certain people at certain times and I'm the only one who can determine all these things with any degree of certainty. My dad drives in with me too. We talk a lot in the car, mainly about this thing I'm going through. He never says it out loud, but I know he's terrified that his daughter could die before him. I cannot tell him otherwise. Some things are too painful for us to talk about. This cancer business has taken over. I cry a lot, but mainly in private. Mood is black, skin is burnt. I am exhausted already and only halfway through this leg of the journey.

The Fall,
and After

Linda Harlos

I am ecstatic about my new job, which provides both intellectual challenge and emotional engagement. I adore my new husband (four years of marriage is still relatively new). After ages of low-maintenance apartment dwelling, I've recently come to cherish the residential mess-in-progress we now call home. For the first time I could remember, no aspect of my forty-something life desperately cried out for major repairs. Gradually, I'd been lulled into enjoying my days without the omnipresent fear of jinxing the future. In the months preceding my diagnosis, I'd catch myself muttering my novel new mantra, "Life is good."

It was October—Breast Cancer Awareness Month—when I, along with about seventeen hundred other Canadian women, became breast-aware with a vengeance. From the beginning of the month, when I first found a small, palpable lump, to Halloween, when I committed to surgery, I was intensely breast-aware every day. In early November, a twelve-by-eleven-by-six-millimetre lump of invasive ductal carcinoma was removed from my left breast.

Lumpectomy alone is no big surgical deal, lending itself to outpatient day surgery under local anaesthetic. The big deal requiring general anesthetic is the slice under the armpit (axillary dissection) to remove lymph nodes to help gauge whether cancer has spread elsewhere in the body. Following this surgery, severed nerves and swelling meant my left arm felt numb and huge. Nerves slowly repaired themselves, replacing numbness with tingling. The closest thing to it that I'd previously experienced was extreme sunburn, albeit never in my armpit. With the swelling, I felt like an involuntary participant in some bizarre novelty race where, instead of having my ankle tethered to another human being, I was obliged to carry a grapefruit under my arm all day. Eventually, zealous performance of the recommended boring exercises yielded results: I lost the grapefruit and the sunburn gradually receded. Within a month, although I would hardly describe things as completely normal, a trip to an indoor driving range inspired me to drag my golf clubs with me to St. Kitts over Christmas.

Taking the opportunity to dip good breast and dented in the Caribbean waters provided a fun distraction. More important, it allowed me to build up a reserve of energy and calm before undergoing my first chemotherapy treatment the day after our return. At this juncture of my adventure tour to the kingdom of the unwell, I calculated that I was probably still hanging around some foreign airport departure lounge. My journey was under way, but the rough stuff hadn't begun yet.

Although my research somewhat prepared me, and I did escape physically unscathed, my first meeting with my oncology team was nonetheless bracing. Because my tumour was relatively small and showed no signs of having spread, I was semi-expecting to be offered "chemo lite."

However, my age and a combination of diagnostic factors pointed in the direction of a full-meal deal. For a combination of reasons (being shit scared probably the strongest), I asked a perfunctory few questions before readily acquiescing to the recommended treatment plan. To extract something resembling informed consent, they then disclosed all of the risks commonly, or rarely, associated with treatment. Some are potentially fatal in their own right (heart damage and leukemia). Others are merely unpleasant, predictable indicators of extreme toxicity.

In addition, chemotherapy offers no guarantees. What an understatement! As my oncologist conceded, there's no guarantee that any individual patient actually requires chemotherapy, since most breast cancer patients are cured by surgery alone. There's currently no reliable way of separating the sheep from the goats. There is also no efficacy guarantee, since the disease spreads and kills some women, despite chemotherapy. Finally, there are no guarantees which, if any, of chemo's side effects will be experienced. It's essentially a crapshoot—you just sign on and take your chances.

Much of what I could look forward to involved ingestion and/or elimination: appetite loss, mouth sores, nausea and/or vomiting, constipation, diarrhea. I wondered how I could suffer from *both* constipation and diarrhea. . . . Would it be one or the other, or would they occur in sequence? Curiosity notwithstanding, I didn't actually want to know.

My husband consoled me with the reminder that no single chemotherapy treatment was likely to make me feel any worse than I had from previous recreational activities. One of my preferred forms of self-inflicted abuse over the past decade has been expeditions to high altitudes, most of them in countries not blessed with North America's bourgeois amenities. Once, my African guide on Mount Kilimanjaro learned enough English-language synonyms for "vomit" to fill a thesaurus over the course of six memorable hours. I've dragged my ass out of a sleeping bag at −20°C, stumbling in the darkness, in a desperate search for a discreet out-of-the-way rock to squat behind. The relief of finding one (kudos to zip-crotch outdoor apparel!) was tempered by the grim realization that if I toppled one way I'd plummet a few thousand metres into Chile, while a fall in the opposite direction would launch me on a similar trajectory into Argentina. Thus, vomiting and diarrhea in a venue with central heating and indoor toilets and no obligation to get up the next day and keep climbing?—*please!*—a walk in the park in fuzzy bunny-head slippers.

The anticipated loss of my limp, thin, mousy hair wasn't cause for vanity tears. I pre-emptively got an extremely short, low-maintenance haircut suitable for expeditions to places lacking running water and mirrors. Chemo then propelled me through stages: first, moulting animal; then, ugly duckling; and finally, bowling ball. When the occasion calls for hair, I now don my blond party head. Friends and near strangers alike assure me that I've traded up. My treatments have managed to rid me of that annoying middle-age shadow moustache and have temporarily made shaving legs and armpits redundant. To help me adjust to cancer's vanity challenges, I attended a seminar that could have been called How to Tart Yourself Up When You Feel Like a Bag of Crap; I left with more free cosmetics than I'd ever owned. Luckily, I still have some eyelashes to which my free mascara can adhere.

Back in 1974, my mother had found a lump larger than mine and underwent more extensive surgery than I did. That era's characteristic secretiveness was part of her package of fears, horrors and burdens. Few facts routinely changed hands in those days, even between family members. The sudden appearance of my mother's wig while she was undergoing treatment led to my juvenile conclusion that her daily trips to the hospital included chemotherapy. Since we didn't discuss it, my private guess was not confirmed. Decades later, while comparing treatment regimens, she surprised me by saying that she hadn't undergone chemotherapy. Her wig, she belatedly assured me, was a result of nothing more dramatic than our genetically shared bad hair.

Keeping secrets costs. Isolation adds immeasurably to the sufferer's pain, so I experienced great relief when I decided to share my lousy news with as many people as was conscionable. I invited recipients of my first widely distributed e-mail on the subject to discuss its contents with mutual friends. One caveat was that they not reverse the intended spirit by talking in hushed tones about "poor Linda." The other was that for the time being, I preferred not to entertain horrific cancer anecdotes. (Once you break the secretiveness taboo, people's sense of what to share can be surprisingly off the wall.)

When e-mails, telephone calls, cards, flowers, gifts and offers of food started arriving after my first mass e-mail, I was initially horrified at the prospect that someone might think I'd shamelessly and opportunistically solicited them by sharing news of my diagnosis. Once the flurry of post-surgical sympathy subsided somewhat, and the ordeal wasn't yet over for me, my only regret was that I lacked the foresight to make my circulation list even larger.

Some difficult and disagreeable life events are inevitably solo experiences, but attending chemotherapy sessions doesn't have to one of them. Friends accompanied me in small swarms, an assortment of amusement devices in tow. During my inaugural treatment we watched *Shrek*. I knew that the anti-nausea drugs were working when, without the slightest flinch, I watched the movie's ogre tuck into a bowl of eyeballs. Between videos and the more or less constant offers of cappuccino, boxes of chocolates and homemade cookies from Tupperware containers, we didn't even get around to playing Scrabble.

I desperately need this cacophony of company, an audience whose existence requires my bravery, even if I have to become a one-dimensional cliché of the perky little survivor to ensure their retention. I need their hugs and casseroles. Someday they may get the full story of this unsettling experience. I don't dare tell it even to myself most days.

What, for example, do I do with the seismic rage? Since the time of my mother's diagnosis, there has been an alarming increase in the number of young women being diagnosed with breast cancer. Inspired by researchers and charities, a cheerleading press reports "amazing cancer breakthroughs" with clockwork regularity. So why do about fifty-five hundred Canadian women still die from breast cancer annually? In the past century, there were at least as many highly publicized wars on cancer as there were major military conflagrations, with approximately the same result as the war to end all wars. Mammography, radiation and chemotherapy have barely budged breast cancer's mortality statistics. (This information so flagrantly violates media reports implying constant progress that I had to read it in not one but two reputable sources before I could believe it.) Most of my friends and relatives, who inhabit the same pink-ribboned hope haze that I did until a few months ago, are incredulous when I tell them. If I notice furrowed brows, wide eyes or frowning mouths, I don't always persist. I need their ongoing support, and hope sells better than fear.

Early on, I had to counsel myself—sometimes daily, sometimes hourly—not to indulge my simmering anger. I need all my emotional energy, and my allies, to persevere through what's still coming. I can't afford to alienate any among my army of caregivers, for whom I am genuinely grateful and on whom I am genuinely dependent. Some sources suggest that anger can distract from recovery. Self-interest suggests that I defer any fits of indignation.

Camouflaged by my periodic fury is something even more disconcerting—immobilizing fear. I'm afraid of dying before I've lived "enough," whatever that means. I'd always assumed, based on longevity in my maternal line, that "enough" included entitlement to a three-digit age. Instead I'm currently struggling with the thought that until now I've been waving hello to the world, while hereafter I'm likely to be waving it a slow, loving goodbye.

Despite apocryphal stories about vile side effects, the worst I've experienced thus far is fatigue, the onset of which is mysteriously inconsistent. Some days I'm a ball of fire; some days I'm an inert blob. But no nausea and nothing else unbearable. And with chemotherapy behind me, the worst is probably over. My surgery was both a technical and a cosmetic success, with healing progressing astonishingly well, according to an assortment of professional and non-professional viewers. The removal of the lump and surrounding margins of healthy tissue initially produced a slight divot. That said, you'd still pick the pair out of a laundry basket as a matched set. (I diligently consumed more than enough ice cream to fill the hollow in the affected breast.) It takes twelve to eighteen months for surgery scars to heal and recede into their permanent state, leaving me plenty of time to decide whether to turn any residual line into a long, thorny stem by having a rosebud tattooed to the end of it.

I've just scanned my screen to see which words the spelling feature doesn't like. It balks at the cancer-specific medical jargon, the same words I wouldn't have recognized just months ago. Should I allege that no one prepared me for this? Or should I admit that before I needed to, anything more than a cursory glance—accompanied by a relieved sigh and a crossing of fingers—at the reality of breast cancer was absolutely nowhere on my priority list?

Lest I'm tempted into Olympic-size self-pity, even a naturally half-empty-glass gal like me can acknowledge that there's room for gratitude amid this crummy experience. There's lots of information and support available. My employer took it on the chin and is cutting me some slack.

My lump placement couldn't have been better for early detection. I had a skilled surgeon and a mercifully quick surgery date. I'm blessed with a sturdy constitution that, remarkably, tolerates and regenerates after each new treatment onslaught. I have a wonderfully supportive spouse, family and friends. I have a secure job, high-quality public health care and two supplementary insurers underwriting everything from prescription drugs to faux hair. I'm aware that not every cancer patient has all these soft landings. I also don't know a single person who hasn't suffered an episode of job hell, or relationship hell, or some version of unsolicited and undeserved misery. Tempting as it is occasionally, nurturing a grievance against the universe would probably be misguided.

By
Choice

Hildegard Martens

When I was a young girl in the 1950s, the thought of getting married was merely a misty, unfocused image in my mind. I never dreamed of a trousseau, a wedding dress or a wedding day. I was struck much more forcibly by the sheer need to survive on our cold and isolated farm in Manitoba. New life and gruesome death seemed to be present everywhere—the horror of witnessing slaughtered animals juxtaposed with the joy of finding a new litter of kittens in the barn loft or seeing a newborn calf.

My parents seemed exhausted much of the time, and we children had an endless list of daily chores—milking cows, feeding calves and chickens, washing the cream separator and the dishes, helping with the cooking and the hoeing in the garden. Electrification did not come to our area until about 1950; this meant melting snow for the wringer washing machine, baking bread in the wood stove in the kitchen and chopping wood or carrying coal from the cellar to feed the Booker stove in the living room.

During this time, I would often look at the postcards and black-and-white photographs my parents had brought from Russia. There were scenes of cherished homes and orchards that had been left in haste, of relatives dressed in quaint clothing looking stoically into the camera and of corpses in open coffins. The pictures spoke to the tragedies my parents had endured when they were still teenagers. My father's oldest brother, mother and father died from typhus they contracted during the flight from their homes following the Russian Revolution of 1917. My mother's family had been well-to-do estate owners who lost everything. Relatives who stayed behind often ended up shot or exiled to Siberia.

I would also study a photograph of my father as a young man in northern Ontario, where he first worked in Canada, holding his baby in his arms and standing beside the open coffin of his first young wife. These pictures both fascinated and frightened me and in a strange way exerted an influence on my life. The potential for tragedy seemed greater than "living happily ever after."

I know now that people who experience horrors of this kind often don't have the emotional energy to deal with their immediate lives but continue to be haunted by their pasts. While saying little about their own lives, my parents would recount incidents about their relatives in Russia over and over again, but in time I tried to shut out their stories and struggled to avoid taking up their burdens.

Psychologists claim that we live out a script, the main outlines of which are set down in childhood. My script seemed to be that of the misunderstood and tragic heroine. I never felt wanted or understood. After a day's work, my parents had little time or emotional resources left over, and as I was the youngest of five, my plea for attention could be the "final straw."

At fifteen I stayed at home to do my Grade 9 by correspondence, at a time when my brothers and sisters had left the farm to attend school or to work. That winter, I became an avid listener of CBC's Metropolitan Opera broadcasts on Saturday afternoons. I particularly liked the romantic tragedies and identified with Desdemona in *Othello* and with Violetta in *La Traviata*—I was capable of a deep, abiding love that I felt sure no man could match.

Boys were certainly in my thoughts throughout my time at residential high school in the late 1950s. My first boyfriend there dumped me with a rather unsentimental letter, so, even in those days, I felt that boys were undependable and innately promiscuous. And perhaps, quite perversely, I wouldn't have been interested in those who were loyal. It felt easier to be the wronged party, perhaps because of the measure of freedom that it afforded.

The only time in my life I ever tried on a white wedding dress was when I was sixteen. I was visiting a girl-friend, who persuaded me to try on her older sister's dress—I remember how its stiff lace scratched my skin and how I felt simultaneously embarrassed and doomed. At the same time, a thrill went through me as I thought of the sexual pleasures I would experience when I married—in the fifties, and in my world, sex before marriage was still a taboo.

By the time I went to university, after a stint of working to earn some money, a second powerful theme began to emerge in my life—equality and financial independence nurtured by the lectures of my favourite professor, a flamboyant Marxist. It seemed to me that the doctrines of Marxism offered an explanation for what had been determining forces in my life. Unequal wealth along with unequal power explained so many things: why, for example, my maternal grandparents in Russia had been stripped of all their wealth by envious poor peasants, and why men, including my father, seemed to think they could simply impose their will on their wives and children.

While I was opening up to a new understanding of my past, boyfriends were still an important part of my life. I was considered pretty, even beautiful, by my classmates who selected me as Snow Queen in my second year of university. The event caused conflicting emotions—pleasure because of the recognition and anguish because I was afraid of being valued primarily for my looks.

Wide reading in feminist literature told me that other women were also chafing against the restrictions and limitations of the times. Books like *The Feminine Mystique* by Betty Friedan and *The Second Sex* by Simone de Beauvoir confirmed my feeling of being trapped by the demands of the traditional female role. The world that opened up through my reading seemed to offer a chance to do what I really wanted—to be financially independent, not beholden to any man; to be an actor in my own life, not a satellite. If someone was to have any glory, I wanted it to be me.

This desire for independence became so strong that it invariably won out whenever I was faced with a choice to marry or not, first with boyfriends in Winnipeg and then again with men in Toronto where I had gone to do a Ph.D. in sociology in 1969. I did agree to marry one man in those early years of graduate school, but I could not accept his notion that if we had children, *his* money would remain *his*, so we parted.

In my mid-thirties, I came up against a problem facing unmarried women of this age who have focused on their careers. What about children? Maternal feelings had been deeply buried for a long time. My lovely Persian cat, who shared my room during my years in student residence at the University of Toronto, returned my mothering with purrs and devotion, but the longing for a human baby would not go away.

I sought out a Gestalt therapy group. Developed by the psychoanalyst Fritz Perls, this therapy was part of the "human potential" movement popular in the sixties and seventies. It seeks to help individuals become fully aware of their wishes, desires and constraints and then to make conscious choices based on this self-knowledge. "Don't tell me what you are thinking," I was told by Gestaltists, "but what are you feeling?" At first, the answer was "nothing." And it seemed that it had been "nothing" for a very long time. After all, who would want to go back to feeling like a wronged heroine?

But Gestalt had an impact, as protective layers were peeled away and I was able to risk feeling vulnerable once again. I subsequently fell in love with an idealistic younger man I met at a Gestalt group meeting and we decided to live together. I felt lucky to have met someone who valued my independence and seemed to want an egalitarian relationship.

The next two years should have been bliss, but they were not. I was thirty-seven and I had my Ph.D., but I felt that time was running out for me to have a baby, and the desire to be a mother was something I couldn't let go. My partner, being seven years younger, did not have these same pressures, and he would not agree to my becoming pregnant. Now I was face to face with a momentous decision. Should I break off this relationship and do it alone, or should I give up my wish to have a baby?

The worst thing I could imagine was to give up my wish to have a baby and then have the relationship with my lover founder several years later. I thought this was a distinct possibility, and that my sacrifice would then have been in vain. We finally separated after wrenching arguments, and while I felt great pain, I also felt a surge of hope. I would do it alone. I didn't have any role models except an early British suffragist, Sylvia Pankhurst, who in 1928, at the age of forty-six, deliberately became pregnant and had a baby boy while single. The chapter in the book *The Fighting Pankhursts* that describes this event is appropriately titled "A Woman of Principle."

I started to put things in place. I secured a good job in government with a pension plan, bought a house and set to furnishing it. I contemplated many methods for becoming pregnant, including asking friends. In fact, one friend considered it briefly but bowed out after consulting his lawyer.

I discussed my plans with a few select women friends and with my oldest sister. Nearly everyone was sympathetic, but most counselled caution. Two friends who were single parents because of divorce pointed out that being a single mother could be difficult; however, my Gestalt therapist, also in her late thirties, gave me her full support, saying, "If this is what you want, do it. Follow your heart." That felt right to me. I did not give a lot of thought to whether this was a socially appropriate course of action. By this stage of my life, I felt that many social conventions were meaningless or even perverse. After all, social conventions had limited women's opportunities for decades.

The end result of my quest to become a single mother was settling on a means I could ethically accept, and in 1983 I gave birth to my son. He is an exceptional person, both intellectually and emotionally, and we share many interests—including a love of Persian cats!

Looking back after nineteen years, I can say that being his mother has brought me the most intense joy imaginable; I have never regretted my decision. In loving my son, I've been able to understand the nature of men in a whole new way. Of course, there have been times when I felt emotionally and physically exhausted—during the nineties I twice became the victim of the "restructuring and downsizing" so commonplace during that decade. My fear of job loss was enormous, not only because I was solely responsible for raising my son, but also because I remembered vividly what it was like to be poor, and how my parents and grandparents had suffered in Russia. And even though, with considerable effort, I was able to find new positions and continue working, those were times when I would have welcomed having an understanding, capable partner.

Did my career suffer because of my choice to become a mother? In many ways it did, primarily because the workplace has largely refused to recognize women's dual roles and to offer more flexible work environments. As well, erroneous assumptions were often made about whether I, a woman with a child, was serious about advancement.

My son may have his own story to tell someday about the extent to which he missed having a father in his life. When he was a little boy, he would often say, "I'm so glad you decided to have me." He certainly knew he was wanted! As he moved into adolescence, we had our share of conflicts, but what is life without differences of opinion?

Ever since my son's birth, my mother, a widow for the past twenty years, has come in the winter to spend a few months with us, visiting, helping out and, in a way, mothering me so that I can in turn mother my son. Even though she is now well into her nineties, her capacity to give to us is undiminished.

Remaining single and becoming a single parent by choice can raise eyebrows even today, and in many ways these topics remain an area of silence in our society. I've seldom been asked why I didn't marry. To those who do ask, especially if I feel they are merely being nosy, I answer, "Just lucky, I guess," although obviously more choice than luck was involved. And as for my choice to become a single mother, very few people ever question me about it. Let's just say if I had to do it all over again, with the same set of circumstances, I would.

Virgin
Crone

Marianne Brandis

Virgin, Mother, Crone. It's a well-recognized triad, the pattern of most women's lives. The Virgin at a certain point becomes a Mother, and eventually a wise woman, a Crone.

But there are some women who bypass the Mother phase and go straight from being a Virgin to being a Crone. This is the kind of woman who, as her younger years pass, reaches an age when she realizes that she is unlikely to marry or, perhaps almost unaware, has chosen not to. She has no children. The woman I'm focusing on lives alone, or virtually alone, so that she has considerable autonomy and solitude. She doesn't fit many of the conditions usually taken to define women's lives. She has a different centre and different priorities.

The Virgin-Mother-Crone triad assumes that the experience of being a Mother is essential to the Crone's wisdom: it's the only kind of experience that's even considered. But what kind of Crone does a woman become who has never been a Mother? What kind of person is the middle-aged woman who is not a Mother but is definitely on the way to

Cronehood? Is the wisdom of the Virgin Crone different from that of the Crone who is a Mother?

It was in my early twenties—in about 1960—that I began thinking about marriage and singleness. I got along well with men; also—but on a different track, as it were—I had frequent and mostly humiliating crushes on them. I disliked the idea of spending the rest of my life alone, but at the same time I was attracted to solitude and independence. I realized that I was most fully myself when studying, researching, reading, writing.

The crushes were an imaginative search for the kind of husband I could visualize having. In spite of vague visions of being married, however, I never pictured myself as a housewife and mother. The only kind of marriage I could contemplate was one without children.

I began to realize that I might remain single. Sometimes I regarded the prospect with a gloomy sense that there was no other possible destiny for someone as awkward and eccentric as I. At other times, I was more positive: if I was single I could travel, be free, live as I wanted to.

Examples of married life were all around me, in real life and in books and movies, but I knew very few older women who were single in the sense that I've defined it. The single and solitary women around me were either young, not yet married but intending and expecting to, or they were widows, mostly with children and grandchildren. Women who had jobs or professions also had husbands and children. None of these were models for the sort of life I was warily contemplating. The one or two older single women I knew didn't talk about their lives, and I didn't ask them. I should have. I should have regarded them as Virgins on the way to becoming Crones, possessors of a wisdom far more rare than that of a Mother.

In my journal I was trying to weigh the alternatives, visualize both kinds of life—the novelist-to-be sketching scenarios, writing imaginary biographies. It would have been helpful to have more images of how a single woman lived, both outwardly and inside herself, images that might have guided me through all the innumerable choices, many of them unconscious and instinctive, that shape a life.

There were very few. Older single women at that time were mostly silent about their lifestyle, knowing that in spite of their professional and other achievements—which might be considerable, and highly respected—they were regarded as living incomplete lives. Nobody articulated this; nobody needed to. With women friends of my own age I talked about men, but never, to my recollection (and according to my journal), did we discuss the possibility that we might remain single. We didn't consider how we would design our lives if (heaven forbid) that was what happened. Being single would mean being a reject: you didn't contemplate that, let alone plan for it, least of all choose it.

Therefore we were living provisional, temporary lives. Sooner or later this transitional period would end and "real life" start. While waiting, some of us had a good time. I did too, occasionally, but as I moved through my twenties I felt increasingly uncertain, unfocused, depressed, desperate. The year of my M.A. studies was particularly bad. Where was I going from here? Should I work toward a Ph.D.? Find a job? What sort of job? Writing, which was what I really wanted to do, would almost certainly not earn me a livelihood, so something else was needed.

There was no one moment when I decided to remain single. None of those men proposed to me, so I never actually said no, though I must have been giving "no" signals to them as well as to myself. I was eccentric and introverted, and for these and other reasons I was probably best suited to single life. Though at the time it was socially impermissible to live according to this inner blueprint, I did remain single, and I did become a writer. While I was half-heartedly trying to do the expected thing, something inside me followed my individual blueprint as much as possible.

I had two assets that helped me to shape a single life. My mother never pushed me into marriage; in fact, she occasionally spoke of the possibility that I might never marry, and she accepted that. Also, we were immigrants; we had come from Holland when I was eight. I had watched my parents draft a new blueprint for us, as all immigrants do, and I knew that it could be done.

At whatever age it is—thirty? thirty-five? forty?—the woman who is still single has to invent a life that's different from the one she had probably expected to have. It requires creativity and courage, as well as common sense.

When I reached that stage, what I needed was a clearer, prouder image of the kind of person I was, the kind of life I wanted. Something in me—no doubt the same part that had been speculating about singleness—had already been collecting ideas. In books, I had come across a few images of unmarried professional women, with briefcases and tailored suits, their lives centred on absorbing and important work. I knew about the Victorian ladies who travelled to out-of-the-way parts of the planet, botanizing, sketching, writing—but they were not all single. And there was the very attractive image of the graduate student, whose life is transitional but acceptably so. Teaching English at Ryerson Polytechnic University in Toronto, and researching and writing books—as I eventually did—had a graduate-student feel about it. My life is still much like that, the transitional quality long ago made permanent.

A few images came from the lives of single men that, especially in literature, tended in past times to be seen in a more attractive light than those of single women. One of my favourites was of a man sitting by a fireplace in the evening, reading. No doubt women did so too, but the picture I have comes from the time when women, especially those leading non-traditional lives, were less visible than they are now. My image was of a man totally absorbed, oblivious to but sheltered and nourished by the atmosphere of books, firelight and lamplight, comfortable and slightly shabby furniture. There's no sign of wife or children. I savoured that image.

These, then, are some of the experiences that a woman like me might bring into Cronehood. Not being "chosen," or being chosen but saying no. Muddling through a decade, more or less, of indecisiveness, unable to shape a very definite life of her own because "anything might happen." Then, gradually or suddenly, realizing that nothing is going to happen, that she had better get on with it, regard as permanent what has been temporary. Perhaps she has a sense that this is second best—not necessarily because she thinks so but because society tells her so—which may lead to a deep-seated feeling of being wrong and unacceptable.

And then, perhaps to her surprise, she may come to accept it and perhaps even rejoice in it, delight in having the opportunity to be as fully as possible what she has it in her to be.

Some of my best times now are spent sitting in my armchair, by the fire, under a lamp, with a book. I've made this image real. This is me, now, and I'm sitting in my own house, by my own fireplace, reading—researcher, writer, perpetual student. The house is full of books and papers and all the clutter of a full-time writer.

I reached this point by indirect ways—oblique and confused on the surface, with many turns that even now I can't label as being right or wrong, but largely guided by that inner sense of what I really needed and wanted. I abandoned the ideas—serious enough at the time—of becoming a media personality or an economics professor. Instead, I worked for four years as a writer for radio, then for twenty-three years taught university English. All along, I was learning to be a writer, and eventually my books began to be published.

I'm self-employed now and work at home; I have to make a point of going out to where the people are, of inviting them here. Social life is extremely important to me, but it is always framed by solitude, and that is how I like it. I sometimes miss the casual companionship that comes from sharing a roof with someone, but I need the solitude and the space. Like a solitary tree, I grow mostly according to my nature and choices, shaped by soil and weather but with an open area around me. Mostly I love that space; what brings on my darker moods is not some simple form of loneliness. Having 360 degrees all to myself can be difficult, but it can also be a pleasure.

I'm not defined by a relationship to a husband and children. I've never had to centre myself on them, nor have I been the centre of their lives. In my adult years I've never lived with anyone for long enough to have my eccentric corners rubbed off. My primary focus is my writing and what's needed to make it possible, which includes the whole structure of house, garden, intellectual stimulation, connections with other people and time spent alone.

Being single means that I'm not always firmly fixed in my age and generation; I often surprise myself by thinking like a younger or an older person. Immigration and many moves within Canada kept me comparatively rootless, and the wide-ranging imagination needed for writing made all connections temporary, provisional.

All these elements are part of who I am now, and I carry them with me into old age. At sixty-three, I'm on the way to becoming a Crone. When I get there, I will have travelled by a different road from that taken by the traditional Crone, for whom the Mother phase is assumed to be central. But the road I took need not be defined in terms of negatives, of things lacking—at least no more so than any other course of life. It has an identity and pattern of its own, and the process of shaping it continues.

Debonding

Faith Johnston

A year ago my husband played seven games of racquetball with his twenty-one-year-old son. Then he drove home, grabbed a pillow from the bedroom and flopped on the living room couch to watch a football game. It was there that I found him hours later. His death was a fluke, a sort of accident. If only he had not been so competitive (he won all seven games). If only he had recognized the symptoms of heart distress (a bottle of antacid was open beside the sink). If only I had been home.

I have a cousin who has been widowed twice. Her first husband was killed in a construction accident. Her second husband died in his sixties, after a series of strokes. Someday, she says, she will draw up a list—the advantages and disadvantages of a sudden death versus a long lingering death. She is a very crusty lady but a sympathetic one, and in the early days after my own husband's death she phoned often and sent me cheery e-mails. She had been out for a walk on a lovely day. She had been to a quilting convention. Life goes on, she seemed to be saying. God is good.

And of course, she's right. We are a resilient species. Even at the moment of finding my husband's body, I had begun the process of reconciling myself to the hard fact of his death. My poor darling, I thought, your life has been stolen away; you will miss so much. But at the same time I told myself that he didn't know, that he hadn't a clue, that there were worse deaths than falling asleep on your living room couch. I still go back to those thoughts, to that night, over and over again. Perhaps that is one of the disadvantages of a sudden death: the tendency to get stuck in that moment, like a car mired in the mud, its wheels spinning. There's no going back, but there's no going forward either.

It was New Year's Eve. I had just arrived home from four days with my own children on the West Coast. All the comings and goings, the logistics of supporting a blended family of five children, so daunting at first, had become almost routine. The children were in their twenties and living on their own. We had been married eight years and considered ourselves extraordinarily lucky.

That luck had changed. I was no longer the woman who had found love again in her forties—a sort of fairy tale we like to believe. ("Do you mind," said a friend, "if I tell your story to my family studies class?") Now I was a widow, and I didn't like that word at all. I felt that I had been thrust into old age prematurely.

My apartment block is full of widows, doughty women who always have a cheerful word when we meet in the elevator or the laundry room. How do they do it, I wondered, year after year—all those dinners eaten alone? "Widows," I said to my daughter, "widows everywhere. Did you know that widowers are seven times more likely to remarry than widows?" She told me I was being morbid and bought me a copy of *Rolling Stone* with a cover photo of Courtney Love, topless. "She's a widow, too," she said.

But I wasn't convinced. It was so clear to me, in those early days, that the best of my life was over. The future seemed entirely bleak. There was the money to travel, to do whatever I wanted to do, but I was sure there would be no pleasure in anything, so what was the point? I thought of the grandchildren yet to come, of taking care of them by myself, half the pleasure lost. I felt a new kinship with all the lonely people in the world. I thought of a friend, childless, widowed in her forties, who tended to latch on to men who treated her badly. I had listened to her sad stories but never really understood. Now I did. There are times, I have discovered, when even a scrap of attention is better than nothing at all.

It was as if I had crossed an invisible line into a new world in which I had more in common with the panhandlers I met on my walks than with my friends who were still in pairs. I was needy not for money but for attention, for love, for hope. I was not depressed in any classic sense. I read late and slept eventually, I had the energy to go for long walks, and I took up again all the activities that were mine alone and had not involved my husband. Still there was a lot of time left, a lot of life left. What would I do with it? Get a job? Buy a house and start a garden? Keep a cat? None of these ideas appealed to me. I had just retired from teaching and had no need, no desire, to reconstruct that phase of my life.

"You must learn to become good company to yourself," a wise friend advised. Yes, I said to myself, take your own interests more seriously. Don't be ruled too much by the need for companionship. But emotionally I seemed to have reverted to adolescence. I bounced around as if on a bungee cord, one minute up, soaring, the next minute entirely glum.

There was a man I would often meet in the mornings when I jogged down the crescent and into a park along the river. He was a slight, bony man with blue eyes, who smiled and said hello and then was off and on his way. He had a jaunty sort of walk. I could imagine him crossing a desert with the same self-assurance, stepping out briskly, wearing his Tilley hat and carrying a newspaper, his springer spaniel following obediently behind. My husband was that sort of man, happy with his routines, energetic, optimistic. I wondered if this man had a wife. Already I could picture the two of us, in our housecoats, sharing the Saturday papers.

Then one day, in the same park, I met a blond woman in a pink shirt throwing a stick for a springer spaniel. The wife! My heart sank, all my fantasies dashed in one blow. But later the same day, I ran across the same pair and realized that it wasn't the right dog at all—far too shaggy and ill kept. There was still hope! I blush to tell you this story now, it's so ridiculous. But there it is—that's how I felt. I wanted a replacement, and even a small grain of hope was enough to set me off.

I've been writing in the past tense as if I have come through and become a more sensible person, but that's not the whole truth. I realize more and more that I am the same person I always was—cool on the surface, but willing to follow my romantic heart wherever it leads me. At twelve I fell in love with the paperboy (and he wasn't the first!). I have never broken the habit of loving men; I've never seriously thought of trying. If the man in the Tilley hat should happen to be single, and if he should one day break his stride and invite me along, I cannot imagine saying no. But in the meantime, I'm not holding my breath.

When you live alone, work comes easily. For play and growth you need other people—close friends who love you despite your annoying quirks (isn't that what husbands are for?). If you knew me, you would say I have many such friends, but still they are not enough. The married ones are busy with families and careers. The single ones have developed their defences. We approach one another warily, fearing excessive demands on our time, fearing rejection. How easy it is to appear needy and ridiculous!

Developing intimate relationships in middle age is daunting, but what is the alternative? Burying myself in books? Becoming a counter? I fear becoming a counter. It seems to run in the family. One of my grandmothers (widowed early) counted the buds on her rosebushes; an old cousin (also widowed early) counted her slights, tallied them up in a long list. Someday others, too, would know what it meant to be alone. Then they would be sorry for neglecting her—and I, of course, was one of the culprits. May I not become a counter.

How will I find that balance of work and play that nourishes us all, whether we are young or old? I don't know yet. It seems that everything in my life has changed, that every relationship is in the process of realignment. It is not a simple matter of replacement, after all. No person can replace another. Perhaps, someday, my husband will become one of my many ghosts, a missing piece of myself, but only a small piece, one I can live without. Meanwhile, I must make every effort to look forward, for I know that if I look back, I will spend the rest of my life loving someone who is dead.

A year after my husband's death, there is a belated New Year's dinner at my sister-in-law's house. Everyone in my husband's family is there, happy to be together again. The feeling of caring and congeniality goes far beyond the usual command performance.

A year ago on this day, we were planning a funeral, and a few nights before that my husband's youngest son smashed his fist into a brick wall when he learned of his father's death. None of us will ever forget that night, but we do not speak about it—it's rather like the war. I was born during the war, but growing up I never heard a thing about it. I'd like to ask my stepson about his father's last hours. What did they talk about? What was my husband thinking? Was he happy? We've had many private conversations in the past year, but I have never dared ask these questions.

The oldest son takes his father's place at the head of the table and carves the ham. When we play cards, he is the scorekeeper. There is no debate about any of this—no discussion at all. It's as if his father were still present, guiding his behaviour. But the appearance of normality is deceptive; our common link has been broken, and we are into something new, into forging a new set of relationships, and though I am not sure what my place in this family will be, I am determined to stay. I had often viewed my stepfamily as a burden, but now I see it more and more as a blessing. Is it possible that in the past year I have grown in wisdom?

I know only that my loneliness and despair are subsiding. I still cannot look back, but I can live fairly comfortably in the present. The merry-go-round of life may have dropped me off, unceremoniously, back where I started, thirty years ago, but I'm not the only one. Like other women whose lives have been filled with people but who are now alone, I am standing here waiting to choose my horse, ready for another go.

In memory of Barry Boothe, 1944–2000

Mother
Interrupted

Sarah Harvey

Good mothers don't want to drop their newborn babies on their heads. I understood that. At thirty-one, I wasn't young, stupid or inexperienced. I had a seven-year-old son I adored. I had wanted a second child, albeit for some fairly dubious reasons, and now I was terrified of her and even more terrified of myself. How had I come to be standing in my kitchen on a perfect autumn day, contemplating infanticide?

It was 1981, and I had been married for eight years to a man I had come to loathe and fear. Isolated from my friends and unwilling to confide in my family, I decided to have another child, since being a mother was the only thing that brought me any joy. My husband was out of work, and we had run out of money and moved in with my parents, whom my husband detested (the feeling was mutual). My daughter was conceived in my parents' four-poster bed while my mother played duets with my son on the grand piano downstairs. Mozart, as I recall, something cheerful and sunny to herald the beginning of what would become a nightmare pregnancy. At five months, I went into labour and was told by an obstetrician that if my baby was born, it would die. Left alone, hooked up to an IV, watching a machine that monitored my baby's heart, I struggled with fear and pain and a powerful desire to rip the IV from my arm and run—away from my husband, my children, my future.

When the contractions finally stopped, I was sent home with strict instructions to spend the rest of my pregnancy lying down. I could forget about working in the garden. Even lifting a full kettle of water was forbidden. I read a lot of biographies that spring and summer—other people's lives being infinitely preferable to my own—and worried about the significance of every passing twinge and pang. I did my best to look after my son, although I failed to play an adequately animated Robin to his Batman. When I was eight months pregnant, he broke his arm in a fall from our backyard apple tree—he was Superman that day—and I cringed when a nurse asked me what I had been doing when he fell. "Lying on the couch," I replied. "Reading a book." When the labour finally began, one day after the due date, it was swift and, if not painless, certainly the most fun I've ever had in a hospital. I was elated. My daughter and I had both survived, my son was happy to have a baby sister, and I could go home and carry on doing what I did best.

A month later, I was wondering what would happen to the baby (and me) if I dropped her on her head. Would I be arrested? Would my son be able to visit me in prison? Would I be able to get a full night's sleep and eat a good meal? As the days wore on and my anxiety deepened, I became utterly unable to care for Fiona—I couldn't nurse her or even be trusted to prepare formula. I cried every time she cried, and even changing her diapers exhausted and repulsed me. A picture of me taken at the time shows a woman I barely recognize—gaunt, unsmiling, standing next to my frowning husband, grimly clutching a crying baby and wearing the ugliest apron in the known universe. I felt no connection with the baby in my skinny arms, only unendurable anxiety, paralyzing shame, unfathomable depression and enormous guilt. Adrienne Rich says that "the first knowledge any woman has of warmth, nourishment, tenderness, security, sensuality, mutuality, comes from her mother." If that was true, my little girl was out of luck.

By the time Fiona was two months old, I was, to put it kindly, a basket case. Well-meaning friends talked about the "baby blues" and predicted I would "snap out of it" as soon as I found my bootstraps and pulled on them. Nevertheless, I sank further into the squid-ink darkness of my depression. My chronically optimistic mother, who was by then looking after both children, agreed with my husband, for the first and last time, that I needed help. When I became incoherent—about the same time dehydration and weight loss gave me the skin of a ninety-year-old and the body of a twelve-year-old—my father, a doctor, quietly had me admitted to hospital under the care of a psychiatrist who was also a family friend. From her accent and her interest in my relationship with my father, I assumed she was a Freudian, but by that point, I was beyond caring who looked after me and where. I would have accepted treatment from Satan himself as long as he gave me something to help me sleep. Preferably all day. Preferably somewhere far away from my crying baby.

I ended up in the local psychiatric facility, and I got my wish—round-the-clock drugs and no baby. I missed my son, but there were routines to learn and group therapy sessions to attend. I learned that you didn't have to get dressed, but that self-loathing increases exponentially with every day that you don't get out of your pyjamas. I learned the secret of pouring tea from cheap metal teapots, a skill that remains useful to this day. I learned the fine art of lining up for meds. I learned which patients were harmless and which were likely to pounce on you as you came out of the shower. I learned that hospital dietitians can be capricious and cruel. I learned that clothes are important even in a mental hospital. I learned that if you reveal something right away in group therapy sessions, it encourages others to speak and you can then be silent. I learned that everybody, from the anorexics to the schizophrenics, from the chronic alcoholics to the guy whose wife had just left him for another woman, thought there was something *really* wrong with a woman who couldn't look after her children.

For the first few days, I lay in bed, sleeping or weeping, waiting for the next round of medication or a visit from my husband, who vacillated between bewilderment and rage. He spoke often about how difficult his life was. The psychiatrist informed my family that I was suffering from an "agitated depression." She told me to get out of bed, get dressed, eat something and prepare myself to have Fiona stay with me until I had bonded with her. Then I could go home. "How will I know when we've bonded?" I asked. "You'll just know" was the enigmatic reply. The thought of my baby in a mental institution propelled me out of bed and down the hall to the nurses' station, where, in an effort to fatten me up, I was fed oddly flavoured protein drinks of a peculiarly viscous consistency. In the evenings, while Fiona slept and everyone else watched television, I managed to complete an Icelandic sweater with an intricate cream-and-black pattern. Why I was allowed to have knitting needles in a psych ward remains a mystery to me, but there I sat, night after night, knitting and purling, counting the stitches, counting the rows, counting the minutes until my next pill.

One evening, a particularly tough female patient glared at me and said, "You're one of them innaleckshuls, aren't you?" It was the first time I had heard the word "intellectual" used as a pejorative, and I dropped a stitch in my rush to deny it. I was curious, however, about what had tipped her off, since I hadn't exactly been dazzling my fellow inmates with my wit and erudition. "It's your pants," she replied. "Only innaleckshuls wear that kinda corduroy." She wandered off, and I laughed for the first time in a month. That day at lunchtime, I took the next step toward freedom: I ate solid food. An unfortunate episode with some parsnips masquerading as french fries set me back a few days, but I persevered and was soon enjoying such delicacies as Jell-O with canned fruit cocktail and soggy tuna casserole.

When Fiona, ten weeks old and by far the cutest resident of the ward, disappeared from my room one morning while I was in the bathroom, I was as frantic as any "normal" mother of a missing child. As I searched the ward for my tiny daughter, it occurred to me that I must love her, after all. Why else would I care where she had gone and who had taken her? Why else would I feel that my heart was about to explode? When I finally found her asleep in the arms of the old fellow in the next room (no bonding problems there), I knew that I was prepared to eat whatever was put in front of me and spill my guts in group therapy if that's what it took to get home.

Two weeks passed, then three. I was eating and sleeping and missing my son, who hated visiting the hospital. I went home on day passes and took my meds. Only one person, an elderly pediatrician, told me not to worry so much about bonding with my baby. No one suggested there might be a hormonal component to my condition. No one asked me about my miserable marriage. No one informed me that postpartum depression often disappears with the simple passage of time and the judicious use of appropriate antidepressants. No one told me I was a good mother. After I'd spent a month in the hospital, my bond with Fiona was deemed sufficiently strengthened, and I was allowed to go home. I was calmer (and heavier) when I left the hospital but still terrified, this time of losing everything I loved.

In the months following my release, I cared for my children with a passion bordering on the paranoid, certain that one day they would denounce me. I imagined Fiona standing in her crib in her pink OshKosh overalls, pointing a pudgy finger at me: *"J'accuse."* But every bedtime story, every trip to the library, every messy meal, every new word, every sandcastle, every card game, every swimming lesson reinforced my sense that I could be a good, if not particularly patient, mother. I began to enjoy my children again and enjoy myself with them. My confidence grew, and two years after Fiona was born, I left my marriage, taking the children with me.

The years that followed tested my resolve on a daily basis. What I lacked in patience I made up for in tenacity. My somewhat perverse sense of humour became my greatest asset in the struggle to raise two children alone. When I made tough decisions, I knew that no judgment could ever be as harsh as my own. My son's teenage years were particularly arduous—for both of us—but when I ask what he remembers about that time, he says, quite simply, "You were always there." Not "there for me," just "there," which was often all I could manage. People sometimes ask me if I have forgiven myself for abandoning my children. I ask them if a mother with pneumonia should have to forgive herself for seeking medical attention. I was sick, I received the treatment deemed appropriate at the time and I eventually recovered. End—and beginning—of story.

Because of me and in spite of me, my children are amazing individuals who continue to challenge, educate, infuriate and delight me. My son has no recollection of my temporary absence from his life. My daughter is mystified and somewhat annoyed at the suggestion that we may not have bonded, since all evidence points to the contrary. In the two decades since my "lapse" in mothering, I've come to see that terrible time as a pivotal point in my life, an event that shocked me, defined me and ultimately inspired me to choose the possibility of joy over the certainty of despair. Every day I wear a ring inscribed with the words *Amor Omnia Vincit*—Love Conquers All. Most days I believe it.

They Didn't Come
with Instructions

C.J. Papoutsis

When I was five, someone gave me a toy iron and ironing board for Christmas. That was in the 1950s, when we played with gender-specific toys—dolls, toy stoves and tiny plastic dishes—and little girls expected to get married, have babies and be homemakers.

My mother said that one day I would find a kind, generous man to look after me. We would get married, I would clean his house, cook and have babies. That's what women did. It never occurred to me, or my mother, that I might not enjoy cleaning, cooking or babies, or that there might be other choices.

I did marry a kind, generous man. He came from Athens, Greece, with strong opinions about who in the family did what, but time passed and our roles became blurred. Laundry, housework and cooking got done—by whom didn't matter after a while.

Growing up as an only child, I'd never had much to do with babies. My mother's stories about the miracle of birth and instant bonding didn't prepare me for reality. I bombed out of motherhood when the delivery room nurse gave me our daughter to hold, moments after her birth. My frail self-esteem crumpled when she scowled and pushed me away with the strength of a wrestler. The veins on her head stood out and her face turned bright red. She opened her mouth back to her ears and shrieked like a dentist's drill with sporadic gasping noises. By the end of my first week of mothering, my main impressions were that babies were loud, smelly, sticky and felt as if they were broken. I also discovered that although my talents were many, non-stop nurturing and caregiving weren't among them.

Our new family member forced us to live without sleep. Every night around eleven-thirty we bundled her up and hit the road in our drafty 1961 Buick Electra convertible. It had a hole in its muffler and sounded like footage from a Hell's Angels movie. The little despot slept as long as we kept moving and started screaming again the minute we returned home and shut off the engine. Our landlord disliked our wailing baby and our raucous Buick, so he evicted us.

I had given up trying to pacify our daughter. My husband had no luck either. Everyone said she had colic, but nobody could tell me what colic was or what to do about it. Woodward's Gripe Water was supposed to help, but dipping her soother in wine was the only thing that worked.

I lived in fear of Sudden Infant Death Syndrome. If the baby wasn't screaming, I'd jiggle the pram to make sure she was breathing. Then she'd wake up and howl for another two hours. The kid had me figured out. She knew I was frightened and incompetent. Her job was to expose me as an impostor, and she took her work seriously.

I cried, raged and hated myself. I felt like a tired, used-up loser in a saggy, stretched-out body and wanted my pre-baby figure back. My husband wondered who this woman from hell was and what I'd done with his wife. He loved me. We had a healthy, beautiful daughter. What *was* my problem?

I hated being a mother. Being responsible for someone's life gave me anxiety attacks and a dependency on Rolaids. I was a spoiled, immature twenty-year-old and scared stiff something awful would happen to my child and everyone would blame me. Motherhood was the final exam; I hadn't studied and got caught cheating. My emotions terrified me, but I couldn't tell anyone because such feelings were considered unnatural back then.

When I arrived for my six-week checkup in tears, raving about suicide as a community service, my doctor decided I had "baby blues," a euphemism for post-natal depression. He prescribed Valium. That's what doctors did in 1969. Valium didn't cure post-natal depression. I still had it. I just didn't care.

Nobody told me that babies start growing teeth at three months with a whole new repertoire of symptoms. We tried teething rings and oral jellies, but an old Greek lady told me to dip my finger in brandy and rub it on the baby's gums. There's probably something in the Criminal Code now for people who do that. Brandy wasn't an instant cure, but it gave me a chance to gather my frayed wits occasionally and may have saved our daughter from shaken baby syndrome, something we hear about often these days. She hasn't become an alcoholic either.

It took me eight months to recover from post-natal depression. Just in time to get pregnant again. Our daughter was seventeen months old when our son joined the family. His arrival was less traumatic because our daughter had already broken us in. We had surrendered to sleep deprivation and were sliding toward full-on psychosis, but then this little guy liked to sleep and only cried when he had a good reason. My post-natal depression lasted three months. This time I took up yoga, not Valium.

Meanwhile our eldest, not to be upstaged by her baby brother, developed a red, scaly diaper rash that conjured up images of jungle body rot. She was allergic to the first two creams the dermatologist prescribed, and in a few days the rash covered her entire body. Strangers peering into the pram jumped back, demanding to know if she was infectious. It took three weeks to get the rash under control so we could take her out in public without attracting a crowd.

Our daughter was allergic to dust, animals, some drugs and many foods. My husband, who grew up hungry during wartime in Greece, couldn't understand anyone, especially his child, being allergic to food and thought it was down-right ungrateful to be allergic to medicine.

The year our children were four and five, we decided to give our first family portrait as Christmas gifts. Both kids woke up with pink eye the day of our photographer's appointment. My husband thought we should admit defeat and cancel, but I spent all morning applying warm camomile tea bags to the children's crusty, swollen eyes, hoping they might look human by picture time. A few distant relatives still remember us as those rumpled people with their two sad children squinting at the camera through red, half-closed eyes. It took us twenty-five years to gather enough courage to sit for another family portrait.

By the time our son was two, I'd been a homemaker long enough. Never good at repetitive tasks, I completely lost it over potty training. Spending two months teaching someone to pee in a container wasn't mentally stimulating enough, so I got an entry-level government job, which was kind of like potty training but with pay. My first year working, half of my monthly salary paid for daycare. Since I enjoyed the social contact, I justified the economic disaster by calling it an investment in mental health. It was, except for the guilt. Dropping the children at daycare every morning made me feel I was abandoning them so I could have fun and get paid for it. It was like saying, Here, I don't want these kids any more. You take them and I'll give you money.

My guilt never went away. It roiled just below the surface, then washed over me without warning. When the children were older and we left them at school, I felt bereft when our little shapeless bundles of winter clothing waved goodbye from behind the chain-link fence in the schoolyard. They could have been poster children for a refugee camp.

187

As a supporter of the women's liberation movement, I had earned myself the right to work full-time, keep a perfect house, cook gourmet meals and raise exceptional kids. I was a pioneer. One of the first generation of superwomen raising the first generation of superchildren. To ease my guilt and prove my kids weren't disadvantaged because their mother worked, I nagged, tricked and bribed them to swim before they walked, read before they started school, excel at sports, play musical instruments, look good in designer clothes and graduate in the top 10 percent of their class, even if it was only kindergarten. I wanted to give them a head start in this cutthroat world, to give them a competitive edge—hopefully without pushing them over one.

When my mother cautioned, "Children whose mothers work spend all their time on street corners and become criminals," I had to prove her wrong. Our kids were twelve years old before they ever crossed a street by themselves.

Our daughter started ballet lessons when she was three. Our son was a member at two golf courses when he was ten. They played soccer, hockey, basketball, baseball, volleyball— if it was round, they chased it, threw it, kicked it or hit it with a stick. Our kids had no time to daydream or gaze into space. Their lives were so structured that we only saw them in the car on the way to and from school, games or classes. We lived like gypsies, except instead of a caravan we drove around in an old station wagon full of ballet costumes, sports equipment, fast-food wrappers and half-eaten fruit. When our son's teacher complained about the messy handwriting in his homework assignments, he told her, "I can't help it, my dad takes the corners too fast."

I loved my kids but never enjoyed them—their vulnerability intimidated me. I wanted to do everything right but didn't know how. They didn't come with instructions.

I had no idea what fear was until I had children. Fear for someone you love is a thousand times worse than fear for yourself.

Some people are born with a strong nurturing instinct. Some of us have to learn it. When I finally grew up and stopped beating myself over the head for not being wife and mother of the year, I realized we had been blessed.

Our adult children are gifted in different ways; one is artistic, one is business-minded. More important, they are loving, kind and never miss a chance to laugh. How this happened is both a miracle and a mystery. You need a licence to drive a car, own a dog or buy a gun. Any fool can have a baby. Many have three or four. Some parents do everything right and their children grow up to be axe murderers. We had no idea what we were doing, and ours turned out just fine.

Glimpses

On the
Water's Edge

Ingeborg Boyens

Monday morning at an aging public pool in Winnipeg. I am wearing a black polyester bathing suit, built for functionality if not style. The chlorine vapours envelop me as I walk along the pool's edge, diligently focused on the business of not falling on the damp tiles. With one hand skimming the wall—nonchalantly, I hope—I pick my way through the neon-coloured Styrofoam "noodles" abandoned by the last aquasize class. As I walk down the stairs into the water, I feel its liquid coolness inching up my ankles . . . calves . . . knees . . . thighs. . . . In my imagination, my serviceable black suit is transformed into a diaphanous silk skirt pooling on the surface of the water. I slide in, elegance personified, as the water flushes away the pain and awkwardness of my former dry-land stumbling.

Welcome to my weekly Aquasize for MS class. I was diagnosed with multiple sclerosis about fifteen years ago. The orders my brain issues to my errant body misfire and lurch down nerves scarred where their protective sheathing has worn away. My body, which is supposed to be lithe and beautiful in its feminine prime, is mere ballast outside this pool. I am in my mid-forties, but I totter and stumble through life like one of those frail women in her mid-eighties we used to see timidly teetering along the aisles of the old Eaton's. I walk on invisible stilts; the mere flapping of a butterfly's wings a mile away will inexplicably upset my precarious balance. My hands are muffled in oven mitts; my handwriting has deteriorated to an awkward scrawl that even I can no longer read. My mouth is filled with marbles; the words I try to enunciate come out rattled and slurred.

It wasn't always like this. I used to swim laps, ride bicycles and dance until I dropped. In the flush of youthful conceit, I used to stride about with never a thought for the simple task of locomotion. I took my body for granted, assumed it would pilot me on an adventuresome course through life. However, the hazards of unseen geological events have detoured my route. Yawning, volcanic fissures often split the sidewalk, mountain ranges dredged up by the snowplough appear along winter streets and giant rolling hills emerge from a buckled carpet. Daily life with chronic illness has become a course in extreme adventuring.

It is some small consolation that I am not alone. I know there are thousands of victims of chronic disease who, like me, muddle along trying to figure out how to live a life largely defined by its losses. My medical encyclopedia lists with numbing repetition how chronic illness—usually auto-immune disease—affects women more frequently than men, and typically in the prime of their lives: arthritis, irritable bowel syndrome, scleroderma, systemic lupus erythematosus, fibromyalgia, chronic fatigue syndrome, seasonal affective disorder and my own personal brand of disability, MS.

I wish there were comfort in the sisterhood of the sick. But even if there were, I still would yearn to fit into a society that doesn't really have a place for me. It's a society that celebrates youth, beauty and sexiness. The ugly walking shoes and the unsightly industrial canes that are the backdrop of my life are a reminder that someone whose body is flawed by chronic illness has no business thinking of herself in those terms. Our society also expects a woman to be the chief caregiver, the one who kisses the skinned knee and applies the Band-Aid. What happens when it is the caregiver who needs the care? And in a society that encourages women to "do it all," a woman is also supposed to be the household manager and a productive member of the working world. How can I be a part of this world? I have no children and no job, and I have always been an unenthusiastic housekeeper.

I remember how life with my illness began. I was in my early thirties, with a new husband and a stimulating job as a television reporter. My life was ordinary in every way. Like many other women, I had walked down the aisle, gone camping in the rain, backpacked through Europe. But then I began to feel an odd tingling in my hands and feet. On the courts, my racquet missed the ball more than usual. I was curiously dizzy as I tried to write my TV scripts in the passenger seat of the CBC van as the camera operator raced us back to the station. Stress, I thought, in that familiar chorus of dismissal. But then came the day when my weekly game of racquetball fell apart completely. Not only did I lose— which was indignity enough—but I collapsed. My hands and feet simply refused to obey the commands I issued.

My neurologist knew something was wrong when he called on me to do a simple dexterity test. My task was to touch my finger to his and then touch my nose. I managed to reach his fingertip just fine, but the return trip was more problematic. I stuck my finger directly into my eye. That triggered a round of those high-tech tests with the peculiar acronyms. And then came the diagnosis. "It is not fatal," the doctor said, no doubt thinking he was passing on good news. He told me MS was an incurable chronic degenerative disorder of the central nervous system in which the myelin sheath that coats the nerves like insulation on a wire is eaten away and replaced by scar tissue that interrupts the nerves' signals. The menu of symptoms I could expect included pain, malaise, fatigue, dizziness, numbness, slurring, tremours, lack of co-ordination and balance, visual problems, paralysis, loss of bladder and bowel control, sexual disability and maybe cognitive dysfunction. He told me the disease could be virtually benign or could put me in a wheelchair for life. It could come and go or it could relentlessly progress. We would know its course better in about five years. "Good luck," he said.

After those not-so-consoling words came the assignment of learning to live with the solitary reality of chronic illness. At first I thought about it incessantly, worrying about the unpredictable nature of the disease, wondering if I would be able to walk the next morning. But that grew tiresome. MS didn't land me in hospital or a wheelchair. Instead, it became my private torment, something I was unwilling to share with my employers or my acquaintances.

Five years later, I still walked the four blocks to work, though I arrived sweaty and exhausted. I still lived in a two-storey house, though I had to clutch the handrail going down the stairs. But I felt it could have been so much worse. I played the Pollyanna Glad Game. Oh, I'm glad I'm not in a wheelchair, I thought. I can do this.

But there were inevitable costs. Five years of limbo, of marking time, ruined the chance of having a family. I hadn't wanted to saddle my husband with children if I should be too disabled to play a full role in their care. By the time we had both adjusted to my illness, most of my thirties were behind me. We could not defy nature. I was fated to look at other people's children playing outside the front window. I would never hold a newborn of mine in my untrustworthy hands.

The next casualty was my job. By then I was a documentary producer and I had convinced myself—and my bosses—that I was doing okay. But all that self-deception collapsed when a friend told me a colleague of mine had asked her if I had a drinking problem. A few days later, while I was on an out-of-town shoot, a farmer bluntly asked me what was wrong with me. I found myself sobbing uncontrollably. It was obvious that it was time to begin weaning myself off the working world. I started by reducing my hours. And then, with the guidance of a sympathetic human resources officer at the CBC, I finally admitted to myself I could no longer manage.

Family, career—that's how many women measure their self-worth. Those were now gone for me. However, the story of chronic disease is also told in smaller losses. It hurt that I had to give away my bike after admitting to myself that not even training wheels would help me keep my balance. And I hated having to abandon those early-morning neighbourhood jaunts with the dog. I finally recognized the problem was not that Brigadier couldn't walk on a lead, the problem was I couldn't walk on the other end of it.

I have been spared those horrible attacks that some people with relapsing-remitting MS suffer. Instead, my version of the disease has seen a slow and steady worsening punctuated only by periods of crippling self-pity. These days, I have an uneasy relationship with my disobedient body. I can no longer sew on a button, pick up a toddler, or braid my hair. I walk with a cane, equipped with a macabre spike for Winnipeg winters. My eyes are cast down, focused on my feet and the sudden challenge a crack in the sidewalk or swell in the snow might pose. I pick my way down the stairs, clinging desperately to the handrail, legs wide for stability. I bounce off walls, miss doorways and smash into doorframes in a fashion worthy of *The Three Stooges*. I try to remember to laugh.

Spontaneity has disappeared from my life. I visualize what I am going to wear, how I am going to get to where I am going and where the bathrooms are. Much to the toe-tapping frustration of my husband, it takes forever to fasten my jacket zipper or to tie my recalcitrant shoelaces.

My adventures are small these days, limited to the unexplained falls that leave onlookers perplexed and me embarrassed. Like the other night at the dog park when I unceremoniously tipped over. Solicitous hands reached out to hoist me up. There were the inevitable questions: "Did you trip?" "Did some dog bump you?" From my vantage point prone on the snow I saw my dog, ridiculously sturdy on his four feet, turning his snooty Airedale head away. Could that be canine embarrassment?

Like my dog, our human society also operates on the principle of denial. People don't want to confront my failings, so they apply a quick, dismissive label in their minds. The simple stamp ("she has MS!") renders me essentially invisible. MS looms large in my life, but I am not the personification of a disease. I want to shout out, I still buy sanitary napkins, fuss about "good fats" and "bad fats" and worry about the ever-deepening wrinkles around my eyes . . . just like everyone else! However, I resolved years ago that I would play by the rules. After all, nobody likes a grumpy cripple. I've learned the correct answer to the question "How are you doing?" is a simple, bright "Fine. And you?"

It is only the children, who have yet to learn the rules of polite discourse, who are direct in acknowledging my frailties. It is the precocious five-year-old next door who asks with admirable curiosity, "Why do you have that cane?" At a suburban restaurant, I find the three-year-old at the next table staring at me with unchecked, round-eyed inquisitiveness. I am an oddity: sitting alone at a table for four that typically would be occupied by a mother, a grandmother and two kids. His brown eyes widen into open fascination as I heave myself up with my trusty cane and wobble out of the restaurant. I can hear his mother hissing at him, "Sshh. Don't say anything."

The fact is, I am an ordinary person trying hard not to let this stupid condition overwhelm my life. I have tried all of those pointless and desperate attempts at a "cure." I have applied good nutrition, moderate exercise, a healthy lifestyle and old-fashioned determination to my "problem." I have taken all the "wellness" courses. I have seen naturopaths, homeopaths, physical therapists, massage therapists—the works. I know the comfortable clichés that are supposed to banish the troubles of chronic illness: "the glass is half full," "live each day as if it is your last," "take pleasure in the small things." There is some truth in all these philosophical encouragements. Yet the bitter reality is that every new symptom brings another flush of panic, along with the cold fear of the further loss of independence and the requirement for yet another accommodation. A friend with MS told me she had managed to find relief from her symptoms . . . when she was undergoing chemotherapy for breast cancer.

I have learned—sort of—to accept the frailties of my blemished body. Not to love the embarrassments they cause me but perhaps to accept them. I recognize there are compensations. The forced immobility of MS has brought me to this computer and re-awakened my love of writing. I doubt I ever could have written two books if I was galloping from adventure to adventure, without a thought for the more reflective moments that make up a life examined.

I think my physical failings have softened the brittle edges of my personality and made me more open to the shortcomings in others. I am more sympathetic, thanks to MS, and less easily disappointed. Are these the qualities, I wonder, that have convinced my husband to overlook the tedium, the worry and the extra work that MS brings to a relationship? I am well aware that dismally few marriages

199

survive the test of chronic disease. I am so grateful that mine, somehow, has beaten the odds.

I have come to recognize that other people can be just as awkward, clumsy or gauche as I. Just this bleary-eyed morning, in an effort to open a new pack of coffee, my husband, Gregg, speared the scissors into it, spraying ground coffee across the sink, counter, stove, toaster and coffee maker. Hours later, when I found still more coffee on the kitchen floor, I realized I didn't have a monopoly on MS-style blunders.

Chronic disease defies normal storytelling principles. There may be a beginning, but there is no climax or satisfying ending. MS is just a long, boring accumulation of losses that no one wants to hear about. I still hope for a cure, a chance to re-engage a life as a participant rather than an observer. But I would settle for learning how to live life—particularly a downsized one—well.

And once a week, at my aquasize class, I shed the awkward body that has redefined my life. In the pool, my twitching muscles are salved by the grace of water. In the pool, we victims become athletes—the canes, walkers and wheelchairs of dry land left behind. Freed of the constraints of gravity, I reclaim the form I lost. Strong. Subtle. Lithe. In my element, I am a mermaid cutting fluidly through the water, my legs turned tail, slapping the water in pure exuberance.

Nobody
Needs to Know

Mary J. Breen

I started out as a nine-month secret. It was 1944, and my mother at forty-one discovered she was pregnant with me, her first and only child. Instead of openly rejoicing, my parents decided to tell no one but the village doctor—not one person in their families, not one of their friends. So well did my mother fool people by standing very straight and continuing to wear her sturdy corset that when I was born, the village busybody travelled all the way to the city hospital to see for herself; she couldn't believe that Mrs. Breen was in the maternity ward.

My mother considered their close-mouthed behaviour a perfect model for me to follow. Secrets were the norm; "nobody needs to know" was the rule. There were no end of things I was not to mention, from who had been over playing bridge the night before, to what my father's family had done for a living, to where we'd gone on a holiday. The one really big thing I was *never, ever* to tell anyone was this: my parents had owned and run a prosperous movie theatre for six years when I was a young child. Then television arrived, and everyone stopped coming because they preferred staying home to watch *Hockey Night in Canada* and *I Love Lucy*. Our theatre, like thousands across North America, closed its doors. Soon afterwards, we moved to another town, where my father returned to high school teaching, and I was told to keep my vivid memories of the theatre to myself. It was as if I'd been put in a witness protection program, and my real past had been erased. So strong was this taboo that as I write these words now, forty-five years later, my stomach tightens up, and I want to beg you never to tell a soul.

None of the other things I was forbidden to speak of seemed at all important. They weren't the "good" secrets I had heard whispered in the schoolyard, the kind that are irresistibly better passed on than kept to oneself. Nor were they the life-or-death ones I read about in books—no murders or spies or mad relatives in the attic—but just stories of ordinary people doing ordinary things. I couldn't understand how we could be hurt by anyone knowing that the Breens had been farmers, or that my father had been scouted by a major league baseball team (but had turned it down for some unspoken reason), or that he had had a job other than teaching. It was like being told to hold my breath forever.

I obeyed their secrecy rule, but I didn't like it, and I certainly didn't understand it. I assumed it was somehow connected to their ominous reminders that since we were Catholics in a Protestant town, we needed to keep things close to the chest. Perhaps "they" weren't exactly the enemy, but on the other hand, "they" didn't need to know our business. (This old kind of Irish Catholicism may seem strange now, but just thirty years earlier, my parents had experienced the bigotry of Toronto's "No Irish Need Apply" signs, and for them, your religion was still the test of whose side you were on.)

Gradually it became clear to me that not only was I to keep many things secret but many things were being kept secret from me as well, especially about my father. "She doesn't need to know" was the other half of their rule. Although I heard many stories about my mother's family, I learned next to nothing about my father's. Every evening when we said the rosary, we prayed for the repose of the souls of his parents, aunts and uncles, and a sister, people he spoke of with great fondness—but little detail. The only contacts with his two brothers and one sister were Christmas cards and occasional letters that, of course, I wasn't allowed to read. We didn't visit them, and they didn't visit us. Once, and only once, a brother came for a short visit. Even though I was only eight or nine at the time, I couldn't help sensing the tangle of love and pity my father felt toward his favourite brother. Of course, I wasn't told why; I was just told not to ask any questions.

I loved my father in the unconditional way children do when they are with someone who gives them endless approval. He was a gentle, handsome, loving man who always had time for me. We spent hours and hours together—playing cards, painting, playing ball, going for walks, fishing, making up math quizzes, doing homework, reading bedtime stories, as well as going to daily Mass and saying our prayers. I have a photo of the two of us, me about eight, my father close to fifty. My hand is in his, and I'm grinning up at the camera, certain that life is full of only good things. That's how I felt around him—except when I'd ask him about his early life. Then his manner would change. Instead of his usual comfortable way, his answers would become brief and uninformative. He wouldn't get cross with me, but until the topic changed, I felt as if a door had closed between us. I was always left hungry to know more.

Of course, memories have a way of popping up unbidden, and sometimes little things did come out. I remember he started calling me Genevieve, his sister's name, when we played cards because he said I teased him exactly as she had done. And once he told me about taking out a new Arabian horse against his father's orders, an unbroken stallion that had thrown and nearly killed him. I also remember one Christmas, as I sat surrounded by gifts, his telling me that when he was young, he and his siblings had received only one orange each. Then there was the story, one he and I both loved, of a boarding house where the woman owner would tuck a loaf of bread right up into her armpit while she cut off chunks and then flung them off the end of her knife to the men. These are not remarkable stories in themselves; what's remarkable is that despite how much time I spent with my father, this was almost all I knew of his past.

The summer I turned sixteen, my parents and I visited his first cousins near the family homestead in the Ottawa Valley. I was astonished to be immediately loved and accepted just because I was his daughter. The only puzzling thing was they all called him Leonard, whereas I thought his name was Larry—short for Lawrence. My mother's explanation was that Leonard was just another of his given names. Despite how happy my father was there, laughing and playing cards in the farmhouse kitchen that had been his home, this was our only visit. It was almost twenty years before I saw any of those cousins again.

I went to university, then off to Malaysia with CUSO. Then came the unthinkable. Instead of heading for a convent as my father had always hoped, I got pregnant, then married in a Protestant church, and—to make it all worse— soon after divorced. I went from being their good child, their top-student-pride-and-joy daughter whom even the priest praised for her "good works" overseas to a fallen Catholic, a divorcée. My father was shattered. When I returned home six months pregnant, he barely spoke. He couldn't even look at me.

I was heartbroken with my own loss and with knowing the anguish I was causing him. I knew his strict Irish Catholicism left him little choice except disapproval and disappointment, but I was still surprised by the extent of his pain. All I could hope was that he wouldn't turn away from me forever, and that his tenderness toward his little grand-daughter would remind him of how he'd once felt about me. I also thought we had lots of time. But I was wrong.

Three years later, while I was living in B.C., he was diagnosed with cancer. Despite painful treatments, he was dying. I returned home, and on the day he died, he hadn't the energy—and I hope no longer the will—to stay turned away from me. He lay in his narrow hospital bed, unable to see more than shadows, and assured me he had left us a little money in his will. As I cried, he held my hand, and for a few minutes I had my father back, back in his old role as my protector, trying to comfort me for all I was about to lose.

Despite our brief reconciliation, the pain and confusion of his rejection never went away; I just put it away, over to the side of my life, not quite in focus, but never out of the picture.

When my mother died seven years later, I took over sending Christmas cards to my father's cousins, and I even managed a few visits. During one of these visits, one of the older women asked me to look through a stack of old photograph albums with her. I was nodding off over page after page of photos of blurry strangers when she nudged me and said, "Look, there's Leonard!" I opened my eyes to see her pointing to a small photo of my father wearing a long black robe.

"But . . . what's he wearing?" I asked, and with that, I was given the key to much of who he was: for nine years, my father had been Brother Lawrence; he had been a Christian Brother!

The earth's plates shifted and resettled; some things now fitted together perfectly, and some were forever upended.

Here it was, an explanation for so much—his extensive knowledge of Latin, his assumptions that I would attend Mass with him every morning and that we would pray four times a day, his use of the name Lawrence. More important, I knew immediately that this was a huge piece of why I had upset him so much.

I pestered every relative and old friend of my parents to learn more, but I've found out only this: he'd entered the Christian Brothers as a boy of sixteen, just after an uncle in the Order, a Brother Lawrence, had died. Brother Lawrence was a man of great promise and drive, and the assumption was that my father would soon fill his shoes, even though he was so young, his personality and interests entirely different. My father went along with the plans of his superiors, even taking the same religious name, but just before his final vows nine years later, he decided to leave that world of teaching, prayer, and obedience. The only explanation for his leaving came from one of his cousins: "I think he met your mother, dear." It's true that my parents were friends by this time, having met several years earlier during teacher training at Toronto Normal School, but if he did leave because of her— and he certainly did love her—they didn't marry for another ten years. Maybe he left because the expectations were too great, or maybe he realized he didn't have a vocation. Maybe something much darker happened. I was given a photo of him at seventeen, and I can barely look at it: this beautiful young man has the saddest eyes I have ever seen.

I was told his sister took to her bed for three days on hearing the news of his leaving the Order, so perhaps he expected the same shock and disapproval from everyone, even from me. Or maybe he was unable to discard the rule within the Order of keeping personal things to oneself—a habit that stayed with him long after he'd left behind the long, black one he'd worn all those nine years. Or maybe he recognized in the choices I made in my life that same ability to put one's own will ahead of God's, and they seemed all too close to the choices he had made forty years earlier; after all, we were so alike.

If only my parents could have seen that this secret, so rooted in attitudes about sexuality, pleasure and will, was going to grow like another member of the family, planted squarely between my father and me. If only they could have known how it would affect his ability to love me.

Perhaps I'm wrong, letting the light of day shine on this secret part of my father's life; maybe nobody *does* need to know, but oh, how important this discovery has been. It's given me a way to understand the depth of his pain, and so, a way to forgive him. But, most of all, it's given me a way to feel my father's love again; it's given me a way to heal my heart.

Toe-Ring

Jennifer L. Schulz

When I close my eyes and imagine myself in five years, I see the *woman-in-the-distance*. She is an elegant, acclaimed academic, firmly placed in the life of intellectual pursuits. She has been shimmering on the horizon of my mind for years, beckoning me. I'm sure that one day, if I work hard enough, I will meet her—I will become her.

This is new for me, openly acknowledging her existence, and already I'm worrying about how this revelation will be received. I'm more accustomed to keeping her to myself because of what I know about the boundaries of female conversation—and what it takes to keep within them. Lately, I've been trying to respect the boundaries without always observing them, so the *woman-in-the-distance* is, as of now, out in the open.

She has been with me for a while. When I was fourteen, I travelled through England with my family. I stood on the banks of the River Cam, near the Bridge of Sighs, at St. John's College, University of Cambridge, and told my parents, "One day, I'll go to school here." Ten years later, on a gorgeous sunny day, walking past the Bridge of Sighs to my grad house with a year's worth of luggage in tow, I felt invincible—full of the potential for scholarly accomplishments. Surrounded by hundreds of years of intellectual prowess, I tried on my first academic gown. That was when I first glimpsed the *woman-in-the-distance* in the mirror. I knew I belonged.

Ever since I was small, intellectual pursuits were my thing. Perhaps I was a strange kid, but I loved school more than anything else, more than ballet, skating, piano—you name it. The other kids would play outside, and I would stay in and read. I loved to learn and still do. There is an exhilarating click for me whenever I master something new and can pass it on to others. This excitement for learning and teaching probably came in part from growing up in an academic home where family trips were fun *and* educational and flash cards were the expected in-car entertainment. At eight, I was the only kid on my block with her own set of encyclopedias, and I was proud of it. At ten, I received my first school-wide prize for academic achievement.

It was the end of Grade 4. I sat with my friends and classmates on the floor in the school gym and watched as other students were called up, class by class, to claim their prizes—certificates for academic accomplishment, most improved academic performance and best school spirit. My name wasn't called. I was crushed. Each year before, I had won a prize for the highest marks in my class. My girlfriends noticed my disappointment and tried to comfort me with their hands on my shoulders and murmurs of reassurance. Then, an award I had never heard of was announced: the John Pritchard Award for top academic achievement in the entire school. My name was called—I had it! Beaming, I strode to the podium and accepted my prize. When I returned to my part of the floor, there were no comments from my friends, no hands on my shoulders. I said, "Isn't this great? I'm so happy." No response. That was when I learned not to talk about my academic successes. Two weeks later, when our report cards came out, I knew I shouldn't mention my grades.

I don't remember whether I made the complete connection when I was ten that no prize meant personal disappointment but comfort from my young female friends, while the top prize meant personal jubilation and a cloud of silence from those same friends. Looking back at that incident now, I see that two significant realizations were cemented for me: the importance of being recognized for my academic interests and accomplishments, and an equally strong need for support and validation from my close female friends. I know I need both, but it has been hard to reconcile the two.

When we were inseparable teenagers, the balance was tipped in favour of support. So many of our successes were the same that it was easy to celebrate them together. Our interest in guys and our "triumphs" with them provided fertile ground for many special connections. We shared so much with each other that it didn't matter that we never talked about school performance. We had each other's support. Between learning how to shave ("use the pink Daisy, and don't shave past your knees"), planning boyfriend-attraction strategies, buying our first tampons ("ick, the scented ones are gross") and relating French-kissing debacles, lifelong friendships were formed. Later, in university, my friends and I met every day in the student centre for lunch and continued our intimate conversations. To demonstrate our bond, we bought toe-rings. Not just any toe-rings—no plain, silver, slightly etched toe-rings for us. We bought sparkly, gem-encrusted toe-rings, and we wore them all the time. Especially during our daily soap-opera-watching ritual. Toe-ring on foot and remote control in hand, each of us knew what our favourite characters and villains were up to, because we had time enough to attend classes, philosophize and watch TV. Although I continued to observe my silence around academic accomplishments—even through law school, I steadfastly avoided comparing marks and discussing class rankings—our boundless connections made our conversational bounds less important.

The bounds matter to me now. The importance of talking about my academic pursuits with my women friends has grown for me since I became a professor in a faculty of law. As my friends have married and had children, we have moved from talking about boys to talking about birthing boys, but the silence around my interests persists.

Our primary topics of conversation are children, religion and money—none of which relate directly to my life. We talk about children, even though I don't have any. Why? Maybe it's because I always ask about them. I ask because their kids are cute, because I really am interested and because I'm afraid we won't have anything else to talk about. If I don't ask about their children, we might talk about religion. Then I'd have to reveal that I neither practice our religion nor am I clear that I believe in God—heretical, I fear, in a group where we all went to Sunday school together. So, fine then, on to money.

Well, without children, my partner and I do not worry as much about economic planning and financial forfeiting, so the topic of money is not as central in our house. (In fact, it's not even a house; we live in a converted loft. Living in a loft with no children and no plans for any apparently does not compute.) Besides, we have separate money—there are no consultations before we spend, and consequently there are no issues, at least none for us. For some of my friends, this lack of shared money is bewildering and indicative of a lack of a "plan." "Without a plan, how can you be stable, together, united?" I am left with nothing on the approved list of topics to talk about.

Why do wonderful, intelligent women feel free to discuss athletic, artistic or birthing success, but not brain success? Why the silence around intellectual and academic achievements? Full-time moms are expected to be proud of and talk about their achievements—their children. That's part of the job of good mothering, and we celebrate it. On the other hand, descriptions of intellectual success are *not* encouraged. I am not expected to talk about my successes and am not celebrated for them in the same way. Perhaps a focus on academic accomplishments is just that—academic. It might be too removed from the daily activities of full-time mothering, or perhaps it is too much a part of the world of men. What I do know is that there is very little space in which to talk about my professional interests, and as a result, validation from some of my women friends is hard to come by.

And then there is the problem that talking about intellectual success is seen as bragging, especially if you are a woman. (Remember Mom's good advice to keep the bragging in the family?) Intellectual ability seems to be accepted as something we are born with, not something we work for—and we shouldn't boast about the things we're born with. So it's a double whammy: first, such accomplishments fit better in the world of men, and second, if we are lucky enough to garner some despite that, we shouldn't display pride in them. Since there is no control over brains and we don't work for them, we must be silent about our "brain" accomplishments.

Woman can, though, it seems to me, trumpet success in areas of struggle. If we are born thin and stay thin, we don't boast about it—we didn't work to get there. But if a woman was overweight and then loses seventy pounds, she can flaunt that because everyone knows she worked for it. Similarly, women seem able to recount their athletic and artistic successes because these accomplishments involve struggle in an obvious way. Athletes must exercise, train and sweat, so their successes are deserved. Being artistic also involves toil—the sculptor laments the loss of her funding in her chilly garret. Even the new mother can describe the pain that culminated in her drug-free birthing success. But cerebral success? I get the impression that some think it takes no particular skill, is innate and involves no struggle. Well, like metabolic rate, there is something to be said for heredity, and yes, some of us got lucky; however, it takes tremendous effort to translate that initial advantage into something tangible in the world.

Pursuing intellectual and academic dreams, publishing regularly and commuting hundreds of kilometres to teach every week, as I do, is real work. It's taxing, and it doesn't leave a lot of time for other things. Because there is always more to read, more to write and more to present, the work expands to fit the time available. Consequently, I am always working, always pursuing head-related goals. According to goddess psychology, I would be classified as a brilliant Athena (warrior woman in the world) and a lousy Aphrodite (golden goddess of love). Or, as an old boyfriend once wrote, a person who spends "far too much time over-utilizing that key cerebral organ to decide matters that are best left to that key circulatory organ." But this geographically challenging, intellectually stimulating life of mine works because I'm stuck in my head, not in my heart. I am proud of this, but it has come with some sadness—another area of silence.

I've found that it is impossible to pursue my dreams without leaving at least some relationship wreckage behind. Intellectual strength makes some relationship weakness inevitable. If you think "too much," analyze "too much" or just generally assert your own way "too much," things get tricky. When you are devoted to the *woman-in-the-distance*, you are not devoted to a man. This, quite simply, is problematic in heterosexual relationships. The pursuit of the *woman-in-the-distance* means you can conceive of life without your partner. This can be dangerous or might be liberating, but it most assuredly leaves wreckage in its wake.

When that wreckage begins to pile up, I feel I have failed, and I do not want to admit that to anyone—least of all to some of my women friends, who might not appreciate my life decisions.

I have changed without my long-time women friends. I have lived away from them for years now, and although at first we talked incessantly on the phone and visited frequently, we now miss one another less. When we visit, it's harder to reconnect. Too much time is spent on catching up and getting the news rather than really speaking intimately. Our divergent personal choices have altered our talk, altered our friendships. I don't want the same things they want. Is this because I moved away? I don't think so. More likely I have always wanted different things from many of my women friends, and time, distance and my spouse have helped put that into clearer focus. I did not want a father for potential future children; I wanted a partner. Nor did I want a house in the suburbs. A flat over a bakery in Paris would be more like it. Here in my new city, I have met women who seem to understand these things. We've formed a book club—not a mere book club, though, a salon, as in Coco Chanel, semiotics, oenology and Rodin. (Some of the men we know are threatened; they call us the Sisters of Satan.) Perhaps it is the diversity of the salon—a lawyer, an artist, an accountant, a Wiccan, a Jew, some Christians and a few agnostics—that allows us to applaud one anothers' successes. When success is measured in different ways, one woman's need not intimidate the others.

The conversational taboos diminish when the reference points are different. My friends from home—all mothers, all married, all Mennonite, all homeowners—have matching reference points; they share many of the same traditional indicators of success for women. I've come to realize that a circle of homogeneous girlfriends can silence.

That silence scares me. I think it may mean the end of some of my long-term, much valued friendships, at least on some levels. We have difficulties sharing our successes; it's hard to share the exhilaration of winning Professor of the Year with someone who is disciplining her child and washing the dishes while she listens. And when I'm lost in the minutiae of legal footnoting, my appreciation of the sheer elation over finding the perfect preschool is not nearly as enthusiastic as it should be. I may never connect with the physicality of their love for their children because I may never have a child. They may never connect with my *woman-in-the-distance* because she may not be important to them. But maybe what's important is that one day I will.

I have one eye trained on her at all times, and I am closing the distance. In the meantime, I continue my work, begin doctoral study and keep envisaging. And in between, there are flashes—fantastic, midnight, red-wine conversations that make me think no time has passed. My friends and I talk, for a while, the way we used to. We occasionally even watch our old soap opera, just to make fun of it over the phone. We all still hate the villain, we definitely do not want to work at the cosmetics conglomerate and we laugh together. I look down at my feet. There is the toe-ring. I have a toehold after all.

A Place on
the Pavement

Debbie Culbertson

My father holds my new second-hand bike steady on the cracked sidewalk in front of our grey stucco house. He has just come home from work at the sewing machine store. His bow tie is gone, and his white pressed shirt is open at the neck. I can smell du Maurier cigarettes and Old Spice as I climb onto the bike's smooth black seat and reach for the handlebars. My father smiles as my feet find the pedals. Then I'm gliding along while he runs beside me, one hand resting on the back fender. I'm laughing and my hair is flying in the air while his stays Brylcreemed to his scalp. Suddenly he lets go of the bike, and I glide, wobble and bump over broken sidewalks, whirring past wide front porches, grape-vined gardens and rusty Chevys. When I stop, my feet dragging on the broken concrete, I turn and look back. He is gone.

That fall, my father leaves my mother and disappears from our lives. My stay-at-home mother finds work in a canning factory, goes back to school and cries at night. There are no new school clothes, and the fridge is often empty. I make a promise to myself that if I ever have children, I will never leave them and will always be there to catch their backward glances.

In my teens I pursue a kind of working-class normalcy. I am going to be a secretary, marry a nice boy and have a houseful of children. I take typing and shorthand, date boys who drive fast cars on back roads, cut classes to walk along the railroad tracks. Panic sets in as my eighteenth birthday draws closer. I want to be in control of my life but have created a situation where I will be as economically dependent on men as my mother has been.

I become a model student. I study hard, cram four wasted years in high school into a few months. Although I am accepted into university, I cannot entirely escape, cannot reach for the ring without wearing one. At eighteen, uncertain about survival on my own, I marry my best friend. We become one of the thousands of young Canadian couples who survive on married-student loans in the late 1970s.

When Jonathan is born, I'm in the second semester of my master's degree. It's a time when women play tapes of Beethoven next to their pregnant bellies and prepare flash cards for their infant children. I read *Free to Be You and Me*, tape *National Geographic* maps on the wall beside Jon's crib and lay him on sheets printed with primary colours.

It is the height of the second wave of feminism. I nurse Jonathan while writing papers on women's history, rock him to sleep while reading Adrienne Rich's *Of Woman Born*. Sometimes he attends classes with me, zippered into a front carrier next to my heart. Later, we walk hand in hand to the co-op daycare where the faded names of 1960s children are still crayoned on some walls. As my son plays in the sandbox,

I wonder whatever happened to the children named Moonbeam and Summer Skye.

On a warm spring night, I leave Jon with his dad and walk with a thin corridor of women along Toronto's back streets to protest violence against women. We wear black T-shirts emblazoned with "Women Unite, Take Back the Night." I feel a kinship with the women who march beside me, as if we had cut our thumbs and mixed our blood, pledging a lifetime of protests together.

In the summer, Jonathan sleeps in his stroller as I push it along in a massive Toronto peace rally. I walk next to an elderly woman who has been marching for peace since the 1950s, when there were only handfuls of protesters. "We were called names then," she says. "Some of us got beaten up." As we talk, a plastic bag filled with water explodes in front of Jon's stroller. It has been aimed at us from an apartment high above our route.

Some friends and I crowd into a packed lecture hall at the Ontario Institute for Studies in Education. Mary Daly is the featured speaker. The lesbian feminist author of the new book *Gyn/Ecology* delivers a searing condemnation of those institutions she terms patriarchal—the church, the nuclear family and heterosexuality. Her solution is a radical kind of separatism—a women's-only community, a kind of sanctuary and fortress against the dominant society. At the end of the lecture, she invites questions. I raise my hand. "What about women with sons?" I ask. A ripple of laughter runs through the crowd. "I'm afraid I can't help you with that one," she says with a broad smile.

At university I encounter other lesbians. At first, I intellectualize my interest in them, treat my curiosity like a graduate school assignment. I stumble into a conference on lesbian sexuality fresh from my part-time job, wearing a blouse and skirt, high heels and panty hose. Among the sparkling scarves, blue jeans and flannel shirts, I am the odd one out.

I meet a woman who has left her husband to be with another woman. In the process, she has given up custody of her young son. This shocks me more than the fact of her orientation. I am again seeing the empty place on the pavement where my father once stood. How could she give up her child?

Then, I begin to understand part of the reason she may have made that sacrifice. I feel an overwhelming, unexplained need to separate myself from my husband and, sometimes, even my child; I want to see myself more clearly outside of the brass-framed photograph of the three of us that sits on top of my bookcase. That picture reveals a wife and mother. I need to know if there are other relationships that might define who I am. My husband and I separate, and Jon is sent back and forth between us like a laughing and trusting yo-yo.

I date women for the first time. Susan, a tiny brown-eyed young woman I met at the sexuality conference, takes me to my first lesbian bar on Toronto's Church Street. Until this moment, I have seen women dance together only at weddings, when elderly widows enjoyed a waltz or two together. But here, on a smoky, blue-lit dance floor, women of many ages are dancing as if their lives depend on it. Some are fresh from the overflowing typing pools on Bay Street, wearing short skirts and silk blouses, their thick hair teased into lions' manes. Others stand with feet apart, cigarettes smoking between strong fingers, hair cropped short, wearing crisp cotton shirts and Levi's. I don't want to stare, but I can't help myself. I watch the women dance and touch, my heart pounding and mouth going dry from longing, my beer getting warm while I hold on to it with both hands.

A creamy white envelope comes in the mail. "Congratulations. You have been accepted into the doctoral program. . . ." I am offered fellowships to study at a university in Evanston, just outside of Chicago. I leave Jonathan with his father and travel to the United States. At first it feels like a vacation, a release from responsibilities and a new freedom. The euphoria wears off quickly as I settle into the daily routine of seminars, papers and endless studying. Soon I am longing for my son. I remember the lesbian who gave up her child, and Mary Daly's dismissal of any woman whose bond with her child is greater than her own desire. I stop dating the new women I have met, afraid of what it might mean for my son and me.

The cost is higher than I expect. No more salty chicken dinners with Emilie in her Chicago apartment, while a block away the last train leaves for Evanston and Tracy Chapman spins out her love songs on the turntable. No more intimate intellectual conversations about "queer" politics with Kitty while she pushes at her glasses and uses the other hand to juggle the tilting tower of books she carries into our feminist theory class. Instead, I spend long nights in libraries, take solitary jogs along quiet back streets and make long-distance phone calls to a child who asks me when I'll be coming home.

At a local laundromat, a young actor starts a conversation with me as I dump my wet clothes into the dryer. He invites me to his opening night, and we begin a relationship that will last for the next five years. I become pregnant and we move in together. I put my feelings for women firmly into the back of our bedroom closet and take the eight-hour train ride back to Canada to reclaim my son. Now that I have a male partner, it will be difficult for anyone to claim that I should be barred from parenting by virtue of whom I choose to love. My new partner and I marry; I am once more tightly framed within an "acceptable" family pattern.

By the time our daughter is born, my relationship with my husband is cold and strained. We move to Ontario, and our marriage slowly begins to fall apart. We often fight; he swears at me, throws chairs down the stairs, breaks the glass of a childhood picture. A short time later, Jon tells me that my husband has hit him; a hard slap that has frightened him and broken his trust. A friend asks, "Are you afraid of your husband?" When I realize that the answer is yes, I know it is time for me to leave.

I begin to date women again. It is like returning home after being a refugee in a land where I was not welcome and would never feel at ease. With women I can again speak my own language, feel that stir of recognition and celebrate that, yes, I survived and isn't it good to be among *my people* again.

I meet Heather, a hazel-eyed strong-shouldered woman from Alberta. While we bathe together in the hot springs in the shadow of the Rocky Mountains, her sweet voice reaches into me and calls out my spirit to meet her own. This time I do not turn away, do not deny the passion that draws me to her.

In the summer of 1996, I move from Ontario to Alberta with fourteen-year-old Jonathan and nine-year-old Rachel. We begin a new life with Heather in a rural town a stone's throw from the North Saskatchewan River. Together we buy a cedar house on five acres of aspen trees and pasture. A slough (Easterners call it a marsh) cuts through our land.

Our move here brings a sense of peace and wholeness to my life. I take time to walk the gravel roads and sit with my feet hanging over our dock. Away from the steel and concrete of Ontario, I reflect on the twists and turns that have brought me to this place. I begin to accept myself as a lesbian and a mother.

As I begin life with Heather, I know that some people will say I am placing Jonathan and Rachel at risk. They will argue that in our intolerant society, my children may be the objects of abuse because of their mother's choices. Yet denying my own identity and submerging myself in marriage did not preserve them from harm.

During our first summer in Alberta, Rachel makes friends with a girl who lives a quarter of a mile down the road. Like a New Age Huck Finn and Tom Sawyer, they are inseparable. With torn butterfly nets slung over their shoulders, they go in search of minnows, discover salamanders under rocks and listen to the rattle of cattails and orchestra of frogs.

One day, Rachel slams open the back door and tearfully announces that her new friend is no longer allowed to visit our home. She cannot come for sleepovers or share meals with us. After we calm Rachel down, Heather and I take a walk over to the girl's house. When her mother answers the door, we are not invited over the threshold. The woman tells us that a mutual acquaintance informed her that we are lesbians. She is angry that Heather and I had not "warned" her about our orientation. Nothing we can say will shake the woman's conviction that her daughter should not be exposed to "sinners" like us.

We return home from that encounter, expecting Rachel to blame us for the loss of her first friendship in her new home. But it is Rachel who keeps the faith. "I don't want to be friends with anyone who doesn't like my family," she says.

Before fall arrives, we visit the large country school that Jonathan and Rachel will attend. We tell the principal that we are an "alternative" family and are concerned that our children may be subjected to the prejudice of others—teachers or peers. She reassures us with a smile, saying that she will not allow any such behaviour. We are filled with hope that Jon and Rachel will skim through school without a care, like the "whirligig" beetles that glide across the surface of our blue-green slough.

Despite the best intentions of the principal and our own efforts as parents, we cannot prevent Jonathan from making his own mistakes. Within a week of starting school, he gets into a fight with another boy. We are confronted with the fact that Jon has used his fists to let other boys know he's just as tough as they are. In our female-headed, pacifist household, how can we help him express his masculinity? We take Jon jogging behind Heather as she pedals her bike for miles along dirt roads. We buy him drums, and he starts taking music lessons. Better for Jon to "beat the skins" than fight with his fists.

Jon and Rachel carry signs bearing the words "Hatred Is Not a Family Value" as we stand on the Alberta legislature grounds among the crowd of drag queens, pink-haired twenty-year-olds and office workers. We are all here to support Delwyn Vriend, a young man who lost his job at a local college because he is gay. The province's human rights commission refused to investigate Vriend's dismissal, claiming that prejudice against gays and lesbians was not covered in provincial legislation. He challenged that refusal, eventually taking his case to the Supreme Court. The justices agreed with Vriend, ruling that homophobia must be read into Alberta's human rights laws.

Unfortunately, the Supreme Court ruling is not enough for those who believe that it's a sin to be gay. In letters that drip with condemnation and promises of violence against "sexual perverts," they lobby Premier Ralph Klein to invoke the notwithstanding clause, a legal loophole in the Constitution that gives provinces the right to opt out of national legislation.

In front of the closed wooden doors of Alberta's stately Parliament buildings, speakers demand that the government refrain from overturning the Supreme Court decision. Our children laugh and cheer, but Heather and I, ever watchful, scan the crowd for any sign that words of hate might be transformed into action.

The high school holds an open house when Jon is in Grade 11. He proudly takes Heather and me on a tour of his classrooms. One of the teachers asks him to introduce us. Without hesitation, Jon responds, "These are my two mothers." The woman stares for a moment and then says slowly, "You can't have two mothers, Jon." He meets her gaze and says evenly, "Yes, I can." The teacher is still shaking her head as we leave.

Today, thirty-two years after my father disappeared from my life, twenty-year-old Jonathan has the same wide smile, dark hair and sea-blue eyes as the man who once ran beside my bike. He sits at the kitchen table, wolfs down a plate full of pasta and tells us about the rock band he drums for, his job as a short-order cook and his life as a university student. His long-haired, teenage sister sits beside him, laughing and teasing her brother.

When Jon told us that he was moving out to live in the city and share a home with friends, a voice inside me shouted, No—you can't leave! Then I knew. I no longer needed to protect and support him. I can let him go without letting him down. I can wave goodbye to my son. And this time, Heather and I will be there when he turns back to wave.

We Are More
Than Our Problems

Wanda Wuttunee

Memory: I'm in Fort Resolution, a tiny community of several hundred in the Northwest Territories. I awake to a hot, blue-sky summer day in July. The only place for toast is the pool hall up the dirt road, about a five-minute walk. I know how to blend in as a woman alone in these communities—no makeup, nondescript clothes, low-key behaviour—so I'm a bit startled when all of a sudden there's a young man on a bicycle beside me. I didn't hear him coming. "Hi. You're Cree, aren't you?" he asks. No one has ever guessed my heritage so quickly. I think for a moment and point to my face—"Fat cheeks?" He nods. He balances well in the rutty road as he rides beside me. Just before I turn into the pool hall, he says, "If I don't find someone to drink with soon, I am going to blow my head off." All I can think to say is "It sure is a beautiful day. Enjoy it." After breakfast, I go to the school to work with three locals who have a vision for themselves and their community. As part of a research project on economic development in First Nations communities, I am there to help these people get small businesses started so their youth have options other than the ones there for the young man on the bicycle.

Another memory: Jacqueline, a young woman in Haines Junction, Yukon, has chauffeured me around for a weekend while I visit her community to help local people who yearn for small businesses. She is an artist and also works as an economic development officer. We're staying at her family's cabin. On this soft June evening just before the sun goes down, we can hear the rhythmic thumping of the grouse immersed in their mating rituals. An energetic granny is looking after the meals for the workshop. When Jacqueline tells her about the grouse and the thumping, the granny says with a twinkle in her eye, "You know what he is saying?" She starts flapping her arms and strutting, "I feel like chicken tonight!" Jacqueline's laughter rings out in the warm evening air. Later, when she tells me of the devastating impact of the suicides in her family—one after the other, after the other— her personal courage and integrity astound me. After tears, we laugh again. Government statistics cannot measure the resilience of that human spirit.

And another community. Nestled in the northeast portion of the province of Manitoba is the small fly-in community of St. Theresa Point. A mall houses the "economic heart" of this isolated place—a Northern Store, a chain retail outlet, a fast-food business, and a convenience store that is closed all the time that I am there. To deal with the 80 to 90 percent unemployment, there is one economic development officer and two staff members. It's December when I arrive to interview these people and other community members to find out about their vision for community development. The place where I stay used to house the nuns. The windows are covered in plastic for insulation that doesn't work too well, so while I fit in some marking for the Native studies course I teach at university, I'm on my bed huddled beneath five quilts.

And yet, my strongest memory is of the joy I share with these First Nations people. We gather at a radio station to play music and help raise money for a local charity. The big question is what designer made my socks—as a guest in town, I'm an object of much interest. We get caller after caller flinging answers at us. The fifth caller in wins a bingo card with the answer—Calvin Klein! In this remote little community, where the lineup stretches 150 feet down the mall at 9:00 a.m. on welfare day, the laughter flows freely, people get engaged in a guessing game for charity and they know about a designer from New York. We finish off the day with a ceremony honouring the elders. Smiling faces in a community known in the outside world by a single statistic—unemployment.

St. Theresa Point, Manitoba. Haines Junction, Yukon. Fort Resolution, Northwest Territories. Tiny dots on the map. Hardly worth noticing. The people living in these places are some of the faces behind the statistics that any non-Aboriginal Canadian might know about from the "newspaper reality"—headlines about our problems, about Aboriginal people being at greater risk for a wide range of medical problems, including infectious and cardiovascular diseases, as well as chronic conditions such as diabetes and tuberculosis; about how life expectancy for our people is seven to eight years fewer than for other Canadians; about the frequency of alcohol and substance abuse, family violence and suicide, which alone is two to three times higher for First Nations people than for other Canadians.

I am a teacher. While my training is in management studies, I teach at a university in the Native Studies department. I hold two degrees in business and a law degree. In 2000, I finished a Ph.D. on Aboriginal economy. One of the first things I say to my students when we meet in the classroom is that my goal is to help them see beyond these "problem" statistics and to move the understanding of my people from their heads—the logical, rational and objective place that universities ask us to operate from—to their hearts. That is, I believe, the beginning of true knowledge, wisdom and understanding. Those are the teachings that I follow.

Logic dictates that people with huge obstacles that go to the essence of their existence are too far down a dark hole to have any kind of hope for significant and lasting change. That has not been my experience. That is not what I teach my students. These statistics do point to huge problems that we have to come to grips with—but are they the whole picture? Where am I in those statistics? Where are my colleagues and some of my relatives? Where are the ones who live their lives with courage, pride and delight? Like Auntie Maggie, a trapper woman who laughs through hardships and celebrates life and its natural ending after outliving three husbands in northern Manitoba. Like Jane Priscilla Wuttunee, my granny, a healer and mother of twelve. Like James Wuttunee, my grandfather, who fed and clothed his family with grace, good heart and hard, hard work. We've been the invisible ones and, for far too long, the silent.

We are more than our problems, and the chorus of our voices is getting stronger. In the work I do, I witness the positive changes happening in individuals, families and communities. I know other statistics that balance those we read in the daily newspapers, the ones that represent the inroads we are making in education and business: currently there are over forty thousand Aboriginals enrolled in colleges and universities in Canada, up from a total of sixty in 1961; and there are over twenty-two thousand viable Aboriginal-owned Canadian businesses, up from a total of eighty-five hundred in 1981. But statistics can never get to the heart of who we are; for that we need others to know the stories of individual Aboriginal people who stand out in our communities—people like my father, William Wuttunee.

William, of Cree, Irish and Scottish heritage, was born in 1928 on Red Pheasant Reserve, Saskatchewan, a tiny place of about thirty-six square miles—typical, dirt poor and filled with people who do the best they can in trying circumstances. He had eight brothers and sisters (three others died) who were born to Priscilla and James Wuttunee. James made the decision to move his family from the reserve to the nearby small town, Battleford. He felt he had to give up his status as an Indian in order to provide his family with a better life; he did not, however, give up who he was or his integrity as an Indian.

My father attended residential school for two years, with the resulting emotional scars suffered by any ten-year-old who feels as though school turned out to be "a prison for unknown crimes." After earning the highest marks across Canada in Grade 12, my father won a scholarship to McGill University. He studied law and eventually completed his studies at the University of Saskatchewan. He met my mother in Regina, married despite the opposition at that time from my mother's Caucasian, strict Catholic family and had five children. I am the eldest.

My father entered into a pact with one of his brothers: they would raise their children without the burden of anger and shame from our history. No passing down of the outrage against the injustices suffered by our people. Supported by my mother, who feels strongly connected to Aboriginal culture, my siblings and I learned the positive, beautiful things about being Indian. My father taught us about our relatives: we knew our aunts, uncles and cousins; we visited the reserve regularly and learned to take pride in our culture. These heart gifts are part of me.

Did you read about my father or about my family in the newspaper this morning? We are part of the reality that isn't often reported on. Newspapers don't tell the whole story, but they may well be the main source of information for most

239

Canadians on the pulse of Indian country. Even if these stories run alongside ones about other "problem" circumstances
or people in Canada, somehow they take on a different hue
if they are about Aboriginal peoples. They sit differently.
Reaction is often, Why waste money on a losing proposition?
Why isn't anything changing? Sometimes those attitudes
colour encounters we have with others.

One particularly memorable encounter for me was with
a man from a business-support program in B.C. who was
attending a conference on entrepreneurship that I, as an
M.B.A. student, was also attending. We began talking over
lunch, and for some reason, this man felt he should advise
me that I had three strikes against me. He stated matter-of-
factly that my age (thirty-two) and the facts that I was female
and Aboriginal were deterrents to my becoming successful in
business.

I consider those traits my biggest assets.

It may be hard to have hope for us when so many are surrounded by a darkness born out of painful personal experiences. But there is hope. I carry hope because of what I see
happening in individual lives, what I witness in small, isolated
communities and because of the many gifts I have been
given by my father and my mother—pride in my heritage,
an ability to see the beauty of the human spirit and a belief
in myself. I see the hope, the dreams and the reality that are
not measured by those statistics you read in the newspaper. I
see the bright lights shining across this country. They are the
heart and soul of my people. This story is my gift to them.

Bettina's
Hat

Linda Rogers

A few years ago my friend the fabric artist Bettina Matzkuhn was putting together a show of reversible hats painted with personal totems; she'd asked a number of her friends to provide primal images for her to work with. Her question to me was whether I had a "comfort fetish," something like an old blanket I depended on at those times when children suck their thumbs and twirl their hair. "Don't be silly," I said. "I'm a grown-up." Then I remembered—the mantra I always resort to in times of stress or illness: "I want my mother."

When the catalogue of Bettina's hats arrived, I saw that my mantra had been translated into a breast with legs painted on the crown of a hat. It took a hat with a nipple to make me realize I'd come a long way from wanting to be an honorary boy—girls were too passive and weak—to understanding how much I loved and needed my tribe.

Initiation into the tribe of women wasn't easy for me, growing up in the fifties. "Mother tongue" was an oxymoron then; our mothers' tongues were tied as surely as their breasts and hips were shackled in products by Maidenform. My mother, using her "man's" mind in the woman's world of advocacy for social causes, managed almost every arts and humanitarian organization in Vancouver, but even intelligent, socially aware mothers like her were complicit in the conspiracy to separate girls from their bodies and from each other. Because our mothers wanted to protect us, they taught us to dissemble, to squeeze into moulds as constricting as girdles.

Part of the moulding involved constraints on language. There were words we did not utter in my family, and for me, the only daughter, the list was long. My parents never used what they termed "vulgar" language, which included the correct names of body parts that were considered private. I never heard any word at all for "vagina." In fact, I didn't know I had one until I menstruated!

In sharp contrast to the blank space in language for female genitals, there was a plethora of ridiculous, "underground" terms for the penis, like "peeper," "dingus," and "dewey." The subversive language indicated that this body part was dirty, for peeing, never the instrument of desire and ultimately pleasure. On the way home from school one day when I was about nine years old, my friend and I were stopped by a man in a car, who wanted to show us "something." We knew what the something was but didn't have a word we were allowed to use. I took his licence number and reported him to my mother, who called the Royal Canadian Mounted Police. When the constable came to our house, I was reading. I don't think I looked up past his boots once.

"Do you know what a penis is?" the policeman asked. I said no. Young ladies, nice girls, did not know words like that, and if they did, they certainly wouldn't admit it to a cop. He informed my mother I wouldn't be asked to testify because of the limitations of my vocabulary. My mother accepted this as a testament to her effective daughter-rearing. But surely it must have struck both of us as ironic that someone who had already wormed her way through a large chunk of English literature should be described as word challenged.

And yet, my father, who was a lawyer, taught me that language was the key that would unlock every mystery, whether it was legal, philosophical, theological or anthropological. Why was it, then, that I kept bumping into words and concepts that might as well have had a big red line through them, indicating DO NOT GO THERE? I was given free rein in my parents' magnificent library, where I devoured my father's grown-up books, even though I certainly didn't understand everything I read. I knew better than to ask them about words I'd never heard mentioned in the house and did not appear in my dictionary; instead, I drew my own conclusions or interrogated one of the worldly boys at school. In *Tender Is the Night*, Dick Diver comments on bad sex with his wife, Nicole, saying he never made love to dry loins. What did that mean? Certainly he wasn't kissing overcooked lamb chops. I assumed it was a typo and transposed two letters so it read "lions." Henry Miller uses the word "cunt" in the first sentence of *The Tropic of Cancer*. I got a detention in French class for whispering a query to a classmate who might have known what that word meant.

Much of the terminology we did have access to reinforced rigid division between good and evil. This was a time when humans were separated along gender lines—beer parlours were divided into "Men's" and "Ladies and Escorts"—and our sex seemed to be further split into "good girls" and "bad girls." Bad girls were easy. They wore feather earrings and tight skirts and rode sidesaddle on their boyfriends' motorcycles. Bad girls advertised: they looked cheap. Good girls didn't. They were to be "young ladies" who wore gloves, went to Sunday school, crossed their legs at the ankles (never the knees) and ignored the prospect of intercourse, that most secret of all activities. I knew I was supposed to be a "good girl." What I didn't know was the real meaning of the changes in my body and that it wasn't *bad* to grow into my sexuality; in fact, that it was essential to my becoming a woman.

In those days when the dumbing of young people was a wide social practice, firmly ensconced in homes, schools and churches, we were also dished out misinformation. As a child, I had a nanny who tied my left hand behind my back to force me to use my right one. She also warned me not to cross my eyes or they'd stay that way. I suppose that being left-handed and female was bad enough without adding crossed eyes to the sinister mix. "Children who indulge in self-abuse go blind," the nuns at Our Lady of Perpetual Help School told my Catholic friend. My friends and I weren't sure exactly what self-abuse was, other than it happened below the waist—a place that some people called "down there"—but we knew it was a sin. These were the days before the excesses of some of the Catholic clergy were reported, and we all bought the story that the holy Catholic Church was the chief arbiter on what constituted a sin, which included any form of sexual pleasure before marriage, let alone a self-induced one.

Later I accompanied my mother to Jericho Hill School for the Deaf and Blind, where she read to blind children. By then, schoolyard talk had filled me in a bit, so I assumed all these kids were suffering the consequences of sexual self-abuse. Even at that time, it was hard for me to believe all these perfectly nice children deserved such a terrible punishment. And then I began to worry about my paternal grand-mother, pillar of the Church of England, who reportedly went blind from diabetes. Was she also guilty of indulging in the solitary pleasures of the flesh?

There were also stories about pregnant, unmarried girls being sent "to visit their aunts" because they had been "led down the garden path." Putting together my own observations

and the story of Eve's expulsion from Eden, I began to associate gardens with trouble, their earthly delights an invitation
to transgress any one of a number of social laws.

In the well-groomed gardens of my neighbourhood,
no one ever talked about the pleasure of being a woman.
The cautionary tales, the horror stories we were told were the
electric prods used to control young females, to keep us in
line. I am astonished by what I didn't know, given that I was
insatiably curious. It's so much easier these days to call yourself "sexually liberated." That means your sexuality—heterosexual, homosexual, autoerotic—is your own damn business.

The one thing I did know was that if I wanted to marry
within the Lucky Sperm Club, people "entitled" by birth into
upper-class families, I had to be cautious and play the game. I
had an appetite, but nice girls hid their hunger. "Greed" and
"ambition" were words appropriate to men. My father told me
a girl shouldn't compete in sports or in school and should
never be "hungry." A hungry woman was by definition hungry for men. That would have made me an insatiable nympho-
maniac—a word that hung over my neck like a sharpened
guillotine—and would have resulted in social death.

Rejecting the tightrope civilities of the good girl and
the civilized gardens we were to be confined in, I decided it
was safer to be a tomboy. The beginning of my adolescent
rebellion against female stereotypes was contempt for those
I perceived to be "girly" girls with flabby pastel minds the
colour of their cashmere twin sets. When hormones transformed us into devious dissemblers, a half-dozen female
friends and I—warriors, we liked to call ourselves—were
determined to explore and name the forbidden territory
"down there," but not within the parameters patrolled by
our careful parents. Since the civilized world of house, garden, school, church and the language that defined them
were all mined with potential sin and judgment, my gang
took over the wilderness beyond. That was our Promised

Land, uncharted, unclaimed territory where we could explore our inner savages.

In the ravines and bushes of the university woods, we devious dissemblers ate as many berries as we liked. We cursed and wanked and pissed on leaves, out-boyed the boys. One of the girls brought Vaseline. Her mother had been a nurse in England during the war. She told us they put Vaseline on burn victims to encourage the growth of body hair. We covered our "private parts" and waited to evolve from young ladies to hairy wild women. In the wild, we did all the things boys got to do, especially bonding with one another in a physical way.

One summer afternoon, bored with stealing apples and smoking smuggled cigarettes, we kidnapped a boy, took him to the woods and undressed him. Because I drew the longest blade of grass, I was blindfolded and allowed to touch him between the legs, where his member responded. None of us had been informed about that. Aha! Perhaps boys scorned girls because of this transformative power we didn't know we had.

"Penis!" we yelled at the top of our lungs as the kidnapped boy ran away, out of the woods back to the civilized gardens. "Penis! Penis!" Our mothers couldn't hear us. Our Sunday school teachers couldn't hear us. The police couldn't hear us. We were free in the forest, armed with the understanding that sexual power is the real reason men fear women.

Not long after we witnessed our first glorious erection, I was in a Holiday Theatre production of *The Emperor's New Clothes*. The emperor had a day job as a substitute teacher. He came to my school and taught English literature and drama, and even though he was smart enough to remember his lines and his blocking, which included expressing surprise that he was doing stark-naked walkabouts, he didn't seem to have assimilated the information that girls under the age of sixteen were jailbait. During lunch hour, he invited me to a picnic in the woods. Having been there with my warrior friends, I saw no problem and went with him to the edge of the forest, where he began peeling off his transparent schoolteacher's disguise. Eureka! There it was, another fully erect penis.

Caught between the forest and the garden, I was paralyzed by the transfixing adult phallus nuzzling against my thighs. But the gang, emerging from the woods behind the school, saw him poised over me and ran toward us, shouting "Penis!" in unison. "Penis!" I yelled with them, all of us once again bringing the word out of the forest, scaring away the naked emperor, who was never seen at the school again, having been exiled to the theatre but not to jail, where he should have been sent.

I was saved by the lost language of women. In rebellion I gained something essential that had been denied to me as a "good girl." Rediscovering the deeper roots of woman-speak in the woods, where we were empowered to explore and understand our own bodies, my tribe retrieved a legacy for our daughters and granddaughters. Nowadays they can say "penis" and "vagina." They have the language of pleasure and know how to protect and enjoy themselves, privileges denied to us because the whole social order rested on our ignorance. What we didn't know and couldn't talk about separated mother from daughter and daughter from herself.

Now I wear my mother, my friends, my daughters-in-law and my granddaughter on my head. Bettina's astonishing hat has brought me fully into a club that is beautiful and various and has ownership of the language that makes us unique. "Breast" is the chakra of pride and reconciliation. After so many years of rooting around in the dark with other girls from the bottle-fed generation, I found what I already had, the mother word for pleasure and belonging.

Don't Say
Anything

Michele Landsberg

My mother believed in white, and only white, cotton under-wear; in one green and one yellow vegetable with each meal, lightly cooked; in wiping from front to back; in washing hands scrupulously after the toilet and before eating; in never sharing a drinking glass; in not sitting on the cold cement of the front stoop (bad for the kidneys) to read your library books; in "little ladies" not whistling or chewing gum. Beyond the physical rules of the perpetual struggle for survival and against germs, in those days before antibiotics, there were also strict codes of conduct for each gender. The bedrock principles boiled down to "Boys will be boys" (for my brothers), and for me, the youngest and only girl, "If you don't have anything nice to say, don't say anything."

Not saying anything at all was my mother's only way of coping with all the not-nice parts of life.

In this, I later came to see, she perfectly mirrored the genteel Toronto way of being in the 1940s, the years of my childhood. Above all, we did not talk about sex or race.

They were not Nice. This was more than dropped threads; this was an entire fabric of experience that could not be spoken of.

When I was eleven, and was nabbed by the teacher with a hot copy of my hand-printed TinyTown Newspaper—complete with headlines, ruled columns and letters painstakingly embellished with serifs—I was sent home in disgrace to find my mother lying down in a darkened room in a state of speechless horror. How could I have written such . . . such . . . filth? It's true, there were doltishly lame little jokes referring to menstruation and underpants. But because I had to stand beside my mother's bed in an agony of shame while my choked self-justifications were waved into silence, I could never explain that the newspaper had started out as an innocent pastime. It was only when my classmates showed utter indifference to my straitlaced items of classroom news (aah, the downward path to pornography) that I began to spice up the classified section with prepubescent smut.

This incident precipitated my mother's boldest step in sex education. Some months later, she managed to find a discreet pamphlet. Blushingly, she mentioned to my brother and me that we would find something interesting to read on a side table in the living room. But I already knew I must not ask about such things. That had been made quite clear several years before when the older kids on the street repeatedly taunted the younger ones—out there under the street lamps in the wild moments of daring at dusk—that our fathers had had to fuck our mothers to create us. I had no idea what "fuck" meant, but clearly it was loathsome, a deed so repugnant that it cast all our origins into a muck of disgrace. I absolutely could not believe that our parents had done something dirty. But the big kids had seemed so sneeringly sure. . . . After weeks of bothered perplexity, I chose a moment when I was setting the table for dinner. "Fork" reminded me of that mysterious word. "Daddy," I asked in my best seven-year-old tone of polite inquiry, "Did you really have to fuck Mummy to get us?"

The impact was stunning. My father thundered into the kitchen, roaring at the top of his lungs, "Lee! Lee! Did you hear what your daughter said?"

"*My* daughter! She's no daughter of mine!" exclaimed my mother, near tears as she frantically stirred the soup.

The counterpoint disownings continued for some time, followed by a profound silence, and I didn't find out the answer to my question for several years.

When urgently pressed to express something, my mother would resort to clichés. At thirteen, I sullenly donned the almost-compulsory 1950s outfit: long-line bra, rubber panty girdle, saddle shoes, bobby socks, pleated skirt and Peter Pan blouse. But I drew the line at lipstick. Beside herself with anxiety that I would go on and on like this, and ultimately fail to "marry well," my mother memorably exclaimed, "But Michele! Even Nature adorns herself!" Later, when I teased her about this ornate utterance, she blushed and explained that she thought she was appealing to my love of Beauty.

Despite this overlay of reticence, reluctance, shyness and propriety, my mother and I had an almost electric current of understanding that flashed between us at critical moments.

The medium was not words but our hands touching.

In 1944, in a moment of profound silence, I learned that it was dangerous to be a Jew. I was oblivious to the war, having been born the year it began, and my parents didn't speak much about our Jewishness. But when my mother took me to Allenby Public School to register me for kindergarten, she held my hand as we stood before the secretary in the principal's outer office. Perkily, the secretary recorded our names, address and phone number, filling in the spaces on a form.

"Religion?" she asked, looking up brightly, pencil poised.

My mother, the soul of social politeness, didn't answer. The silence hung there. At last: "Hebrew," she said, and her hand tightened painfully on mine.

Hebrew? This was a word I had never heard before. I knew it was wrong and that my mother certainly knew better. In the long moment before the secretary nodded and bent to complete the form, and as my mother squeezed my hand tighter and tighter, I absorbed the knowledge that just to say the word "Jew" aloud was dangerous, even for a grown-up like my mother.

My experiences at Allenby confirmed that first signal. There were few Jewish children in the school, and the principal was an open anti-Semite. In kindergarten, while the others sang lustily, "Jesus loves me!" I mouthed the terrifying words to myself—I knew already that it was in the name of Jesus that the other children would taunt and hit—until my father taught me to sing subversively.

"Jesus loves me, Yes he does—ve-e-e-ry kind of Jesus!" No one ever caught me whispering the sarcasm. It was a kind of private consolation.

It seems odd now to speak of anti-Semitism as an unspoken menace in Toronto of the 1940s and 1950s, when the dominant culture hardly tried to conceal its bigotry. The sting in the scorpion's tail was that we, the Jews, were not allowed to speak of anti-Semitism. If we named it, rejected it, spoke out against it, we were doubly reviled as despicable slanderers and outrageous liars.

For this reason, it was impossible to tell my parents about the daily humiliations and perils of being a Jewish child in a mostly gentile public school. How difficult it was to sing those Christmas carols and Easter hymns, praising the foreign God in whose name I was attacked in the schoolyard. Forced to sing them, I nearly choked on fear and shame, convinced that I was betraying my parents. How frightening was principal Kerush, who marched me furiously to his office and threatened me with the strap when I was nine. I had finally summoned the courage not to raise my hand to vow to pray to Jesus every day, in the annual assembly convened by the Gideon Bible Society in the stuffy basement audio-visual Room.

How silencing, above all, was the weekly music class. Mr. Housen, the music teacher, explained to us in Grade 1 that Jews were not musical and that it was well known that Jews could not carry a tune. Therefore, any Jews in the class—except for Marilyn Goldstein, who had perfect pitch and was often asked to sing the opening note—were to mouth the words to all the songs in complete silence, especially when the music inspector came. Seven years of this, and I was made incapable of singing in public for the rest of my life.

Eventually—after the war—some of the other parents finally learned of the open anti-Semitism in the school and complained to the school board. Mr. Kerush was quietly removed to Rose Avenue School in Cabbagetown, then a slum.

A few years back, I took the trouble to do some research in the Toronto Public School Archives. Evidently, silence still muffled the vices of earlier times: the school board minutes of that historic meeting were somehow missing, and the Allenby School bulletin, fondly bidding farewell to Mr. Kerush, who would always think of Allenby as "his" school, made no mention of the reason for the transfer. How tidily the record was swept clean.

But then, the anti-Jewish sentiment of the day was supposed to be our own fault, not theirs. I remember another, perhaps the last, of those wordless hand-to-hand communications between my mother and me. I was thirteen and frustrated by the boredom of my high school curriculum. I nagged my mother to let me go to a private school where, I imagined, the classrooms seethed with intellectual intensity. My brother had been admitted to the University of Toronto Schools, a public but exclusive boys' school for the sons of

257

the upper crust, plus a handful of bright strivers. The principal there had made it clear that although the Jewish quota was filled, my brother—with his blond hair, blue eyes, snub nose and athletic abilities—could just be fitted in. I was passionately envious of his chance at academic challenge.

Reluctantly, at last, my mother made an appointment with the principal of Havergal College, a private girls' school on Avenue Road in Toronto. It was the early 1950s. We were barely clinging to the lower rungs of the lower middle classes, and in fact, there was no possibility of our paying school fees. Nevertheless, she must have decided to make the attempt in the frail hope of a scholarship.

From the first moment of our stiff little interview, the lady principal held her head back with a pained expression, as though we had brought a distasteful odour into the office with us. My mother made her hesitant explanation of my good marks, my poetry writing, my professional work as a radio and stage actress. The principal gave a small surprised laugh, astonished at our temerity. "No, no, it's quite impossible," she said. "We already have two Jewish girls this year, and that is absolutely our quota."

My mother's hand was tight on mine as we crossed what seemed a mile of polished lobby floor to the exit.

Anti-Semitism was the shard of glass in the pale custard of Toronto society. It became subtler after the war, unacknowledged and, to the untutored, invisible. If you were unwary, you forgot it was there or even learned to deny that it existed. You could be (as I was) turned away from graduate school at the University of Toronto, shunned by a new neighbour or mysteriously disliked by a colleague and never fathom the reason until much, much later, when some friendly snitch told you the truth.

But no Jew could ever mention the existence of anti-Semitism. That was the rule. I forgot the rule a few years back when a female "master" of Massey College at the University of Toronto invited me to sit at what they called "High Table" for dinner one night. Massey, an elite graduate college, still trails clouds of the old Toronto. At first, in the 1960s, it was for male students only. Even in the 1990s, when I had dinner there, Christian prayers were said in Latin before dinner, while students of every colour and creed sat docilely below at long refectory tables.

259

Prayers done, I engaged in conversation with my table-mates. One, then head of the University of Toronto law school, asked me where I had attended primary school. He was surprised to learn that we had both attended Allenby. Rashly, I then committed the social faux pas of mentioning my overriding memories of anti-Semitism there. As I spoke, I saw the tight expression on the face of another professor, a prolific and conservative Canadian historian, sitting beside the law dean. I realized that I had once more spoken the unspeakable in the presence of a gentile Torontonian.

The dean of law, a Jew, then promptly reminded me of the rules.

"Anti-Semitism? You are certainly mistaken! I remember nothing of the sort—even though it's true I did move away from there after Grade 2."

The conservative historian smiled a repressed, malicious smile. It was uncannily like the smile on the face of the Havergal principal.

I coped with this embarrassment in the only way I had been trained. I fell silent. I had nothing Nice to say.

My Secret Life
as a Mother

Susan Swan

"You'll never write again," my grandmother told me when I described the difficulties of combining mothering with writing. I remember the satisfaction in her voice when she said this. It was as if she were admitting me to a private club of non-doing.

In those days, I didn't see raising children as an achievement. I gave birth to my daughter in 1974, at a time when some feminists were encouraging young women like me to avoid family life, declaring that marriage and heterosexual relationships had limited female potential historically, in virtually all areas of public life. So confusion abounded over the value of motherhood. Some of that confusion was coming from voices in the women's movement, and I believed them. That is, I claimed I did. My grandmother's warning came after she had given me a statue of a mother holding a small child against her breast. Vowing that she'd eat her words, I hid the statue away. I was rebelling against the notion that mothers should give up professional work for their children.

But I felt too superstitious to throw out the statue; I worried that my grandmother was probably right, that I wouldn't be able to write after my daughter was born, and although I vowed I'd do both, this warning hovered for years in the psychic air around my mothering.

My mother's warning was more sophisticated and chilling. "Doctors shouldn't have wives," she liked to say, a phrase that evoked my country-doctor father who gave most of his life to his practice. As a child, I'd encountered first-hand what his dedication to his community meant: no time for me. In my mother's view, it was better if dedicated professionals went it alone, without dragging in unsuspecting family members who didn't sign on for the sacrifice of time that intense personal ambition demands. My mother's generation came to adulthood around the time of *The Red Shoes*, a film about a dancer who threw herself under a train because she couldn't square off the demands between art and love. Still, my mother's perspective as a doctor's wife was uniquely hers, and mine.

Seeing into my own nature, I knew I shared my father's temperament and drive. Did this mean I shouldn't have a child? Or personal relationships? These questions made me uneasy. As a woman, I wanted both, but in those days there were no voices, male or female, that said it was wise, or even possible, to be a mother and a writer. God knows, Virginia Woolf hadn't raised children. And Elizabeth Smart, author of *By Grand Central Station, I Sat Down and Wept*, had issued a warning—very like my grandmother's—in her poem "The Muse: His & Hers."

Guilt drove him on.
Guilt held her down.
She hadn't a wife
To lean upon

In the late seventies, I met Smart in her cottage in the dell near Flixton, Suffolk, and she told me that seeking "honourable discharge," she had put off her writing until her children were raised. She said as long as she could keep her grammar and syntax, she felt she'd be all right. But she wasn't. I saw an older woman suffering from a horrendous case of writer's block, partly brought on by the forty-year separation from the publication of her first novel to her next book. During this time, Rose, the youngest of Smart's children (she raised all four on her own by working in magazine publishing), came back to live with Elizabeth, bringing along a grandchild. When Rose died, Elizabeth blamed herself for failing as a mother.

Reconsidering my life as a single mother, I see that I was continuously trying to fit into one dogma or the other (and sometimes both at the same time) and never succeeding. The feminist dogma that personal relationships weren't as important as a career didn't accurately suit my life. Although I paid lip service to the notion that such things hampered my literary work, I was privately profligate with the hours spent on my child, my lover, and my friends. I was also doing my best to behave like a man publicly—at least the way I thought WASP men behaved, which was to be stoical, to deny my feelings, to get on with making a livelihood, to do well in my work and, God forbid, to never get caught short by my own femininity.

My journals reflect anxious days of writing fiction, working to meet deadlines as a professional journalist and struggling to be domestic and nurturing. When I picked up my daughter from daycare at the end of the day, I understood why my father wanted to hide behind his newspaper before supper, and I felt fresh respect for my mother's patience.

I sometimes wrote out lengthy conversations I had with a nasty internal voice that kept whispering I wasn't working hard enough at my writing. Isn't this because you have no talent, the nasty voice asked in its insinuating way. But most of my feverishly scribbled entries described practical daily matters like going to Metro Services to talk about my daycare subsidy, or convincing my plucky two-year-old daughter to leave the slides outside her Toronto daycare and come home. Here's a sample from those writerly congeries of self-doubt and domestic impasse.

June 8, 1975. Today I took Sam to daycare on the subway. She was in her stroller. Over 90 today. Apple juice spilled over her sweet little orange jumper. As we got off at the St. George subway station, I stopped and looked up at the stairs in amazement. They went on forever. My eyes filling with tears, I bent down and carried her up three levels.

I wish I could say I had written about how angry I was, or that I had asked why my culture made it so hard for me, a single parent, to get my daughter to school. Did I say, Here I am, a mother, doing an important job, and why doesn't anyone know what I am going through? Or ask why my daughter and I should suffer because the architect who designed the station hadn't given a thought to parents with small children? No, I was too tired. And don't forget, I saw raising my daughter as an activity that I should take care of (with help from my kindly mother) secretly, quietly, effortlessly.

In those days, I was earning about $6,000 a year as a freelance journalist. How hard to believe that is now! I had declassed myself by leaving a prosperous marriage and taking my daughter with me to live in a co-op on Elgin Avenue in Toronto. It was an old, rundown mansion filled with choreographers and musicians. At least, I had babysitters if I went out at night because they all delighted in my daughter, the only baby. She used to sit in the kitchen in her high chair and offer her milk bottle to anyone who came in. That impressed the house members, who said they learned from her generosity.

My low income meant that her daycare space was subsidized. Every six months, I would go down to the Metro Services office at Shuter Street, and a counsellor would go over with me what I'd spent in the past six months. It was a humiliating experience to have a bureaucrat question my purchases as if I were a child. I felt like Bob Cratchit in Dickens's *A Christmas Carol*. If I'd kept my full-time job as a journalist, I would have brought in a higher income, but I was freelancing so that I could write fiction on the side. In those early years, my ex-husband was sharing childcare and not financial expenses. Tough as this was, my situation came out of personal choices I had made, and this gave me confidence.

Meanwhile, the attitudes of the officials in Metro Services to women like me were not welcoming. Women whose boyfriends occasionally stayed over in their apartments had daycare subsidies withdrawn. In a reform school atmosphere, we mothers sat in our seats, subdued, heads down, waiting to be told how poorly we were managing our finances, how lucky we were to be getting government assistance for daycare. If our incomes went up, our daycare subsidies dropped. It was possible to get a raise at work and grow still poorer because Metro Services decided the raise meant we should pay more for our child's daycare spot. These government requirements keep us on an endless treadmill and do a lot to increase our sense of hopelessness.

During one visit, I gazed blearily at the other women in the room, wondering if they were single mothers too. No fathers were present, just one male counsellor and several female employees of the City of Toronto. The morning wore on; most of the mothers had been sitting for several hours with small babies on their laps, others with cranky toddlers playing about their feet. In an unexpected burst of energy, I jumped to my feet and shouted, "This is outrageous! We're mothers! We shouldn't be treated like this!"

To my surprise, the women around me stood up and began to echo my words: "That's right! Why are we being treated so badly? You have no right to act like this toward us!"

The city employees put down their pencils and questionnaires and stared at us, shock and fear on their faces. "Let me speak to the head of the department," I demanded. "I want to know the philosophy behind this kind of treatment."

It was a wonderful moment. Someone exited and returned with the owl-faced assistant to the head of Metro Services. Suddenly exhausted, I sat back down, gaping as he explained that the government had done its best to accommodate us.

Later that day I told a friend of mine about the experience. It occurred to me I should organize a lobby of mothers on daycare subsidy. My friend said that sounded like too much work for a single parent with a small child. I thought about having a few of the women over to tea, but time slipped by and I didn't do it—inviting them over required a political energy that was beyond me at that time.

How did I get through the drastic dichotomies of mothering and writing? Slowly, I became aware that mothering was vital human work, deserving social support, instead of a side project done by private female labour. There were and are far too many cultural pressures that continue to deny mothers, and by extension all parents, the value of their jobs.

However, the demands of child raising made me better organized. I learned to say no and to structure my time so every minute counted. Knowing what mammoth undertakings I was managing without any public acknowledgment also made me proud and gave me an energizing moral fuel. One evening, after a day at the filming of a television program I had been hired to promote, I shared a cab home with some of the television producers. These men began blaming their families for keeping them from writing novels. There was a sudden uncomprehending silence when I told the men they were whining babies and asked the driver to stop.

Slamming the door, I walked all the way home and wrote a chapter of my novel.

Making space in my life for the act of writing also helped my stress. Knowing that good fiction comes from a mentally relaxed place, I made myself sit at my desk every day for four hours and do nothing except write or think about writing. These hours spent in my inner world were a peaceful counterpoint to the rest of my life. Even if I had never published a book, my personal growth would have benefited from that meditative time.

Still, I didn't write about my daughter's presence in my life. Only a few poems and theatre pieces refer obliquely to our situation. In one performance, a choreographer and I imitated little girls talking about their Barbie dolls; in another, we mimed the act of swallowing earthworms. A photograph taken for this performance showed me posing with my head in my kitchen oven, evoking the tragedy of poet Sylvia Plath.

Why didn't I write fiction about us? Did I want to protect my daughter's privacy? Of course I did. But I also wanted to protect myself. Rereading my old journals, I realize one of my pervading feelings then was shame. Shame that I wasn't doing a better job. Shame and fear that my daughter would be harmed. Shame and guilt that I was trying to accomplish too much because I wanted to combine motherhood with writing. Shame and dread that some terrible thing would befall my daughter as a result of my choices.

I felt like a failed mother. I didn't know then that in some sense women with children are all failed mothers, done in by the unfair expectations placed on us by our culture, and by ourselves.

So, looking back, I don't think I could have written about my experience if I'd tried. Video and performance art deal more easily with the recent past than fiction, which is easier to write when the writer has the perspective of greater distance. For me, the difficulties of mothering were immediate and overwhelming, and I had almost no perspective at all on what I was doing. And yet despite the veiled accusations and often misguided assumptions, which had nothing to do with my secret life as a mother, I loved my daughter no less for all that. In one of my old journals, I found this 1983 entry:

Sitting in my chair, in my red Chinese slippers, reading, Sam playing with Emily (cat) on the floor. Snow on the gables of the roofs across the street. Tulips in bloom by the window. Enjoying the peace of my apartment with my daughter. I am happy.

My fear of looking back at our struggles obscured this simple, powerful truth.

Nourishment

Double
Arc

Karen Houle

Tonight, no stars. Snow with a give to it, leaning into March. I walk to the mailbox down the long driveway lined with shivering trees nipping each other's necks like horses. The sky, unbroken dark above, my house lit up like an eight o'clock pumpkin; inside, my two children, small as face-cloths in the bath. Too dark to see into the mailbox. Yet it's there, a thickness my fingers bump into. Too dark to read. It's a weight in my mittened hand, a thing I carry back from the salted road to the house.

By porch light it will become what it is—a bill for furnace oil, or foreign postage, or the town council's book drive. Or Kaetlen's handwriting. She would have been waiting patiently in the mailbox all day. Then she'd be looking right at me, seeing my face break into a smile.

I loved Kaetlen the day I met her. I had had crushes on other girls and women, especially ones with kid gloves and lipstick, but I'd never loved. Loving a woman is like doing new math: sliding the red balls, all at once, to the other side of the abacus. A satisfying, clacking sound—the sound of emphasis falling differently.

We were both at a reception for university entrance scholarship winners. I felt underdressed and hung back, nervous in small talk. We clapped as one by one our names were called. We climbed the stairs, crossed the stage, shook hands with the president, took envelopes containing $4,200 in our left hands and descended the stairs behind the president to our spots. The name Martha Kaetlen Wilson rang out. I saw a boyish young woman with a shock of red hair like a rooster comb, one triangular piece falling down in front, jeans, a worn leather satchel over her shoulder stride across the stage with a quizzical lopsided smile, her hand, confident, stretched out ahead of her. As she neared him, we heard her call out, in a friendly, reassuring sort of voice, "It's Kaetlen, sir, not Martha." And then she shook his hand. He looked confused, hesitated. She repeated, "My name is Kaetlen Wilson, not Martha Wilson." And beamed at him. He cleared his throat and called out again, his manly bell of a voice, to us, to the room; this time not calling *to her* but rather *for her*, introducing her to us, since she stood, rooted and beautiful, right beside him: Kaetlen Wilson. And she nodded, took the envelope, thanked him and skipped down the well-worn stairs.

I had never seen a woman do that, never imagined a woman could *do* that, let alone one with long legs and dyed hair, insist on it being just as she wanted and needed it to be: *hers*. Not letting the moment pass a little crookedly because to straighten it would be bold, inhospitable. Not honing the skill of letting it be right for him and right for the ones clapping blandly but not for her.

We were twenty-year-old women with chemistry labs to do. She lived with her boyfriend, Dave, and her dog, Pete, studying for medical school entrance exams. They had a sunny, shabby apartment with a claw-foot bathtub in the kitchen. We were pure potential, equal parts dance and argument. I didn't know how to dance; she taught me, putting her hands on my hips and swivelling them as if she were prying a tire off a rim. With this swivel I found a boyfriend at the club. He lived with five women and had a mouldy shower. He slept over once in a while. She wasn't impressed with him, but on we danced. Then I got pregnant.

Your eyes fall on the lab report. The doctor's finger taps lightly on the facts: 98,000 units of hCG, human chorionic gonadotropin—the hormones a living human leaks into a woman's bloodstream. The loneliness starts at that moment: there's someone making a beginning far inside you, news of accompaniment, just when you are learning how to do it on your own. Nothing can reverse this news. No pounding on the pubis with a closed fist, no screaming at the street lamps, no guzzled vodka unhooking the muffled, velvet intactness. It cannot be accidentally undone, not in the time you have. It is unlike any other juncture: *To end a relationship now or later? To start the letter or finish the pruning?* Those choices have back doors, hidden compartments, loose ends. When you are pregnant you have only two. And both will pass entirely through your body: you have an abortion or you have a baby.

I was in my third year of university. My boyfriend—a superb dancer—wasn't yet parent material. Nor would he be in the time we had, something I was only required to think about and admit at that moment.

I knocked on his screen door. When he opened it, I told him right away, standing among the scuffed basketball shoes. He hugged me. I didn't know if that hug meant, Wow, we're going to be parents! or Poor you! or Poor me! or How could you? We went upstairs and sat on the edge of his twin bed, facing his Grade 13 girlfriends' pictures pinned up on the crumbling corkboard, and I told him I wasn't going to have a baby with him.

Undergraduate summer research assistants in the physiology department, Kaetlen and I ate lunch on the university lawn each day. She had to shave legs bald and apply electrodes to test muscle conductivity for A.L.S. data. Bic razors clicked in her lab coat pockets. I drugged rabbits and extracted aortas. I ground these up in a coffee-bean-grinder thing, grew the cells again in glass tubes and tested heart medicine on them. Vasoconstriction and vasodilation—silent killers, aging processes. We ate our tuna sandwiches and stretched our legs out in front of us, tilted our faces to the sun or read the newspaper. Her dog, Pete, watched. I can't remember how or where I told her I was pregnant or what she said. I take that lapse in memory as a good thing, a sign that she must have been gentle, must not have rung out words like a bell that would resonate, even now. I do remember that huge tears rolled down her face.

One late August afternoon I walked to the clinic past staring hollyhocks and had my cervix packed with a seaweed expander. Later I lay on my back in the night heat, flicking earwigs off the coverlet, waiting for the morning, when the cab would come with my boyfriend in it, pale and earnest and irrelevant. Then I would lift my hand half-heartedly to him, opened flat out, as I went backward through the double doors of the O.R. I would meet him later, on the other side, in the recovery room. Recovering my own life—smoothed out, emptied, quieted.

As I watched for the cab, the expansion in me unbearable, she came up the walk, that same sure stride, and without knocking came into my room, flowers in the hand outstretched in front of her. I remember them, salmon alstroemerias, their throats filled with bursting exclamation marks of red. Not with stems in the wet earth, not in Chile or Holland or Hamilton, but alive enough to be as beautiful as they ever were.

After graduation, Kaetlen got married and opened a practice in another part of the province. She rented a farmhouse with many bedrooms and a long walk to and from the mailbox. Her dog, Pete, was buried on a ridge to the south of the property. We went there and sat on the grave, eating apples, talking about my twin girls and about her wanting to be a mother. She was with someone she loved, as superb "parent material" as any. They had already been trying to have children for three or four years by then.

An announcement and then a miscarriage. One is like a solar eclipse. It's rare and frightening, and you feel you mustn't look. Talk is indirect, like light seeping out from the edges of the corona. Then, eight months after the first eclipse, a second announcement. Her hopeful voice, lifting slightly. I cradle the phone to my ear, gesturing to my daughters to start eating without me, that I have to take the call. They would have been five by then, able to carry full plates from the kitchen to the garden. Her voice hits notes like bright chimes above her words, the metallic fear partly masked by the sweetness of them: "I'm pregnant. We're pregnant again!" A swell of relief, and we turn again to expecting. A few more months and then a second eclipse. Blood, steady drops in the toilet. Years set the repeating sequence: first, a phone call with the news of pregnancy, and we lean in, hoping. Then the shadowy double, the news that the third and fourth intactnesses have each come unmoored, bumping like slow barges out of her. She, the one with words coming out in dumb muddy clots. I, the one who must hear it said and not flinch, must let the joy and the sadness be pure and new each time. Even when I am pregnant again. An accident, sheer stupidity. As if I could outwit eggs and sperm by ignoring them.

For her, tests upon tests, each charting her unmapped insides. Talking was hard, not wanting to ask her how much of what was shoved where at what degrees Fahrenheit and at what angles—this absurd, necessary scientific project, as if a baby might be launched toward, like the moon, with the right starter kit. We couldn't *not* talk about it either. We laughed until tea came out our noses when she showed me the syringe with jelly that must be squirted up "just before ejaculation." And yet, we watched the cindery arc with unbroken attention, wanting it to stay in the sky. How did she keep the quick step, the bold love for herself? Six solid years trying to achieve in her womb what I didn't seem able to stop. Where to speak from? My own tongue split up the centre from two abortions, and then there were my children, running through the sprinkler with their summer noise funnelling into the telephone receiver, toward her.

We spoke our way across. One word at a time. An ice bridge can be built using its own weight. I found myself saying I would bear them a child. They found themselves gently saying no. They were thinking of adoption. If not for her, I didn't want to bear any more children. I only wanted her to have children. I decided to be sterilized, to say no—for *me.* I painted Kaetlen and her husband a banner on white cotton. On it, the words "She is patient. He is patient. We are patient for this child." How delicately I had to proceed, telling her about closing off my womb permanently, deliberately. We moved like caged finches, from the principles of reproductive autonomy to the absurdity of us, and back to a swaying perch. She sat in the green wicker chair, perfect ambiguity. She brought me flowers then too, to celebrate the end of my fertility. And she kissed me, and kissed my children, and waved, backing down the driveway in her blue Toyota.

When she hugged me at my back door almost two years later, I felt the medicine ball nudge of pregnancy under her sensible green coat. I could have held her forever, feeling stubbornness thriving in her, concentrated. Months later, she did efficient laps in the pool and I sat on a hotel deck chair, transfixed. My eyes never left her body. And when she climbed out, awkward as a pelican, those same long legs, water beading off her boyish shoulders, the wide, red mouth smiling, lopsided, she reached her arms up and turned sideways for me, turned and turned again. I had never seen a woman do that, either. Each time, introducing herself to the world, exactly as she wanted. A long walk across the empty stage, turning, composed, to say, "Yes, this is how I want it."

In the porch light, the letter is from her. What I wanted it to be but wasn't asking all that slow, dark walk from the mailbox, just being with the simple, good fact of a letter, carrying whatever it was inside, letting the momentary stillness and the unknowing be a strength. Just as, on the long arc of two lives, we carry each other.

Ten Beauty Tips You
Never Asked For

Elizabeth Hay

When I was small and in love with Perry Como, I would sit on my mother's bed and watch her put on her clothes exactly as she took them off: in one fell swoop. Overnight those multiple layers of undershirt inside blouse inside sweater upon sweater cooled off and in the morning, when she slid them over her head, they were icy. What kind of mother was this? Where was the makeup? The high heels? The romance? It pretty much broke my heart that I didn't have a beautiful mother.

Sometimes I would suggest that she wear one of her suits, and she would, but not until late in the day—she had the habit of wearing the same old clothes all day long and then changing into something better before my father came home. There was the butterscotch-coloured suit with a matching frilly blouse, and the soft greeny-blue suit with the cream-coloured blouse. Both jackets came in at the waist, both suits were a joy to behold. But two suits was not a lot of suits.

In those days I had a friend with a glamorous, vividly high-strung mother who lived for playing the piano and going to Toronto, which she called *the city*, where she shopped on Bloor Street at the Colonnade. I will never forget the way she looked down at her new suede shoes, and, spotting a scuff on the side, said, "Look at that scuff! I'm going to have to get a new pair!" Nor will I forget the sight of her playing piano with such concentration that her beautiful face screwed up into a monkey's.

Beauty Tip #1: Don't grimace when you play piano.

At eighty, my mother—your grandmother—had become so beautiful that I couldn't stop looking at her. Her thick hair—her crowning glory, as she called it with amused derision—was the colour of fine silver. Her old satiny skin was walnut brown. Her hands with the Henry Moore thumbs—curving into backward C's as befits a sculptor, or, in her case, a painter—were gnarled but arthritis-free. She became beautiful after her four kids left home and she no longer had to pretend she was so damned happy about being a mother. She would dispute this, she always has disputed it, but I am the one writing this piece. Her cross face relaxed, her 1950s glasses came off in favour of gold-rimmed specs and she stopped putting her naturally curly hair into tight curlers.

Beauty Tip #2: It is never too late, as Churchill kept telling Garbo.

In the meantime, you came along. At the age of six you sat on my bed and said to me, "You always wear pants, and you always wear the same pants."

Beauty Tip #3: Listen to your daughter.

If anything, my interest in beauty has only increased with the years. I notice skin more avidly than ever. The way many women work their skin with their fingertips, especially during the cold winter months, rubbing and tugging at it as if it were cheap dry goods. The overripe watermelon gleam that swollen old female knees acquire. The fine cross-hatching

that afflicts blondes who swim in chlorinated pools, the furrowed upper lip that plagues auburns above all. In the name
of research, I ask perfect strangers what they use on their
skin, and they tell me. The ruddy newspaperwoman who
pulled a wagon of *Ottawa Citizen*s behind her bicycle, no
matter the weather, said, "That vitamin E cream you get in
the pharmacy."

"Vitamin E?"

"Yeah. Or C."

The cleaning ladies who were tromping up somebody
else's steps, laden with buckets and mops, said, "Neutrogena
when we can afford it, but usually Lubriderm." The
Cambodian wagon vendor who was selling French fries during the ice storm said, "Vaseline. In Cambodia too." There's
Vaseline in Cambodia? "Everywhere. All over the world."
And you needed it over there? "There it's worse, so cold and
dry that even our cheeks would split." The thin, elderly
woman working in a health food store on a hot summer's day
said, "For years I couldn't have a bath. I'm going to get that
fly"—she was holding a swatter up in the air. "I'd have a bath
and in the middle of the night I'd be scratching here"—
across her belly—"so hard I'd bleed. Then we moved into the
country and I realized I was allergic to the chlorine in city
water. But I still couldn't be in the sun. I'd be in the sun, and
it was like boiling water thrown over me, I burned so bad.
Then I started reading in these books we have"—she pointed
around the store—"and began to take flaxseed oil capsules,
three of them three times a day, and in two and a half
months I could feel oil on my skin. And this summer I could
be in the sun without burning. This may not look like much
of a tan to you"—stretching out her arm—"but if I held it
up against my breasts you'd see how white the rest of me is.
Now I'm down to one capsule twice a day. My hair looks 100
percent better. And my bowels! I just go into the bathroom
and I'm out again before you know it."

I have tried her method in scaled-down fashion, a variation of my old childhood practice of dipping my finger in the butter dish every time I passed the dining room table. As someone who butters her baguette on both sides, you will be sympathetic. I have even framed Beauty Tip #4: Don't bother with skin cream, just eat oil. And added Beauty Tip #5, my favourite, as a corollary: Don't bathe so often. All a daily shower accomplishes is to remove a body's natural oils that then have to be replenished with expensive lotions, and what this furthers beyond lining the pockets of the beauty industry I don't know. But, in honesty, I have to add something else. As someone with a cupboard full of skin creams from as far away as Cuba and Germany, as someone who took a workshop on how to make my own herbal lotions and has a drawer full of ingredients and a willingness to try anything—motivated as I am by the highest scientific interest—take it from me, this is a shortcut: Beauty Tip #6: Nothing works.

Now on to hair. I have it on good authority that before the war women used to wash their hair no more than twice a month, and it was "a job" conducted not in the bathroom but in the kitchen. With shampoo? I asked your grandmother. "Oh, my dear, no. Hand soap." But didn't your heads get itchy? "We scratched."

She remembers clearly the furor when Mary Martin, starring in *South Pacific*, washed that man right out of her hair every night on stage. "People were concerned that her hair would turn to straw." She remembers, too, the Canadian-Scottish sneering that occurred when the first beauty parlour came to town. This was in the Ottawa Valley in the 1930s. "Such nonsense," everyone said, to go to a beauty parlour to get your hair washed.

When I was a teenager like you, I had tragically oily hair and my own technique for dealing with it, something I was reminded of a year ago when I ran into an old school friend I hadn't seen in thirty years. She wanted to know if I still washed my hair with dish detergent. "No," I answered, "not any more. But I have observed that washing my hair every day is a mistake. It looks better on day two or three." Beauty Tip #7: Hair, like homemade bread, is always better on the second day.

Body hair is something else, and finally I have reached the unspeakable heart of the matter. I could have built a pyramid in the time I've spent regretting my own body hair and forecasting your hairy fate. Oh, the sorrows that await. But this is where the torch I'm ready to pass on gets so wisely refused. You dumbfound me by taking a different approach. At fifteen, when you have to give a speech in French class, you take the point of view of the despised and embattled leg hair: the hair on a woman's leg speaks to the hair on a man's leg, asking why its existence is so much more threatened. You practice your speech in front of our French-speaking neighbour, who actually comes from Greece, and what follows on a beautiful June evening is an outpouring of body-hair confessions as informative as they are heartwarming, a United Nations of body hair enlightenment.

"I am hairy too," announces our Greek neighbour, a pretty thirty-year-old who dresses in revealing tops, petite and slender, though with a hearty appetite (she comes for a drink and stays for supper). "I am a very hairy woman," she says. "It is a curse. The Mediterranean curse of hairiness." She describes her trauma at sixteen when a man made a pointed remark about the hair under her arms. And she gives you the following advice about leg hair. Beauty Tip #8: Don't shave. Never shave. First: wax. Then, when the hair starts to come in again, use a depilatory instrument; they cost $100 at a department store.

She tells you, "Don't be jealous of other women. Well, I am jealous. But don't be."

Then, having accepted another glass of wine, she offers to wax your legs. Stepping back with a smile, she says, "This

289

is not a conspiracy. But if you want . . ." She explains that she has a Greek product no longer available under the new EU restrictions. "Now you can only buy expensive waxes. But this product used to be cheap. It is sugar, lemon and water. You paint it on and pull it off in strips."

"Will it hurt?" you ask.

"If it does, we stop."

You graciously decline. But when Irene moves to Europe to teach advanced linguistics at a famous university, I inherit her instrument, the famous hair plucker, since it operates on a North American current and will be useless to her over there. As a result, I can testify to the stoical thread that unites hairy women, whether they be of Mediterranean or of grim northern stock. Never do I use it without thinking of her and of her gentle, forthright urgings that you not make your life harder for yourself than necessary.

In the end, the delivery of your speech was anticlimactic. Your classmates laughed, but much more moderately than you had hoped, and you came home depressed. Beauty Tip #9: Square your shoulders and remember Irene.

A few other things I'll pass on: Noses grow. They keep growing long after everything else has stopped. This is not an illusion. Moles proliferate. They increase in number as you age and there will be no end to them. Brown ones, beige ones, red ones like flicks from a red paintbrush. They prefer your chest to any other place. Eyebrows flourish. Pubic hair thins. Wens removed from your scalp grow back.

Lately, you have taken to wearing your father's old pants, and I find myself thinking as I look at you, You always wear pants, and you always wear the same pants. I am filled with admiration and an almost atavistic—look it up—sadness, and say nothing.

But last week your father said to me, "If you are going to write about the beauty tips your mother never passed on to you, why don't you pass them on to our daughter?" And this seemed like a revolutionary idea, because, although I've been thinking about beauty for fifty years, it never occurred to me that I had anything to pass on. How wrong I was.

Beauty Tip #10: Check out Audrey Hepburn in pants.

Conjuring Up
a New Life

Carole Sabiston

My arms, thrust into our old costume trunk, are searching for something when my fingers slide into ripples of liquid silk. I pull out the mysterious thing. A white rabbit-fur coat! The height of fashion—Mary Quant, Carnaby Street, 1968, wide horizontal bands of fur and leather, a royal purple satin lining—so glamorous, I believed then. Memories flow back. Some thirty-four years ago, this coat enticed me to run away from my life.

That year, 1968, I was twenty-nine, with thirty looming uncomfortably on the horizon. *Don't trust anyone over thirty* was the mantra of the pop culture. I was divorced—rarer then—with a four-year-old son. My life seemed caught in a hypocritical net of dated correctness. Daily life was full with teaching high school art and raising my son, but I met few new people, was occasionally trapped in platonic relationships and travelled nowhere. Self-pity was my easy street. What social life I had was narrow. Woman friends would say "come for tea" and then describe the "married couples only" dinner parties they gave or attended. Their husbands or other men discreetly—and sometimes not so—offered their helpful services.

My parents, immigrant butchers, always concerned with keeping one's place in society, pressured me, an only child, subtly but relentlessly, to be respectable and get settled, which in their minds meant to marry again, quit my job and give up all this art stuff that occupied my non-teaching time. The man I would marry was not a priority; the convention of marriage was.

On the other hand, many aspects of my life were working well. My students were lively and stimulating. My own art-making—painting, collage and textile assemblage—happily consumed me. And, of course, my main focus was my son, Andrew, sunny, engaging and full of four-year-old enthusiasm.

The Feminine Mystique by Betty Friedan and later *The Female Eunuch* by Germaine Greer confirmed my gut feeling that modern women, particularly working women, were far from being on an equal platform with the other half of humanity. Businessmen, for instance, could write off expenses for entertaining and travel, while working mothers, at far lower salaries, were paying hefty fees for daycare with no tax relief at all. Aside from the usual female jobs of nurse, secretary, teacher or telephone operator, no one ever suggested there were more creative possibilities. But as feminist awareness gained momentum, for the first time in my life I actively began dreaming about a wider, more independent and challenging existence. Before I could evolve, though, a moment of insanity was necessary.

It was late December. Joy! I had been invited to a real adult New Year's Eve party—a progressive dinner party—formal and swishy, tuxedos and long gowns. My life was about to brighten up.

About thirty of us were to "progress" from one house to another all across the city. The first stop was for martinis and

canapés, the second for turtle soup and Caesar salad—a cut-
ting-edge menu at that time; the third, for duck à l'orange
and wild rice; the fourth, for pears flambé with Cointreau.
Finally, on to the last house to jive, boogie and twist under
psychedelic strobe lights till dawn.

A city bus was hired for the evening travels, freeing all
from driving—oh clever planning. But wait, there would be
much putting-on and taking-off of coats all evening long.
Wearing my utilitarian everyday khaki raincoat hardly seemed
appropriate over the delicate amethyst brocade gown I had just
sewn from a Vogue Couturier pattern—cloth label included.
The full ensemble must be perfect. Already in place were the
dress, shoes, purse and big gypsy earrings—but no coat!

Ah, the sales had just started—quick, hunt for a coat.
There it was at Gibson's Ladies Wear on a clearance rack for
only $99. Blowing my budget by 200 percent, I bagged the
white rabbit-fur coat. For days the bounty hung on the outside of the closet door where I could admire and stroke it,
burying my face into its sweet, sensuous fur, anticipating the
good time to come. And indeed it did. The party, merry and
amusing, was a great success, and because of a rare Victoria
snowfall, the last eve of 1968 became a fantasy night.
Trudging through deep, silent snow between houses, I
became Dr. Zhivago's Lara.

January 1, 1969. As the late morning sun poked around
the blinds in my bedroom, my eyes homed in on a great
white mass—the fur coat—puffed up on its hanger, glowing
from its previous night of glory. A new year, but something
felt wrong—a letdown, a promise unfulfilled, an emptiness.
What was there to celebrate?

All that day, pacing in our apartment, I found a question
taking shape. What was I *not* doing with my life? What *could*
I do? That damn rabbit-fur coat was the catalyst, of course.
It seemed to mock me. To squander precious dollars on a
stylish garment destined to spend most of its life in a dark

closet was pathetic. Then a moment of clarity—an epiphany! *I* needed to change my life's direction. Time to take charge.

Yes, the coat had provided the answer—take a leave of absence from teaching, travel to a faraway land, live frugally, perhaps primitively, and escape all convention. As I had an invitation to hold a solo exhibition of my textile wall hangings in Toronto the following year, this could be the solution to finding maximum preparation time.

I phoned my friend Betty and announced my decision, assigning her the watchdog role of preventing any attempted retraction.

"Where will you go? To Provence?" she suggests, having just returned from there.

But I knew my inadequate French would paralyze me. "Maybe a Spanish-speaking country—Mexico or Spain," I imagine spontaneously.

"Then have you seen the latest *Maclean's*?"

"Not yet."

"Well, whip out and get it—I'll say no more," she concludes, leaving me in suspense.

The article with intriguing colour photographs radiated from the pages: *Ibiza*—a small island in the Mediterranean, off the Spanish coast—*Islas Balearos*. Our destination—Andrew's and mine—was decided at that moment.

With a purpose and new direction I found it was easy to sell, scrimp and save from that January to June, amassing a small fortune of $1,500—enough for the coming year. Spanish lessons at night school began to give me a taste for the flamboyance of *olé*.

Late on a September evening, we arrived at Ibiza's then primitive, open airport. Everyone, except Andrew and me, was whisked away by family or friends. Suddenly, the two of us were alone in the dark oleander-scented air. As his little hand slowly began to squeeze tighter in mine, panic, then remorse, gripped me. I must be completely irresponsible to embark on this selfish adventure. The lone remaining taxi driver took us to his cousin's *pension* in Santa Eulalia del Río. (I fancied that village for its pretty name.) Two weeks later, a small tiled flat in Es Caná, high on a cliff overlooking an inviting white sand beach, became our home.

It wasn't long before I stopped winding my clock and lived by the Mediterranean sun's predictability. Every day became an adventure—playing on the beaches, exploring the ancient countryside, indulging in aromatic markets, making art all day or socializing with new friends at the outdoor cafés. Often there would be four or five languages spoken at one table—a European cross-section. My limitations were frustrating. Not so for Andrew. He quickly found little friends speaking Ibithenco, Spanish, French, German or English, who all blended their words together, creating a new, efficient play-world language.

Perhaps some might question my taking a small child on this unknown year. At first I did, too, until I saw him flourishing. His name became Andres, *el rubio* (the blond one). Hands ruffled his white locks. Families appeared and included us in their everyday Ibithenco lives. He absorbed the new experiences with wide-eyed exuberance—seeming to understand that the world is a thrilling and diversified place. I learned much through my child's eyes.

New senses awakened. My practical schoolmarm clothes were shed for leather, lace, beads, tie-dyes and shawls—it was flower-child time, after all. A nearby gypsy camp filled the night air with poignant flamenco rhythms. A neighbouring farmhouse, clearly seen from our third floor, had its annual hog slaughter, attended by a lively extended family who had jointly fed the beast all year. The squealing, celebrating and sausage-making carried on for days.

My taste buds continuously met new flavours and textures. Fresh-caught octopus, squid and finger-size turquoise and orange fish that sizzled in local olive oil; brilliant saffron yellow paella; huge country lemons and oranges, then green and black figs—yes, pluck them off any tree, any time; the ubiquitous potato frittatas; the local olives and almonds; and the all-pervasive scent of wild rosemary.

But it was the colour, the stunning colour, that shifted my visual perceptions from familiar muted Pacific Coast hues—slate blues, grey-greens, grey-browns in soft light—to the explosion of glowing vibrancy that made my eyes dance: cobalt skies, copper red soil, turquoise seas, valleys of shimmering pink-white almond blossoms and always the singing vermilion of wild geranium bushes against the blinding white farmhouses. I would never be afraid of red again.

After living by my wits for a year, I knew I could choose a freer life for the future. Living on that small island—with only a short trip back to Toronto for a successful art exhibition—and some weeks travelling with a Eurail Pass left me with a lifelong taste for exploring the world. But more important, I also recognized the need to reconnect with the Canadian me. Time to go home.

Three years later, I had finally left teaching to work full-time in a downtown studio loft, taking on progressively larger architectural commissions for textile wall hangings, occasionally employing up to six assistants at a time. My own exhibition work has travelled internationally, with titles like *Sailing, Flying* and *Parachuting*—all directly connected with the concept of travel and metaphorical escape.

Like others who choose a life in art, I have the privileges of no boss, no set hours and freedom to express myself, constantly pursuing the quest to solve the next self-imposed problem, both visual and financial. Conversely, there is no dental plan, no pension, no day of retirement for most of us in the arts.

As well, women artists of my generation, and before, if married and with children, invariably put domestic chores ahead of the "stolen" time to create, whereas our male colleagues usually have wives or partners to run the household. I have always admired Emily Carr's resolve to remain a "spinster." Her genius might never have been revealed had she accepted a standard domestic life. Bravely she chose singular, personal hardship and, likely, profound loneliness in order for her artist soul to soar.

Eventually I did marry again, understanding what choice means. With my husband's youngest daughter and my son, we became an instant blended family. They and their friends quickly commandeered the white-rabbit fur coat for dressing up. Now, still in the costume trunk, it sleeps, between generations, awaiting discovery by our grandchildren.

301

New
Voices

Flora MacDonald

Quite often people ask me, "Don't you miss politics?" and I usually respond politely by saying, "Well, I find I'm still pretty busy." But that's a cop-out because I haven't really answered the question. Once my political umbilical cord had been cut—in 1988 I lost my position as minister of communications and Member of Parliament when my seat was won by the Liberal candidate—I didn't spend much time wondering if I would miss politics; I was too busy trying to cope with the humiliation of defeat, the pain of being dismissed. Rejection is not something human beings readily embrace. For a while I considered my defeat a personal insult. It meant I was no longer needed. No doubt it had something to do with personal ego, the idea that the attention I was used to getting would no longer be there—wounded vanity and all that.

But that mood didn't last long. Several non-governmental groups, charitable organizations working with destitute and marginalized people in developing countries, suggested I become involved with them. I did, and I can truthfully say these past fourteen years of "life after politics" have provided some of the richest experiences of my life. If someone had made that forecast while I was still in the political circle, I would have laughed at it. I liked what I was doing, I revelled in the stimulation of a knife-edge existence and I didn't think anything could be better.

What a surprise, then, to be caught up in events as challenging and inspiring as any I've encountered. Monitoring elections in newly independent Namibia, in wartorn Sri Lanka and, most movingly, in turbulent South Africa when Nelson Mandela became president—experiences like these helped me make the transition from active politics to a deeper appreciation of the struggles many countries must go through to achieve their independence.

But it's the women I've met who have provided the most profound and lasting impressions: members of a women's organization in drought-stricken western Zimbabwe who, while government officials were paralyzed by the magnitude of the disaster, went from village to village to co-ordinate the daily provision of a nutritious meal for 600,000 children; an elderly woman in Kosovo who, when her village was almost completely destroyed by Serb forces, remained openly defiant and determined to play a leadership role in rebuilding her community; a group of poverty-stricken, illiterate war widows in Afghanistan who worked tirelessly to scrape together sufficient funds to pay a teacher for two hours each day to help them and their children become literate.

I can best describe the impact such experiences have had on me by recounting the personal story of one of the amazing women I've encountered. When I see what she has managed to achieve in the face of horrendous difficulties, my admiration knows no bounds. Nor does my resolve to continue working with her and others like her. Her name is Biri Mema and she lives in Palin, in the remote Indian state of Arunachal Pradesh (AP).

AP is the most northeasterly state of India, wedged between Tibet and Burma and up against the border with China. It has been designated prohibited territory because of the potential threat of invasion from China—the last time that occurred was in 1962. Few outsiders manage to penetrate the jungle vastness of AP. A recent edition of the *Times of India* referred to it as "The Forgotten State." But within its borders is one of the richest concentrations of biodiversity in the world. Various tribal groups reside in the deep and fertile valleys in the high mountains of the eastern Himalayas; to reach them we travelled along the Brahmaputra River in a small Zodiac for hundreds of miles, sleeping on the riverbanks at night. As members of the small NGO, Future Generations, we work with and provide training for villagers in health, hygiene and environmental programs.

As has occurred in other countries of the developing world, health initiatives have proven the most effective entry point when trying to encourage greater community development and stability; AP needs both, torn as it is by tribal struggles and uncontrolled and irrational development practices.

For five years now, a number of local women in AP have been involved in amazing health care work. They have no specialized training as nurses or doctors; indeed, many of them are illiterate. All of them have the unending responsibilities that women around the world share—co-ordinating the many members of their families, organizing their household food and finances and working long hours in the fields. They carry out their many tasks without the benefit of running water and electricity. But regardless of these handicaps, they are cramming into their very full days the added responsibilities of being the village health care workers. They do so in an environment that is heavily male dominated and where women's lives are highly restricted and tightly controlled. Biri Mema is one of these women, and through a translator she told us her story:

"I don't know when I was married, but I must have been six or seven years old because I remember my baby teeth falling out when I was in the house of the in-laws. My husband was already old. Those days were nightmares for me—I don't even want to recall them. I was prepared to do any amount of hard work by day, but the very thought of spending the night with my husband sent chills down my spine. Growing up, I was extremely shy and introverted. I couldn't utter a single word in front of other people. My life was a monotonous routine of toiling in the fields during the days and carrying out the household chores in the mornings and evenings. I never went around my neighbourhood—I didn't know the goings-on in my next-door neighbour's house, let alone in the rest of the village. I was taught to take local beer with my husband. He was such a drunkard that he sometimes had difficulty reaching home at night and slept on the roadside. Before I was twenty, I had lost two children as babies and a third was stillborn.

"One day I saw some people having a meeting; most of them were women. Out of curiosity I went near to find out what the women were talking about—it was about keeping oneself healthy, taking care of the children and keeping fit during pregnancy. I stood there listening, and then they came and asked me to join the group and work for the village.

"I found myself changing slowly—I started talking to the other women in the group, even though my husband felt all my time should be spent either working in the fields or in the house. One day there was talk of a training program being organized in the state capital, Itanagar. I was selected to attend. But when I came back to Palin, my husband was very angry with me. He chopped a pig in two, shrieking that he intended to do that to me. Full of fear, I told my husband the things I had learned in Itanagar and how the knowledge could be useful for us.

"A year later, I was selected to go to Jamkhed on the other side of India for further training. I was illiterate, so I refused. Even then, my friends forced me to attend. That training session was an eye-opener for me. The other women trainees were known as the Village Welfare Workers; most of them were also illiterate, but they were doing excellent jobs. Some of them had even learned to read and write when they were adults.

"On my return I was chosen as the team co-ordinator for my area. In order to serve my village more effectively, I started attending adult education classes, and I'm now able to read and write.

"That led to my being named field associate for the site, a paying job. I can now help others with their reports, then I prepare records and reports for the whole region every month. I started working for my community with renewed vigour. After I met with some of the local teachers, they agreed to give an hour or two several nights a week to instruct other illiterate women how to read and write. And I've even been successful in persuading my husband to give up drinking. He now helps me with my work, and he has become the head *gaon bura* (leader) of our village. He is proud of me and I am proud of him."

I can't tell you what a great joy it is for me to visit the nearby villages with Biri Mema. The woman who five years ago was too shy, too fearful, to venture anywhere but to work in the fields and take care of her own small house is now welcomed by people throughout the entire area as someone who can help them in community development. She speaks at meetings in a calm and measured way, encouraging women to be more active and to take on more responsibilities. She points to her own struggles and what she has accomplished:

"Today I am getting a decent salary for my job; my work has given me a status in the community. More important, I have discovered the joy of the company of others and the satisfaction of helping the people in the villages."

The work of women like these does not see them reporting to some medical accreditation agency; except for the field associates like Biri, they are not on salary from some governmental or non-governmental organization; they are selected by their neighbours because they have already demonstrated leadership qualities in their villages. Once selected, they are sent off for a short period of training, which is upgraded annually, with another two-week training period. They first learn how to carry out surveys in their villages to gather information and data about the basic state of health. They are taught the importance of keeping accurate records. Then they are instructed in the treatment of such illnesses as diarrhea, the number-one killer in their villages, and in the diagnosis and treatment of childhood pneumonia, the number-two killer. They also learn how to give immunization injections and how to treat the many traumas that are part of village life. And finally, they are trained to provide advice for better nutrition during pregnancy and how to assist with childbirth.

In the villages of Arunachal Pradesh, you cannot take your child to a doctor; there is no special clinic building to shelter the worried parent; there are no white-coated workers. When a child gets sick, treatment has to be performed at home. If treatment is not performed quickly and effectively, the illnesses become life-threatening. Children die. They die by the dozens.

In Arunachal it is frequently the case that a woman will have twelve pregnancies during her life. Of these, data show that maybe two will be stillborn, four will die of diarrhea, two of pneumonia and one of other causes; typically, three may survive. This type of health condition brings stress to women's lives. It brings alienation into families. Is it any wonder that many children are not given a name until they reach their first birthdays? Why get too close to a child who might die?

In the most recent data collected in the three sites where Future Generations Arunachal carries out its health care projects, infant mortality cases in 1997 totalled slightly more than two hundred. Last year, thanks to the training and the efforts of Biri Mema and her colleagues—the volunteer Village Welfare Workers—the number of fatalities was reduced to twenty.

Such is the kind of work being carried out in Arunachal Pradesh and in many developing countries as a result of partnerships between dedicated non-governmental organizations and committed local people. Unfortunately our main media outlets seldom cover such worthwhile stories.

So what have Biri Mema and the women of Arunachal Pradesh meant to me? I think back to the hurdles and obstacles that confronted me when I first contemplated getting into the political arena. I had proven I could run campaigns for others, but to be the person out front, the one who was the focus of attention, was something I had to steel myself to do. It didn't come easily—what if I made a mess of it and let my supporters down? And how was I to disprove the never spoken but ever-present, insidious questions: Can a woman really do this? Will she have the staying power, the fortitude, the guts to make tough political decisions? These issues of confidence and gender are among the obstacles that continue to impede women's efforts. The barriers I faced in politics thirty years ago still exist for many women in Canada today. I often griped about these man-made obstacles—I still do. But when I consider what Biri Mema and others like her have managed to accomplish, given the difficulties they face on a daily basis, I know that my road was easy by comparison. Biri has shown me that once the qualities of indomitable courage and determination are given free rein, there is nothing women cannot tackle. She and her colleagues are transforming their small corner of the world— such things as greater equality, recognition of the role of women, better health care and greater protection of the environment are slowly becoming the norm.

There's no doubt that the defeat I suffered in my last political campaign was traumatic. My glory days were over. I fancied myself relegated to some historical dustbin. And I wasn't prepared for it. But the old adage still applies: when one door closes, another opens. These past years have richly rewarded me; to be sure, I've had adventure and fun, but also I've had the satisfaction of helping out in a very direct way. What more can one ask for? I've been fortunate to meet people like Biri Mema and am determined to do whatever I can to help her and her Village Welfare Workers. Telling you her story is one such way.

Life with an
Overeager Conscience

Sandra Beardsall

It was probably predictable that a person with a relentless sense of social responsibility should find herself, at age thirty-one, walking down the dusty road that leads to the village of Vaikalpalayam. The people of this hamlet are Dalits, or "Untouchables," India's social and economic outcasts. When an opportunity arose to attend a work-study camp exploring issues of human rights and religion and helping to build a community centre in this village, how could my do-gooder heart resist? Despite the aura of the exotic that filled my every step in the hot red sand, perhaps I should have guessed that this village and I would someday meet. What I could not have imagined was the way that this small encounter would weave itself into my world-view.

"Well, I never saw a child with such a conscience!" Aunt Violet exclaimed to my parents, when I was about three. No one remembers what I had done to evoke my great-aunt's comment, but her authority, as one who had cared for many children, was deemed impeccable. Apparently, then, my passion for the right and the good was kindled early and needed only a bit of fanning to begin to blaze. My middle-class family was respectful and caring. We attended the United Church and helped others; the idea of writing up the Ten Commandments on two tablet-shaped sheets of paper and taping them to my bedroom bookcase, however, was entirely my own. I doubt I knew at age eight what a "graven image" was, let alone "adultery." But the French provincial gold trim on the two bookcase doors looked irresistibly like Moses' stone tablets, as rendered in my red leatherette illustrated Bible. It seemed as right and natural to ponder these ancient, obscure injunctions on my bookcase as to gaze at the graceful ballerinas twirling on my pink bedroom wallpaper.

I learned that a keen conscience never goes on vacation. In 1970, when I was ten, we took a one-week family trip to Myrtle Beach, South Carolina. I not only noticed that all the hotel guests were white and all the maids were black, I obsessed about it. I watched these women in their green cotton uniforms line up to board the city bus that would take them away from the beach to . . . well, I had no idea, but I was sure it was not to comfort and luxury. Their weary eyes worried my soul. I decided, as grandly as a ten-year-old could, that the racial construction of the American South needed immediate and serious attention. As a start, I left little notes for the maids who cleaned our room each day: "You are very nice." "White people and black people are equal." The maids did not reply.

Undaunted, and assisted by the "Stories of Famous People" volume of my family's *Children's Encyclopedia* set, I took as my hero Harriet Tubman, the amazing Underground Railroad organizer. That year in Grade 5, I made her the subject of my speech for the annual school public-speaking contest. No one got as fired up about Harriet as I had hoped, but I felt some satisfaction in getting the word out. The American South may or may not have felt the benefit of my zeal.

It was in these elementary-school speaking contests that I realized the first thing I had not been told. When I gave speeches on freedom fighters and racial prejudice, I got a lukewarm response. When, in Grade 8, I spoke on the joys and trials of living with siblings, I won all the way to the county level, where I took second prize. I also took the point: people prefer whimsy to moral rant. I had no idea that my noble ideals of truth and justice, which were linked for me to a sweeping love of humanity, would in fact alienate me from many people. I began to realize that I would never be entirely at home in the world as long as my care for it involved my inexorable conscience.

There was no turning back, though. Others aided and abetted. When I was a young teen, someone at church suggested that I should consider becoming an ordained minister. I resisted as long as I could—it was hard enough being an uncool teenager without this further embarrassment. I was not a pious believer, and I did not know how to deal with the Bible's contradictions. A few religious studies courses later, both piety and the Bible were duly deconstructed, and I was hooked. The more I studied, the more I got involved in the life of the United Church and the wider social struggle, the more I learned to analyze critically my beloved world—all for its own good, of course. I became more truly what I had always been, *a woman who loves the world too much*—with nary a self-help book to guide me.

So began my real life of alienation. While I was still studying theology, two former school classmates, young men who had, as far as I could tell, never taken any interest in me whatsoever, took me aside at a class reunion, sat me down and tried to talk me out of my vocational choice.

"You have real talents," they insisted. "We still remember the siblings speech. Don't throw your life away like this!" The pleading in their voices told me they were sure I was about to follow a charismatic leader into a distant forest and drink poisoned Kool-Aid.

Once ordained, I became, for some, a member of the "moral police," those unpleasant people who take offence at raunchy jokes and censure alcohol consumption. Not that I do either, but the assumption that clergy exist to make people feel guilty is entrenched in a culture that has long abandoned any actual fear of organized religion. How many times have I suffered through the phrase "I know I shouldn't swear in front of a minister, but . . . ?" What I would like to say, but don't, is that I don't mind the swearing, but would they please apologize for driving those gas-guzzling, air-polluting sport-utility vehicles?

For others, my affiliation with a progressive religious group means that I represent a lot of bleeding-heart causes like feminism, gay/lesbian ordination and women's reproductive choice. Nearly everything I stand for could be off-putting to a good number of people, especially other Christians. I could not possibly have Jesus Christ as my personal saviour and call God "Mother," could I? Like many of my United Church minister colleagues, I became wary of telling airline seatmates and other strangers in close quarters my true profession. Like other leftists, I learned not to announce my political preferences unless I wanted a battle. It is harder, though, to hide the fact that one has ordered the vegetarian meal.

Something else happened as I entered theological school. I learned that I was not alone, that in fact many of us are carried through life by overeager consciences. I met people even more zealous than I, people who viewed my lifestyle and commitments as practically wanton. I discovered groups whose members crusade for their causes with a boldness that I could never match. Animal lovers, tree huggers, pacifist communists, anti-poverty activists—they had shaped what for me had been half formed, private anxieties into organizations that could issue tax receipts!

Of course, the problem with finding fellow travellers of this sort is that we tend to complicate one another's lives and together alienate ourselves even further from everyone else. Every cause embraced adds to the list of products to boycott, meetings to attend and things to fret over. We exhaust one another with conscientious possibilities, even as we revel in our common quest. There is also the challenge from outside, from the Powers That Be who would delight to see us split with each other over some matter of principle. Still, what a gift to find myself a part of a long and vital legacy, to learn that I did not invent, but only inherited this overwhelming sense of moral duty. A second-century document describing the Christian ethical life told followers of this new religion to live as "resident aliens" in the Roman Empire. And so some of us do.

It did not take India long to remind me of my small place in the order of resident aliens. I already knew that this sub-continent features whole religions shaped around views of life's sanctity that would put my non-killing ways to shame. India defeated an empire with non-violent resistance. I already knew that I had much more to learn than to teach here. My first glimpse of this ancient land, awash in humanity—people walking, riding, pedalling, peeing, praying, begging, meditating—confirmed that this place was far too complex for any analysis I might attempt in several years, let alone two weeks. Even in the midst of the deepest poverty I had ever seen, even as the West rained terror just over the northwestern horizon in the opening volleys of the Gulf War, India invited my well-worked conscience to take a holiday. And then it gently taught me its special lesson.

The residents of Vaikalpalayam speak Tamil. On our first visit, an interpreter facilitated the introductions. The women of the village had a question that the interpreter hesitated to translate. Why, they wanted to know, do you women wear such ugly clothes? Sure enough, our sensible beige pants and drab T-shirts paled in the face of the Indian women's saris, threadbare but bold in blue, purple and green prints. Tiny girls, already seasoned labourers, wore delicate pink flowers in their hair as they headed to work in the fields. One of the women produced a small red dot, a *bindi*, and pulling me close, fixed it on my forehead. Yes, the women agreed, that was a start.

The next day, I visited the village on my own. We used sign language and my few feeble words of Tamil to converse. I learned that one of the women was named Shandra, which means "moon," and sounded much like my name, Sandra. This similarity gave us a special affinity. A young girl shook off her plastic bangles and handed them to Shandra, who then slid them over my fingers and onto my wrist. Indeed, the women nodded, that is much better.

On my last day to visit the village, I walked there slowly, not quite ready to say goodbye, or even *poitavarum*—"I go, and come again." I stopped to pick up a red hibiscus blossom that was lying in the dust and tried to put it in my hair.

"Hello!" called a voice. I turned and saw a man standing at the gate of his small middle-class home. "Would you like some roses?" he asked. I followed him into his garden, where his wife cut red and pink roses from lush bushes. Then they sat me on a kitchen chair, and the woman expertly attached the roses to my hair.

This latest improvement evoked vigorous nods of approval from the women of the village. *Bindis*, bangles and flowers— finally I was beginning to brighten up. As we bade farewell, Shandra pointed to the sky. She was giving me a token, the moon. It would shine, silver and calm, as a reminder of our brief friendship. Its thin rays would form a fragile link between one of the wealthiest people in the world and one of the poorest. And it would be an emblem of another thing I had not been told, or perhaps the thing I had until then simply failed to hear. With conscience, with solidarity, there is also kindness and beauty; there *must* be kindness and beauty. I tucked that thread into my hair, alongside the roses, and waved goodbye to the wise women of Vaikalpalayam.

One of
a Bunch

Sandra Birdsell

Whenever I'm asked what it was like to grow up in a large family there is nothing I can liken the experience to, so I just reply, "It was interesting." It was not an event like going over Niagara Falls in a barrel, albeit at times the ride was tumultuous. The awareness that my family was large and I was *growing up* in it was a gradual one; however, the experience must have been more than interesting, because when I was twelve years old I attempted to write a novel about a large family—my family, the Bartlettes. I had four brothers and six sisters and shared a room and bed with three of those sisters. Finding the time and space to be alone with a book seemed impossible, so why I thought I might be able to write one is likely attributed to an inherited trait that my father jokingly referred to as "infernal optimism."

The house we lived in, in Morris, Manitoba, was rather ordinary, a two-storey, wood-frame affair with a lean-to porch stuck onto the back where, in summer, we would bathe and our mother would set her loaves of bread to rise.

In fall and winter it was taken over by a mound of skis and skates, boots, snowshoes and occasionally the carcasses of rabbits and fowl hung from the rafters amid the bundles of herbs our mother had strung up to dry in the heat of summer. There had once been a piano back there, an old Steinway with lifting black veneer and chipped ivories—the ones not pried off by little fingers. The keys were marked with large letters, written in grease pencil by a child determined to teach herself the notes. The house overflowed with a clutter of children's belongings; its whole appearance was like a boot, an illustration for the nursery rhyme about the woman who had so many children she didn't know what to do.

I imagined the main character of my novel, the family, as being blocky-shaped, a violet-grey colour with a single head and twenty-two arms and legs sticking out from it. That my parents should be included in this shape hadn't occurred to me yet. Their lives seemed disconnected from ours and were lived off stage. While we, the Bartlette children, ruled the world, our father worked at his poolroom barbershop and our mother was a shadowy and often muddled person, a head-and-shoulders study framed by a kitchen window. She would call for us from that window, call all our names, sometimes twice, until she eventually hit on the person she wanted or in a sputter of frustration threw up her hands in defeat.

The perception that our family was a blocky, violet-coloured shape with multiple appendages took hold one Halloween night as we went tramping from door to door. When our shouts for treats subsided and the door opened, I began to notice that invariably the person would exclaim, "Oh, look, it's the Bartlette children! The Bartlette family is here." I had always thought that our numbers made us special; certainly the size of our family made us different from other families in the small town, and I was proud of that difference. And yet I began to feel resentful. As the evening progressed my resentment grew, and when next we were greeted at the door as the Bartlette Family, I made myself taller, poked my head out from the centre of the troop and blurted, "I'm Sandra."

If the woman at the door had heard, my declaration didn't evoke a flicker of response. But from my siblings I felt a sudden stiffness, caught their looks of disapproval, and as we went down the sidewalk their pointed silence left me feeling stranded. We returned home and gathered in the dining room to empty our loot bags on the floor; gradually their miffed tightness dissipated. Under the supervision of the oldest sister, our Halloween treats were divided equally, down to cutting up sticks of chewing gum. I received my share, knowing I'd been forgiven for the crime of wanting to be noticed apart from them. That was when I envisioned our family's blocky shape and colour, felt that I was melded into the unit, safe, but invisible.

Then a stay in bed for an entire winter with rheumatic fever gave me the opportunity to read novels and entertain the idea that my position of fifth child among eleven siblings afforded the best vantage point to view a family and write about it. A particular brother figured prominently in my first work in progress, selected perhaps for his verve and charm. Unlike my oldest brother, he rode one of those narrow-wheeled bicycles that were just beginning to make an appearance in the windows of hardware stores. My oldest brother had opted for a sturdier bicycle with proper fenders, balloon tires and a wide, sprung saddle. I noticed how one brother was fleet-footed, a rolling stone, while the other went about in a quiet determination to learn to play whatever musical instrument he could earn money to buy.

Beyond my bedroom window, a sister climbed a tree and began her watch for unsuspecting pedestrians coming along the sidewalk. Another sister was content to putter in the kitchen and wondered aloud where our mother kept the pinch salt the cookbook called for. I recorded this all while perched uneasily on the side of the bed scribbling in the notebook, feeling more than a pinch of guilt. The doctor had pronounced my heart to be fit as a fiddle, untouched by "romantic fever," as my father called it, and my name had been returned to the roster of the many and varied chores.

The chores were assigned according to how we were bent, and I was bent for the outdoors, for tasks that expended an overabundance of energy. I could stack a woodpile as expertly as my father, chop kindling and spade the garden. On Saturdays there were eleven pairs of shoes that required shining, mud to be scraped from the trousers my brothers wore on a day of fishing at the river. Kitchen chairs were to be hauled outside, upended, leg bottoms pared clean with a knife, scatter mats pounded against the house and dragged through the snow to brighten them. By the time my sisters and I had learned to tie our shoelaces, most hours away from school were occupied with these tasks. I thought that my mother must lie awake at night imagining ways to keep us all busy, to keep *me* from realizing my potential to be a basketball champ, a diva, an acrobatic clown.

Music was an acceptable diversion from these chores. When my oldest and most beautiful sister wasn't hearth keeping, she was at the warped, out-of-tune piano on the porch, playing "Ebb Tide" and wishing for music lessons. Chording to my father's fiddle-jig music on a Saturday night, my oldest brother would be picking on a banjo and puffing on a mouth organ at the same time. A Saturday bath on the porch, a tub of curdled water tipped onto a flower bed, and the lean-to was transformed into a music hall. I imagined the Bartlette music spilling into the street, across the garden, being heard with amazement.

One day a student of music came to visit us. She was from Frankfurt and had come to our town wanting to view the devastation of a recent and terrible flooding of the Red River, as many strangers had done all that summer. A CBC radio producer had also visited and interviewed our mother amid the ruins of our house while we children squatted around tubs of soapy water scrubbing a film of silt from dishes and sealer jars. "Mrs. Bartlette had all the children busy at work," I heard the interviewer report to the country. Mrs. Bartlette had also been written about in a newspaper, a woman stubbornly refusing to vacate her flooded house, finally being forced to leave it from a second-storey window. And so we were not surprised when the German student came knocking at our door.

At the sound of music, we were drawn from all corners of the house and yard to gather at the piano as the student played a Chopin étude, amazed at the music coming from the old Steinway. It was a riveting moment that transported us from the dirt and filth of the floodwaters and the cluttered porch where we stood listening in awe. In the silence that followed, the wooden lean-to suddenly became less than ordinary, and I slunk away along with the others, avoiding the disquiet in one another's eyes. I harboured a growing suspicion that the piano and my most beautiful sister, and perhaps all the rest of us, were not realizing full potential. Unless our parents' budget could allow for special lessons for all, an individual request for such had to be denied.

And yet, I began to notice that we Bartlette children were very different from one another, even the twins who sometimes dressed alike—one had insisted that our father crop her black hair short and feather it in a ducktail, while the other wore her auburn hair in a pageboy style, which she meticulously arranged every morning in front of the only mirror in our bedroom. Photographs the twins had clipped from movie magazines competed for wall space with the artwork of another sister and with my collection of calendars. We bickered over whose taste in art should dominate the walls, whose belongings took more than their share of space in the bureau and closet and whose turn it was to use the mirror. In winter the frozen laundry was brought in from outdoors and hung in rooms throughout the house. Our room became chilly and damp each washday Monday, so one thing that went without any debate was whose turn it was to switch off the bedroom light—a truce became necessary for the sake of needing to snuggle for warmth.

Those thawing bedsheets could also be used as a scrim, illuminated by a flashlight while a sister frightened herself and us with a story of haunting spirits. That one, the story-teller, was scrawny and blond, with warts on the knuckles of a hand. She had already distinguished herself with a summer of hanging upside down from the limbs of a tree beyond our bedroom window, her gobs of spittle—aimed at passersby— spotting the sidewalk below. Then once again, she achieved notoriety by entering and winning a poetry contest. With this sudden vault in status she vacated the sniper's nest and graciously agreed to assist her classmates master the com-plexities of rhymed verse.

The warts on the poet's knuckles were made more appar-ent by the way she attempted to conceal them, hand tucked into her armpit as she climbed the stairs to the stage of the school auditorium to accept her prize. The twin with the pageboy had dressed the poet's hair for the occasion, a style that resembled an octopus lying on top of her head, each of its arms fastened down with a rhinestone-bedecked bobby pin. The prize she accepted was a voucher for five dollars worth of dry cleaning and publication of her winning poem in the school newsletter. Her prize was our prize, too, our prestigious moment, until days later, when a classmate sug-gested that she might have read my sister's winning poem else-where. When questioned, she retreated from her certainty, but by then our poet had been labelled a plagiarist, and the damage had been done.

We fed on one another's indignation, pumped ourselves into a rage that sent us off on a self-righteous march to take revenge. The wounded poet returned to her perch in the tree, while the twins and I lay in wait for her accuser. When she appeared, we descended on her with mud patties, splattering her crisp white blouse. The crime of slander justified the revenge: the soiled blouse, lawn ornaments going missing during the night, a shrub dug up and replanted in a neighbouring yard. When challenged, the Bartlettes had a kind of solidarity that brings an understanding of how wars might begin.

But there were, of course, finer moments when that esprit de corps came into play: in times of illness, when a sibling was struggling at school, when a pre-schooler needed coaching to get a head start, our assistance was carried out with a Samaritan fervour as intense and self-righteous as the desire for revenge.

All too soon, I discovered that my wide-eyed pondering over the nature of our family was shared by others in the town. The minute details of our household and living arrangements were a source of curiosity that, unfortunately, was less than benign. Where did we bathe, wash and brush our teeth? How in heaven's name did our poor mother manage to clothe all of us on my father's income? Mention would be made of a family of two or three children in such a way as to imply that this was a status to be desired, an achievement. And then one day, in my presence, as though I were invisible, I overheard a woman suggest that the reason for our large numbers was that my parents lacked self-control. I began to doubt that we were special and to wonder if we were, in some way, deficient.

The hearth keeper was the first to leave home, and within months I heard her on a live radio broadcast of a *Search for Talent* concert singing "O Danny Boy" in a quavering sweet voice that took my breath away. Then the gadabout brother was gone too, and I was all the poorer for the absence of his laconic wit—and the two bits he'd pay me for shining his shoes before a night out on the town. The eldest brother remained. He'd wait for night, when the house was still, before spreading his textbooks across the dining room table, studying on into the early morning hours. I'd come home, my body shaking with cold and the excitement of a basketball game well played, and find him there. After we had talked and he had given me something good to think about, I sat at the table across from him, going through his medical dictionary and copying the meanings of a list of words he needed to memorize before the night was done. When he acquired his university degree and a president's medal, he too was gone.

Another sister left soon afterwards, as a married woman, and by that time I had given up scrutinizing my siblings and had abandoned the attempt to write about a family. Instead, like many in their teens, I became enamoured of a more fascinating topic—the topic of me.

For a time I imagined becoming a missionary or transforming into "the big-eyed girl" with a ponytail whom the Big Bopper sang about with such sexual zest. Gradually I discovered a profound need for quiet and solitude, which was a surprise to me—and for others who perhaps assumed that a person who grew up in a large family would naturally be gregarious and extroverted, a player of team sports and at home in a crowd. The need to be alone took me far out into the countryside, on walks to neighbouring towns and villages and alongside the Red River, whose yellow current hinted at mystery, at a bygone era, at the people whose birchbark canoes had once plied its surface. One of those walks took me away from home for half a year, and when I was seventeen, another took me away for good.

One by one the Bartlettes left home, and the absence of our body heat and voices made the rooms in the house shrink. The bedroom where my sisters and I had shared the choreography of our nocturnal movements became half its size. Sometimes, when we returned home, we crept up the stairs to look at the room in disbelief and wonder, feeling that we were interlopers and had never slept in the sagging bed and given each other our childhood diseases, shared the afflictions of bed wetting, teeth grinding and growing pains. Likely we had shared an aching need for privacy and quiet, too, even though an expressed desire for privacy had seemed an affront, a lock on a diary a challenge.

We came home on holidays wearing our new identities with a self-conscious stiffness and thinly veiled belligerence that dared a person to question our acquired tastes in fashion, philosophies, religious belief or the apparent lack of one. As the years passed, our mother's dining room proved to be too small for our growing numbers, and banquet tables were set end to end in the basement. Near to thirty, and then forty, adults gathered around the table for meals, while small children ransacked the rooms above and our mother scurried up and down the stairs. With our leavetaking, our father's pocketbook had grown fatter, and our mother's memory improved. She had purchased a diary and recorded the names and birthdates of all her grandchildren and great-grandchildren, and they could expect to receive a birthday card on the appropriate day.

Remember when? Do you remember the time? The storytelling began around the dining room table, but the teller was not allowed to finish because of the number of people interrupting to object, clarify, to change the sequence of events and outcome of the tale, each one intent on his or her own point of view.

By then, I had begun to tell my own stories in earnest, to snatch an hour here and there, writing in a room I shared with the piano, ironing board, sewing machine and television. I would enter it and discover my son's jeans draped over the typewriter in need of a patch, his lovely note signed with hugs and kisses. A daughter's half-finished essay scrolled into the machine. I once found a message—"Dear Mom, people are more important than words. Right?" My youngest child had drawn little squares beneath her note and typed the words, *YES, NO*, beneath them. "Please check one box only," she instructed, a wily girl, no doubt anticipating my struggle with the question.

I never could sit down to write with a sick child in the house or without the beds made, meals planned and the place cleaner than it needed to be. And never without a sense of guilt similar to the one I used to experience while perched on the edge of the bed, when all around me my siblings and parents performed the tasks that were necessary to keep a large family going. The experience of living in a large family has caused me to guard jealously what time I claim as my own, but writing will always feel like a surreptitious act, a covert activity that must be carried on while rightly tending to the more important acts of caring for others.

The Coat I
Left Behind

Maude Barlow

As a Western feminist, I have had to temper my political perspective many times while on international travels. There was my first visit to a Mexican maquiladora free trade zone in Tijuana, where I had to keep my counsel over the cartoon drawings on the factory walls that communicated, in no uncertain terms, that any female worker who got pregnant would be fired. These workers were not even questioning this edict; their struggles were for basic wages and to be able to use the toilet more than once a day.

Then there was the trip to Cochabamba, Bolivia, to show solidarity with the people's uprising against a private water company that had doubled the price of water. High on a dusty slum overlooking the city, I participated in a celebration as the first piped water cascaded out of a tap and held my tongue as the men of the community officiated, gave speeches and generally took charge, while the women, who had always been responsible for fetching the family water, often for miles, stood mutely in the background.

Recently, I stood in quiet anger at a press conference in Tokyo, Japan, where thirty or so journalists—all men— quizzed me in their press club, papered in oversize Marilyn Monroe posters and soft-porn cartoon fantasies. When I gently asked the young women, who had organized the briefing, if they were offended by the heavy male atmosphere of Japanese journalism, they became defensive, and I quickly dropped the subject.

But the exchange that challenged me more than any other to walk non-judgmentally and with complete support in another woman's shoes was my January 1991 trip to Iraq on the eve of the Gulf War. This international women's solidarity peace mission was organized by Margarita Papandreou, the American ex-wife of the former prime minister of Greece, Andreas Papandreou. Margarita had long wanted to bring together a group of women from North America, the (then) Soviet Union and the Middle East to oppose the growing conflict; but only when war seemed imminent did the Iraqi government suddenly allow our mission into the country.

Our hosts were members of the General Federation of Iraqi Women, a government-sanctioned organization that supported, at least in all ways public, the regime of Saddam Hussein. Now, I went to Iraq with no illusions about this man and his methods of keeping order in his country. Saddam took power of the Ba'ath Party by selecting, at the leadership meeting, his rival's key supporters, who were then taken outside and shot. His terrified rival only saved his own life by joining the firing squad. Saddam raised the orphaned children of the men he had killed to become his personal bodyguards and to do his violent bidding, from torture to murder. He had two of his own sons-in-law murdered, despite promising them amnesty if they returned to Iraq after fleeing the country with his terrified daughters.

Yet the members of the General Federation of Iraqi Women, like virtually every single person I met in Iraq, spoke with adoration, even reverence, of their president and would blanch if we criticized him. There were huge posters of Saddam all over their offices—as there are in every home, office and shop in the country—and the women of the federation particularly loved to tell us about how close he was to his wife, when, in fact, he was openly living with another woman. When I asked one federation member about the terrible news photographs we in the West had all seen of dead Kurdish children killed by Iraqi bombs, she turned deathly pale and declared that the photos were all fake.

The federation assigned me a "minder," something all foreign visitors to Iraq must have. My minder was a sweet young woman named Mina, whom of course I called "Mina my Minder" to the other women of our delegation. I was basically a prisoner while there, unable to travel anywhere without Mina or the president's bodyguard who had been assigned to drive me to my daily meetings from the Al Rashid Hotel in downtown Baghdad, where I was staying. Mina would be waiting for me every morning at the elevator and would wave good-night to me each evening as the elevator doors closed. One day, Flora, the Russian delegate, and I tried to saunter on our own out the front door of the hotel. We were immediately surrounded by Iraqi bodyguards and firmly escorted back into the foyer, where Mina and Flora's minder were wringing their hands in distress.

But of course, over the days that followed, we started to see the incredibly brave women inside the armour. They had fought quietly, and at great risk to themselves, to be able to dress in styles of their choosing, and they had the same rights as men in the Iraqi Constitution—more than can be said of the rights of women in Kuwait, which is the U.S. and Canada's "ally." They had just come through the brutal nine-year war with Iran and had all lost sons, husbands and brothers to this dreadful conflagration. They were absolutely terrified about the looming war with George Bush and knew more than anyone in the world what it was going to mean for their lives.

Slowly, we started to bond, particularly when we sat through long meetings with senior government and military leaders who would insist on doing most, if not all, of the talking and who had the exact litany of complaints about the "Great Satan." On more than one occasion, my eye would meet those of Manal, or Azza, and a hint of a conspiratorial smile would dance at the corners of our mouths.

We sat together with a group of international activists at a "peace camp" on the outskirts of the city and recorded their stories on tape recorders. Together on that soft evening, we heard tales of courage and commitment from women as young as fifteen and as old as eighty-five who had come from Australia, France and Florida, among other places, to do what they could to stop the impending war. In the evenings, we would sit in the Al Rashid dining room, which looked like a scene out of *Casablanca*, with its stately old furniture and exotic guests from all over the world, and share personal stories over rapidly dwindling dinner rations. One night, Margarita and I bought everyone a beer (very expensive), and we giggled like a group of schoolgirls staying out after curfew at summer camp. Even sweet Mina took a drink.

One day, they let us visit the fabled monument to the dead of the Iran-Iraq war, which was then off limits to foreigners and local citizens alike. Two giant bronze statues the size of office towers stand on either end of a long tree-lined boulevard. Each is an enormous sculpture of Saddam's arms and hands from the elbows up, holding crossed scimitars against the sky. At the base of each are huge cornucopias, filled to overflowing with the bloodied helmets of thousands of dead Iranians. We stood under Saddam's Swords—Canadians, Americans, Europeans, Russians, Jordanians and Iraqis—and joined our women's hands together in mute tribute to the mothers and wives of the dead Iranians whose blood we could still smell in the air.

We held a press conference, Iraqi women, Western women and Soviet women together, which was amazingly well attended by journalists from all over the world. After all, we were the only Westerners left in Iraq, except for the last embassy people and a few journalists. We said that we thought there were still causes worth living for and called on all sides to stand down. "In the name of justice and for the sake of humanity, we ask you to reject the rivers of blood that will flow in the Gulf region and find a political solution," we begged as one voice. Our message was carried in newspapers all over the Middle East, and I was quoted in the government-controlled Iraqi papers as urging on the war against the "American running-dog imperialists"—hardly a part of my everyday vocabulary.

And then it was all over. On Wednesday, January 9, the Canadian ambassador called me to say that the Canadians were all leaving across country that very day and that he could not vouch for my safety if I did not join them. But I was determined to take my scheduled flight home on January 11 and thanked him for his concern. Except for a few journalists, I would be the last Canadian to leave Iraq before the war.

Friday morning was beautiful, warm and sunny after a week of rain. My Iraqi friends brought their daughters to see us off at the airport. I had lost my coat, a pretty pale grey spring coat with a pastel-coloured scarf, probably left in one of our meetings the day before. I didn't say a word, of course, as it was so unimportant in light of the situation. Sharp-eyed Flora made note of the absence of my coat at the airport, and Azza, one of the women I felt closest to, got all bothered about it. "We'll find it and send it by mail, or I'll have your embassy send it to you." We looked at each other. I couldn't tell her that our embassy was gone. It didn't matter. She knew. We also both knew that there would be no mail in or out of Iraq for a long, long time. "Find the coat, Azza, and keep it as a gift."

We hugged and wept and said goodbye. I knew I could get on a plane and leave this terrible place. These women and their beautiful daughters—who reminded me of my nieces—could not. During the war, when I would see the relentless bombing of Baghdad on television every night, I would have a recurring dream that my coat was keeping some little girl warm in one of those bomb shelters, and the pain would ease a little.

A decade later, I still remember these exceptional women of the federation with great tenderness. And the questions about the meaning of their lives keep coming back. Iraqi women have none of the conventional freedoms Western feminists consider fundamental to a full, self-directed life. Their family customs restrict personal and sexual choices that we now take for granted. Iraqi women have no freedom of speech, freedom of assembly or political choice. They cannot leave the country unless accompanied by a husband or father who is a senior official in the regime. And, of course, they have endured horrible deprivation under the U.S. embargo that has killed so many children and crippled the economy of their country.

Yet when I examine the values of my own culture and country, I am far from happy. Having bought into all the worst aspects of economic globalization, Canada is becoming a society of deepening class divisions, declining social programs and competitive values. The American narrative of survival of the fittest is fast replacing our narrative of sharing for survival. For many, many women in the West, life is a constant struggle.

This tumultuous decade has softened the sharp edges of my feminism, but I still remember, with something akin to longing, the sense of place, purpose and belonging of the women of Iraq. As the miles and the years close around our shared women's bond, I sense that something greater than the sum of any of our lives struggles to be born.

The Boy
Can't Sleep

Ann Dowsett Johnston

The boy can't sleep. He can't sleep because he didn't get the girl. Or rather, he got the girl, but he lost her. And now he can't sleep. Nor can you because he wants to talk.

You try to take it seriously. You try to remember what this felt like. You know you went through this very same thing, at the very same age. But that was so long ago. The summer of 1969, to be exact. The same summer that man first walked on the moon—an event you barely noticed, an event eclipsed by a boy with blond hair and an acoustic guitar and your first trip to Paris.

You try not to say what you're thinking, which is, Thank goodness. You're too young to find "the right girl." You'll find someone better. Smarter. Less selfish. More nuanced. Take your time. This you want to say, but you can't.

So instead you make popcorn. Standing by the stove together in the middle of the night, his tall frame looming close beside yours. Waiting for the first kernel to hiss and sizzle and pop. And as the two of you stand, waiting for the action to start, he bumps into you—a seemingly nonchalant little hip check.

Which is a good sign. This, you've come to understand, is what boys do after they stop hugging and kissing their mothers. A hip check, a knock on the shoulder, a little flick on the wrist. You've learned to decipher these casual little moves, along with the adolescent grunts—the code of a breezy male teenager.

And this you've also learned: the last thing a breezy male teenager wants is to be grilled by his mother. Yes, you would love to know the details of the evening, how it all unfolded, how it led to this middle-of-the-night session in the kitchen. But you resist. You zip your lip and wait for him to talk. Because, as we all know, mothers of sixteen-year-old boys know nothing. Especially about dating. Unless they're asked.

Which isn't to say that the boy has lost faith in you. On the contrary. That's why the two of you are up in the middle of the night making popcorn. He has faith that you will listen. But it's a dance, and this time he's leading.

For years, you led and he followed. As far as he was concerned, adults could fix anything. For starters, they had the power to negotiate with the Easter bunny, a creature he believed had no business being in his bedroom. He trusted you to arrange a front-door drop-off for chocolate. And when, as a toddler, he watched Joe Theismann's leg snap like a matchstick on the football field, he sat in front of the TV, unfazed in his fuzzy yellow sleepers. "Don't worry," he said, as the doctor raced to Theismann's side. "That man will kiss him better."

But over time, his faith in adult magic began to wane. Once, on a vacation by the sea, you stayed up into the night spray-painting seashells with gold paint. You soaked paper in tea and burned the corners with matches, making secret treasure maps that would lead to the loot that you had buried on the beach before breakfast. For years, that "pirate's gold" from Prince Edward Island was lugged to school for show and tell. Years later, when he discovered the true story, he was embarrassed. Unwittingly, you had made him look like a fool.

So tonight, as you stand over the ever-expanding pot of popcorn, you listen as he begins to tell the story of the girl and what happened. You listen carefully, your antennae keen for details. Most of all, you listen for evidence that she might have played him for the fool.

And all the while, you keep your eyes trained on the pot in front of you. If you look him in the eyes, you know the story will stop. Teenage boys retreat easily: you can't approach them head-on.

Of course, this is the same boy who once had a habit of dancing you around the kitchen as you cooked dinner—a boisterous little tango that left you flushed and laughing. This is the same boy who used to stall his bedtime with a series of questions, questions designed to lasso you and keep you close. Do monkeys get periods? What would hurt more: having a baby or porcupine quills up the nose?

But that was before. Now, most nights, the bedroom door is closed, and you are beginning to wonder what it will feel like when he moves away, when he marries. For the past several months, you've carried a poem in your pocket, a dog-eared clipping of "Mother of the Groom" by Seamus Heaney. Which, of course, is silly because he doesn't even have a driver's licence. But when it comes to this boy, you don't like surprises.

Once, you thought that this boy was an egg on a spoon, an egg you could not afford to drop. But now it's clear that he's no egg at all. In fact, he's more than half hatched, and you're no longer holding the spoon. Perhaps you never were.

Still, tonight, as he stands lean and fresh-faced beside you, you'd like to know that his world will unfold as it should. You're tempted to give fate a helping hand, to make sure that no woman ever knocks him sideways—as if you

347

could stop it. Standing in your nightgown, you're tempted to tell him the whole truth about the mating dance of men and women, to spill the beans about all you've learned since that summer in Paris.

But where would you begin? Certainly not by warning him against marrying young. This you've already done, over and over. And besides, it made not one whit of difference when you were told the same thing, when you married his father.

No, you'd start by letting him in on a few secrets. Perhaps you'd begin with the ones women share over long lunches, or late at night, long distance, when others have gone to bed: that the men they love best are not the tallest or the richest or the most suave. The men they love are the ones who make them laugh. The ones who dance them around the kitchen and kiss them on the back of the neck. Most of all, the men they love are the ones who ask questions and then listen to the answers. All this, you're certain, he'll be good at.

And marrying? You'd like to tell him that the right person will *smell* right. His father smelled like April, when the pale green shoots of the trees reach upward, shimmering and electric. But no, that would throw him off. You'd keep it simple: never marry until you're amazed at your own luck, you'd say, paraphrasing Iris Murdoch.

Oh, and that's just the beginning. After the wedding, you must make your own luck. Learn to parse each other's silences; understand the arc of an argument, that it will begin and it will end. Talk to each other in the middle of the night; canoe together. Don't founder on the tiny pebbles of daily life, the ones that trip us all.

No, this you definitely can't say. Not yet; perhaps never. This boy won't know that you too have skinny-dipped under a harvest moon. That you too have tried to fall asleep listening to Neil Young, just as he has tonight. And yes, you too have been played for the fool. Certainly he'll never know just why you learned the hard way how to parse men's silences, to hear what they weren't saying.

No. Instead, you pour the popcorn into the bowl, and he adds the butter—too much for your liking, but you say nothing because right at that moment he has begun to tell you that, actually, there is another girl. One he thinks he likes even better. And she likes him, too. And he wants to know, do you think he should ask her for coffee or a movie on the first date? For the first time, you allow yourself to look him in the eyes and smile.

Tomorrow, once again, you will be invisible: the mother standing at the door, telling him not to forget his sunscreen, to remember to call if he's going to be late. And he will rush down the walk, nodding, not hearing a word you have said. But tonight, the two of you are standing in the kitchen, eating popcorn after midnight because he can't sleep. And nor can you because, right now, he wants to talk.

Speaking
of Dying

Shelagh Rogers

Morning, October 18, 2001

I am in Cape Breton. The CBC Radio program I host, *This Morning*, is in Sydney for a broadcast from a church hall in the centre of the steelworkers' neighbourhood, Whitney Pier. I'm not on the air today, and I'm using this reprieve to tour Whitney Pier and see for myself what the media has dubbed "the notorious toxic Sydney tar ponds" that flank the Pier. It's just past ten-thirty. We're getting into our rented car after a banal errand at the drugstore when I hear on CBC radio that "our friend Kate Carmichael died last night after a brave battle with leukemia. She was fifty-one." The three producers I'm travelling with pat my hand or my shoulder and say they're so sorry. And then unstoppable tears come with the searing realization that Kate has really done it this time. She has died. Just as she kept saying she would.

I first encountered Kate Carmichael on what you might call a blind date. She was in the Halifax studio. I was in Toronto. I could only imagine her through her voice, one with the same properties as champagne—golden, effervescent, lighter than air but powerful and absolutely intoxicating. And she used it to great effect. From our first words, I realized I was beginning a radio love affair. She was playful, opinionated, smart and funny. She said what she meant. No fake politeness. When I asked her in this first conversation, "What did you feel when you learned you only had three months to live?" she said, "I was really pissed off." Knowing that I would get a truckload of mail from some of our more conservative listeners, I rushed in to staunch the flood. "Kate, you mean you were ticked off." Kate said, "No I don't. I was really pissed off. That's the only way to describe it. Look, I knew what it was going to look like when I was going to have a baby, I knew what it was going to look like when I got married. I knew what it was going to look like when I graduated because we talk about those things. Do I know what it's going to look like when I die? No! Why? Because we don't talk about it. So I want to, as much as possible, make it more comfortable for people to talk about it so that people who come behind me can understand what it will look like, what it feels like, what's going on in my head in these months when I think, Will it be tomorrow? Can I make an appointment for next week?"

At the time of our next conversation, about two weeks before Christmas, Kate was going through a bad spell. Her three-month "expiry date" had come and gone. She was hoping to make it through Christmas because, as an active and concerned citizen, she still had a lot of unfinished business in the downtown core. "Kate," I asked, "how are you going to get it all done?" She said, "Well, I have this bit of ammunition. I can call councillors and say, 'Time is kind of an issue for me now. How about we get together and bring this to a conclusion?' And they say, 'Okay, Kate, why don't we get together next Friday?' I say, 'Next Friday? I'm not going to be around, maybe, next Friday. How about tomorrow?' And it works."

Meeting Kate in March 2001

On a whim, I've booked a flight to Halifax. I am going to spend twelve waking hours with Kate and then fly back to Toronto. I have an overwhelming desire to see her in person before it is too late. The night before I meet her, she speaks before Halifax City Council about her three main causes: getting rid of the Cogswell interchange (an ungainly piece of roadway in Halifax), creating a heritage streetscape for downtown and fixing up the infernal parking problem on Barrington Street. Kate Carmichael, against the odds, is very, very alive.

I don't know what she'll be like. Is all that bravado just something she drums up when we're on the radio? Is she as attractive as she says she is? (I love the fact that she knows she's beautiful.) I am nervous about meeting her, about not living up to her expectations. We've been exchanging e-mails that grow more personal with every message. We've written to each other about work and to what degree it defines us both; we've written about children (in her case), childlessness (in mine) and stepchildren (a blessing we both share). We've written and argued about our favourite authors, about our teenage years, about our mothers and fathers. We've also recognized that our friendship is developing at Polaroid speed and how great it would be to go to a Greek island and celebrate it. We have not acknowledged that our relationship will, inevitably, be short. We have an intimacy through our e-mails, but what happens when we leave the virtual world for the real one?

I get off the plane with bed head. I don't wear makeup as a rule but manage to drag some Revlon over my lips. I am wearing my uniform of black top, black pants, black shoes. Oh so Toronto.

My first vision of Kate is in the airport lounge. She is wearing a linen jacket in Popsicle pink with a paler pink shirt and big earrings. Her makeup, her hair and nails are perfect. She has big brown eyes and long legs. In our interviews, she has told me she has used those attributes to get her way. Her husband, Alan, drives us home. We plant ourselves in her sunny yellow den and do not draw breath for the next twelve hours.

Some of our conversation is recorded for broadcast on March 21, 2001.

SR: I didn't know what to expect. I had a picture of you and now that I meet you, you're just right. You look great.

KC: This is a good time for me. In November Alan was planting some tulips and daffodils. I stood watching him from the dining room window and I thought, Those are bulbs I'll never see in bloom. But you know, I am going to see them bloom and it's interesting. . . . I am going to die soon, but all those negative thoughts I could have parked somewhere. I didn't need to have them. And so I don't have them any more. I have started to buy a few clothes for myself . . .

SR: So you weren't buying clothes . . .

KC: No, I haven't been doing anything that seems like a poor investment. It probably happens to everyone who is dying. . . .

SR: What changed your thinking?

KC: If I can manage six months of this, why can't I manage another six? If I had my choice, I would go from now to dead. I am eternally fearful of lingering and being a burden and sort of fading away. I really want to be this person who can walk down Barrington Street, as we did today. There's a lot of bravado in that. I've lasted this long, so why the hell can't I live another six months?

SR: Hasn't that bravado been very good for you?

KC: Bravado is what has kept me going. There is no question. But on my side of the bravado, there was a sense that things were going to happen quickly and soon. I have a very sore mouth, but other than that there are no changes. . . .

SR: What do you do when it hurts?

KC: Nothing. Just keep going. . . . Look, no need to do anything about it. Just keep on going. What I'd like to know is why is *my* dying interesting?

SR: I'd like to tell you. You've made me interested in dying and the kind of dying you are doing, I've been able to talk about death, which I couldn't do before, and not just with you but also with other people. You've found the power in it.

KC: I still don't get it. I don't necessarily agree with you. Why isn't anybody else talking about it?

SR: Why did you choose to do it?

KC: Well, it didn't start out as talking about dying. I started out talking about blood collection because we need it, because I need it. I need blood. Dying scares me. It frightens me. And I'm not comfortable with anything frightening me. When things frighten me, I'm inclined to ask questions so that I can be more comfortable. But there was nowhere to go, nobody talking. People were uncomfortable and didn't know what to say to me. . . . As frightened as I am about the act of dying, I wanted to get the best out of it, milk it for all it was worth. I have a feeling it can be a very powerful experience both for me, the dying person, and the people around me if I plan it properly rather than see it as something that needs to be put in the corner and not talked about.

The other part of it is that I want to make it as comfortable as possible for my children. It's hard to sit down and have this kind of conversation with children. I thought if they could read about it or hear about it in the media, that would help them understand their mother. But I have to say I continued to be floored by the media interest.

SR: You are dying publicly?

KC: That's right—I am sharing it. Yeah. Sometimes a difficult thing to do because there is no question that with each of these interviews a little bit of me goes with it because it's such a personal thing. You're opening up your skin to the world. For somebody like me who tries very hard to be a strong achiever, showing my frailties and my fears in public goes against everything in my personality. But the rewards are far greater than the risks.

SR: When you are alone and you're not being strong for interviews or feature articles in magazines, what gives you comfort when you need it?

KC: This is really a hard thing to answer. There are times when it's really hard to keep up the bravado, when things hurt. I try to calm myself down and think about the good things. Think about what's left to do. Think about people who are in far worse places than I. It's an immediate sort of kick in the ass. Smarten up, Kate. I cry once in a while when

I'm by myself, for about thirty seconds or so, but I snap myself out of it. Feeling frail and feeling sorry for myself doesn't do me any good, so I just smarten up. But there are times when I inject myself in the stomach and I eat these cocktails of pills and I think, I'm just tired of this. Which is stupid because that's what's keeping me alive. But I do think those things sometimes. And I think that's what the end is about. The body just can't do it any more. . . . There'll come a time when a person just doesn't have that oomph to stand up and get out there again. I think that's what will happen to me. I think it's mind over matter. There's a part of me that is terrified when I sit down for those ten or fifteen minutes, when I need that comfort. I wonder if I am losing ground by giving in.

My last conversation on the air with Kate was September 4, 2001. Her voice was frail and dainty, almost like an old woman's. She had good things to tell me—she was winning an award from the Metro Chamber of Commerce in recognition of her outstanding contribution to the downtown of Halifax.

KC: An incredible gift to me to hear these things while I am alive. . . . There is no question that my job has kept me alive that extra year I've gotten. But as far as my health is concerned, I've been on a rather slippery slope this summer. My mouth is very sore.

SR: Does it hurt you to talk?

KC: Yes, it does and it hurts to eat. My tailbone is sore. What happens with the kind of leukemia I have is your white blood cell count goes sky high, which makes your blood very thick and sticky, which makes it hard to get through the body, which eventually is what kills you. And the week before, I had a seizure. It discombobulated me and confused me and set me back. Yesterday and today are the first days I've felt human.

Those kinds of things have happened. So here I am, still here and doing reasonably well, I think, under the circumstances.

SR: What's changed in you because of that seizure?

KC: Scared me, scared me a lot. I decided that what was going to happen at the end is that I was going to stop having transfusions and lie down and just go to sleep and five days later I'd go away. . . . It was a real awakening. It's one thing to talk about it, and here I was—it was actually almost happening. Was I going to be able to pull out of what I was in or was this, the lying-down part, the real clock ticking. . . ? As much as I've been talking about these things, when it comes right down to doing it, it's not as easy as talking about it.

As we end our conversation there is an understanding that this is likely the last time we will talk on the air. I cannot say goodbye and neither can she.

There is a series of "See yas" and "Ciaos" and "Okays" and "Lots of love."

Her husband later told me about Kate's side of that last interview. It's another story of her determination. He told me Kate could barely walk, let alone speak. But she wanted to do it. He took her to the CBC building and guided her to the studio. "She was just going to do it, and that was it," he said. "That was who she was."

Evening, Thursday, October 19, 2001.

I've just returned from dinner with my crew, and I'm back at the City Lodge in Sydney. I'm feeling a splitting pain in my chest as the reality of Kate's death rolls over me like a fog. I open up my bottle of single-malt Scotch and pour three fat fingers into the sanitized plastic glass provided by the motel. The Scotch burns like a hot river as I swallow, but I down it in three gulps. I don't feel any different, so I have another three fingers. And then another. I see myself in the mirror, face blotchy, eyes swollen. I put a towel over the mirror. I lie down on the bed and scream into the pillow. Goddamn God damn Goddamn. There is a knock at my door. I get up, get hold of myself and sit behind the desk. It's my producer, Willy. The door's open, I tell him. He asks, "Are you all right, dear?" and comes over and pats my shoulder. It's 10:00 P.M. We have to be at Ukrainian Parish Hall at 6:45 A.M. to get ready for our live public broadcast. He is responsible for every detail of the show. He needs me to be all right. I have yet to look over the scripts. I have yet to write the opening comments for the show. My head is pounding. I can barely form a sentence. I don't know how I'll host a debate about the closure of the last coal mine in Cape Breton in fewer than twelve hours. I don't think I'll be able to listen to other people's lives without crying about my own loss. At this point, I'm drunk and I feel numb. But I tell Willy I'm fine.

Morning, Friday, October 20, 2001, live on the air, me to the audience, 11:15 A.M.

Yesterday, I was here in Sydney, just getting in the car and I heard Ralph Benmurgui, who is sitting in for me, say Kate Carmichael had died. For the past year I've been introducing all my conversations with Kate with the phrase "Kate Carmichael is dying of leukemia." But because Kate was such a life force and because she was so gorgeous, I never really believed it. Kate was on *This Morning* throughout the past season, talking about what she called "this amazing ride" of living through dying. And over the year, she became my friend. We drank margaritas together, drove way too fast in her car with Tina Turner blaring through the speakers, and we talked endlessly. She talked about the art of dying. But it was, of course, the art of living. And I firmly believe that her spirit cannot be extinguished by death. Her strength, dignity, courage and grace live on.

Kate in her garden, Victoria Day weekend, broadcast on CBC June 4, 2001.

You're gardening and you're in the dirt and the soil is warm, new life, new birth . . . Gardens are about the future, and there isn't much future left. It makes you pensive. . . . As I was being pensive sitting there on my bum, I thought back to a lunch I had the week before with Donna Thompson, a very dear friend who has two children with cystic fibrosis. Cystic fibrosis children don't usually make it through their twenties. Donna's first child died in 1998. He was an athlete, he was well loved in the community, and the community as a whole grieved the passing of Robbie. I asked her to talk to me about the time when he died, for a very selfish reason. I've always been afraid and I continue to be afraid—but I must say now a lot less—of what the end is like. I assumed that a young man with CF gasped for breath, and that's what frightens me the most, gasping for breath. Donna talked about just how peacefully he went away. And there isn't a gift that could be given to anyone in my kind of situation that could be greater than that. The reason is, who is there to talk to about these kind of things? Who can you talk to who has experienced the end? Donna has given me a great gift.

I also asked her where she put his ashes. She told me that she put them in the corner of a crypt, and I asked her, "Do you ever go there to talk to him?" She said, "No I don't. I don't need to go there to talk to him. He's always with me and with the entire family."

Donna gave me the courage to believe that when this body is gone I will still be here in the heads or the thoughts or the conversation of some of the people I've made an impact on. I fear that the moment the body is gone, the spirit is also gone, and the gift that Donna gave me was, number one, the peacefulness of the going. And number two, that there will be times when something will happen in my friends' lives and they will say, Kate did that, she made that happen—the first lilac or a really heavy lilac bloom where the whole bush is just hanging with lilacs—Kate put that there. That's the kind of thing I imagine, that bit of overabundance, that Kate-in-your-face-doing-that-kind-of-stuff. People say to me, "Kate, if there's an afterlife, when you get up there send me a sign." And I always say to them, "You pick a favourite bush in your yard, and if that bush blooms better next year when I'm gone, that's a sign."

AFTERWORD

A dozen or so years ago, a senior colleague treated me with great disrespect and insensitivity. The incident struck me like a blow to the head, though you might think I had been fortunate indeed to have arrived at my mid-fifties without suffering a social injury of this kind.

I registered a protest to the Head of Department but was told nothing could be done. I felt invalidated, baffled, powerless and even became ill for some months, suffering seizures to my neck and shoulder muscles. I could have gone to the dean, who would have set the situation right, but for some reason this didn't occur to me.

Instead, I began to talk about the conflict: to my family, then to my friends. I confess I made rather a drama of it. I told the story twenty times, thirty times, probably fifty times. Each time I told it, the pain lessened slightly. A noticeable dilution took place, and my tale of humiliation developed wavy side curls of absurdity. My tongue became more and more eager to exploit my shame, and I caught myself, oddly, relishing my own anger. Imagine!—I possessed a colleague with whom I was not on speaking terms. Now, that was interesting. Eventually I collapsed the narrative and inserted it into a novel, *The Stone Diaries*, and there it rests, enervated now, incapable of hurting me further.

When I consider the essays in this anthology and those published in its predecessor, I feel the heat rising from the words, and the human relief of having shared a story and thereby mitigating its power. By getting such stories "off our chests," we are lightened and enabled. Frequently we discover that what we believe to be singular is, in fact, universally experienced. No wonder Holocaust survivors seek each other out. No wonder those who have lost a child turn to others who have endured the same loss. We need these conversations desperately.

I remember once sitting in a circle of women who had undergone mastectomies. One of the women was eager to show us her new, light prosthesis, which had replaced one that was heavy and misshapen. She reached inside her shirt and removed it and handed it to the woman next to her. We passed this very private cone of plastic and foam around the circle, each of us admiring it in turn, weighing it in our hands, comprehending it and understanding that this ad hoc ritual linked us together and eased the shared loss of our bodily integrity.

I want to thank each of the women who have brought their stories so bravely to this book. Many of the contributors to the first volume suggested further stories that needed to be told and writers who might be called upon. Susan Roxborough of Random House has encouraged us. Marjorie Anderson has shaped this book lovingly and with great intelligence and tact. Catherine Shields has brought her critical attention to all the manuscripts. Readers across Canada have responded with their own narratives and the knowledge of how women can help each other.

I am honoured to be a part of this ongoing project, which locates itself at the juncture of my two favourite things: language and the company of women. There we can find courage to go forward in our lives.

Carol Shields
May 2002

CONTRIBUTORS

CAROL SHIELDS

Throughout my life, I have been sustained and heartened by women and their courageous resiliency in the face of difficulty. My good fortune has been to observe and document this in my narratives and experience it as a friend and mother. It has been a particular happiness and point of pride to work on *Dropped Threads 2* with the editorial tact and wisdom of my daughter Catherine Shields.

MARJORIE ANDERSON

My life was first made rich by a storytelling father, a wise, gentle mother and seven interesting and interested siblings. After nearly twenty years of the added richness from teaching literature and communication at university, I am leaving that to spend professional time consulting and being immersed in literary projects. My personal joys are still family, including

Gary and our bevy of children and grandchildren, and now the contemplative life at our lake cottage.

MAUDE BARLOW

I am the elected National Chairperson of the Council of Canadians, Canada's largest public advocacy organization, and a director with the International Forum on Globalization, based in San Francisco. I am also the author or co-author of thirteen books, the latest of which is *Blue Gold: The Battle to Stop Corporate Theft of the World's Water.* My early feminist roots have never left me but rather accompanied me on my incredible journey.

SANDRA BEARDSALL

Born in 1959, I grew up in Brampton, Ontario, with my parents, brother, sister and cats. After university studies in Toronto and ordination in the United Church, I spent several years ministering in Labrador and then eastern Ontario. I now live in Saskatoon, working as a professor at St. Andrew's College, and making a home with my spouse, stepson and, of course, the cat.

SANDRA BIRDSELL

Although I grew up wanting to dance, act and clown, writing became my first love. That was twenty years ago. Since then I've published seven books and received accolades and nominations for various awards. Throughout the years I have given up on various hobbies such as sketching, Tai Chi and gourmet cooking. Now I concentrate on gardening, taking vitamins and being what my youngest grandson calls "silly."

INGEBORG BOYENS

I have been lucky enough to spend more than two decades working as a journalist in newspapers, magazines and television across Canada. Then, living in the middle of the country in Winnipeg, on the edge of both urban and rural worlds, I began to focus my writing and interests on food and farming. I have written two books; the second, *Another Season's Promise*, was released by Penguin Canada in 2001.

MARIANNE BRANDIS

As novelist and life-writer, I've specialized in researching, recreating and reimagining the past. I've written five award-winning historical novels for young people and anyone interested in the past, a fictional biography of a long-dead English duchess and two novels set in twentieth-century Canada; I'm just completing a biography of my mother. My latest published work is *Finding Words: A Writer's Memoir*. I live and write full-time in Stratford, Ontario.

MARY J. BREEN

I am a freelance writer and editor, and a former literacy teacher and health worker. As a result of a longtime interest in women's health and in the relationship between literacy and health, I have written two easy-to-read books for women, *Taking Care* and *So Many Changes* (with Lindsay Hall). I have two grown children and one grandson. I live in Peterborough, Ontario, with my husband.

ADRIENNE CLARKSON

My life was shaped by my family and our having come through the crucible of war and loss together. My father and mother were courageous, indomitable and as different as night and day. When I was five, we lived in a tiny rented apartment, and my father told me that some day we would go to the opera together, sit in a box and I would wear a long dark red velvet ball gown. He was right.

MARY JANE COPPS

Born and raised in Timmins, Ontario, I now call Halifax

home. I surround myself with many children, great friends, good books, delightful music, fabulous food and startling words. This is one of several stories that expose the raw emotion of childhood trauma. I've been well published as a journalist, have had fiction published in *The New Quarterly* and *A Room at the Heart of Things* and have written a young adult mystery novel.

DEBBIE CULBERTSON

I am an Alberta writer and editor. My articles have appeared in magazines, including *Alberta Views, Legacy, NeWest Review, Mandate, Compass, Prairie Books Now* and *The Beaver.* I am now working on a biography of Roberta MacAdams, one of Canada's first women legislators. I live with my partner, Heather, and daughter, Rachel, in a small rural community near Edmonton.

BARBARA DEFAGO

I've spent the first half of my life, so far, in Vancouver and now live a few miles away, in Langley. As a therapist, I have been a privileged witness to the stories of others. As a woman, wife, mother, daughter, sister and mother-in-law, I have been blessed. With illness came listening—to myself. I am honoured to be part of this anthology.

ANN DOWSETT JOHNSTON

I grew up in small-town northern Ontario, in a village in South Africa, and on the shores of Georgian Bay, surrounded, for the most part, by women and books. As a journalist, I have been blessed with a profession that has allowed me to continue in the same vein: travelling, talking and exploring the written word. In recent years, I have won a number of National Magazine awards for my work at *Maclean's.* My greatest adventure, by far, has been the eighteen-year journey I have shared with my son Nicholas.

As he heads off into the world to find his voice, I am rediscovering mine: writing on motherhood, modern life and the evolution of the family.

MAGGIE DWYER

I was born in Stratford, raised in southern Ontario and spent twenty interesting years in Winnipeg before moving to Vancouver Island with my second husband. I began writing down the stories that I had long been composing in my head during the afternoons of my years at home with my two daughters. I have published a short story collection, *Misplaced Love*, and am revising a novel.

LISA GREGOIRE

I prefer oceans to mountains. I screen my calls. The first song I ever learned all the lyrics to was *Raindrops Keep Fallin' on My Head* by Billy Joe Thomas—I was five. I knew I was an adult when I started craving vegetables and sleep. I don't hold grudges or life insurance, and the man I married is still my best friend.

LINDA HARLOS

Health crises notwithstanding, I'm generally busy earning a modest, more or less honest living. I'm fortunate to have propelled myself to several of this planet's breathtaking (literally!) venues. Although I'm an avid reader who sometimes fantasized about going through the looking glass, this subject wasn't exactly the publishing debut of my dreams. Love and gratitude to all who accompanied, chauffeured, consoled and/or fed me during my recent ordeal.

SARAH HARVEY

I was born in Chicago but have spent most of my life within spitting distance of the Pacific Ocean. At fifteen I began what has turned out to be a career as a bookseller (with lapses into go-go dancing and clam digging), and I've been writing for the past fourteen years. I have two astonishing children, an assortment of amazing friends, an appreciation of solitude and a desire to learn Latin dancing before I'm too old to safely swivel my hips.

ELIZABETH HAY

I grew up in Ontario, worked for CBC Radio, lived for a time in Mexico and New York City and published my first book when I was thirty-eight. My most recent books are *Small Change* (stories) and *A Student of Weather* (novel). At fifty, I find myself in Ottawa—the part of the world where my mother grew up—with two children who wish they were in New York.

KAREN HOULE

I've spent roughly ten years teaching university (philosophy/women's studies), ten years parenting (twin girls), ten years in graduate school (University of Guelph) and ten years cooking for tree-planting camps. Some of these decade-long activities ran in series, some in parallel current. I wrote this story sitting at my kitchen table looking at the Bay of Fundy and wonder what will take its place in my heart when I'm sitting at my kitchen table in Edmonton next year. My first book of poetry, *Ballast*, was published by House of Anansi Press in April 2000.

FAITH JOHNSTON

I grew up in Winnipeg and returned here to remarry in 1992. My life has been full of passions for many things— for teaching and travel, for learning French and now Spanish, for the history of women and other good feminist causes, for music, for short stories written by women, for two husbands who are no longer in the picture and, most of all, for my children.

KATRINA KOVEN

I love books. I love art. What a joy to have me art on the covers of this book and the original *Dropped Threads*. An added pleasure is that both images come from a collection of my most beloved drawings, *Vinaterta Ladies*. In my mind, these two stylized ladies proudly represent the pair of dear friends who co-created the *Dropped Threads* books: Carol and Marjorie, spirited and creative women whom I thank for inviting me to be part of these unique anthologies.

MICHELE LANDSBERG

I've been writing one thing or another most of my life, including several books—*Women and Children First; Michele Landsberg's Guide to Children's Books; This Is New York, Honey!*—and hundreds of newspaper and magazine articles. For the past twenty-four years, with a few years' hiatus while I lived in New York and wrote for *The Globe and Mail*, I've written a feminist column for *The Toronto Star*. It's a privilege to be able to write about subjects that deeply engage me, heart and mind.

BILLIE LIVINGSTON

After *Going Down Swinging* was published in 2000 (Random House Canada), my first book of poetry, *The Chick at the Back of the Church* (Nightwood Editions) hit the shelves in 2001. These days I'm working on a new novel involving the end of the burlesque world—a fab excuse to take long solo drives through hippie country in Oregon to the Burlesque Hall of Fame in the Mojave Desert.

FLORA MacDONALD

After toiling in the political field for nearly thirty-five years, I've turned my attention to the work being done internationally by non-governmental organizations, UN agencies and dedicated individuals. Travelling with these groups has given me new insight into the challenges faced and often surmounted, particularly by women, in developing countries. It has also fostered a deeper awareness of how fortunate we in Canada are, compared with millions of the world's citizens for whom survival is measured a day at a time.

LISA MAJEAU GORDON

This is my first publication since my piece titled "The Goblin's Revenge" met with great success in the Grade 6 story anthology of 1983–84. A long dry spell. I live in Alberta; I am a prairie spirit. I am fond of gravel roads and open spaces and Labrador retrievers. Last March, my husband, Corey, and I adopted a beautiful baby girl who has filled our hearts to bursting. We call her Grace.

HILDEGARD MARTENS

Toronto has been my home for thirty-plus years. Shortly after receiving my Ph.D. in sociology from the University of Toronto in 1977, I went to work for the Ontario government, where I still work as a senior analyst in labour economics. Previous publications include articles and reviews in academic journals, as well as government reports on a variety of labour market issues. Nineteen years ago I made a right-angle turn in my life when I decided to become a single mother. Now that my son has left home for university and with retirement from the civil service on the horizon, I am once again contemplating a new direction in my life.

SANDRA MARTIN

I am senior arts writer for *The Globe and Mail* and the co-author of three books: *Rupert Brooke in Canada*; *Where Were You: Memorable Events of the 20th Century*; and *Card Tricks: Bankers, Boomers and the Explosion of Plastic Credit*. I've won awards for my magazine articles, and an Atkinson Fellowship in Public Policy, and served as president of PEN

Canada. I live in Toronto with my husband, two children and our cat, Alice.

DANA McNAIRN

I am a writer who—despite having one failed marriage behind me—is open to the possibility and joy of doing it all over again. I'm still all thumbs with gift-wrapping, though. I happily live and write wherever I find myself. In the writing of this essay, a humble thank you goes to Kala Micheal McNairn, for helping me remember.

C.J. PAPOUTSIS

It is an honour to be published in this anthology. Writing is my lifelong passion, despite being held hostage in the body of a civil servant for thirty years. My husband and I raised our two beautiful children on Vancouver Island, home of many writers and artists, where we spend too much time with our umbrellas and plan our next visit to Greece.

LINDA ROGERS

As I am a daughter of word people—a lawyer and a theatrical producer—and descendant of the Trollope family, a literary life was inevitable. I have two brothers and three sons and a mandolinist husband, with whom I collaborate on poetry and music performances. I've been honoured by a number of international awards, including the Governor General's Centennial Medal; the Leacock, Acorn, Livesay and Basmajian awards (Canada); and the Bridport, Kenney and Cardiff prizes (England). My new collection of poetry is *The Bursting Test* and I'm completing a novel, *The Butterfly Tree.*

SHELAGH ROGERS

I am a twenty-two-year veteran of CBC Radio. For the past two years, I've hosted the flagship current affairs program *This Morning*, building a loyal and growing audience. I am one of a small group of recipients of the John Drainie Award for Outstanding Contribution to Canadian Broadcasting. And in the spring of 2002, I received an honorary doctorate from the University of Western Ontario. I live in a bosky village on the Eramosa River in southern Ontario with my husband, Charlie, three miniature schnauzers and, occasionally, my stepchildren.

CAROLE SABISTON

As a child in England and before emigrating, at age eight, I knew that visual expression was to be my connection to the world. Creating artwork by drawing, painting, cutting, stitching and assembling became the core of my life. In 1987 I was elected to the Royal Canadian Academy and also received the Saidye Bronfman Award for Excellence in Fine Craft. My work has been exhibited across Canada and internationally. I live in Victoria with my husband, Jim.

JENNIFER L. SCHULZ

I was born and raised in Winnipeg, encircled by an amazing family and terrific friends. For the past six years I have lived in Toronto with my loving spouse, John, and for the past three have commuted to the University of Windsor to teach law. Now about to embark on an adjunct professorship and doctoral studies at the University of Toronto, I anticipate many new, inspiring, toe-ring-wearing opportunities.

SHIRLEY A. SERVISS

Although I have done many things in my life, the role of stepmother has been a defining one. My first poetry collection, *Model Families*, reflected on my experience in this role, and my second collection, *Reading Between the Lines,* explored the life of another stepmother, Elizabeth Boyd McDougall. I have also co-edited *Study in Grey*, a collection of women's writing on depression. Besides my twenty-year-old stepson, I have a fifteen-year-old daughter who has also taught me tremendously.

PAMELA MALA SINHA

"Hiding" could not have been written without the faith of my loving father, Snehesh. Debashis gave encouragement; Stewart, his belief. From Tina and Shaun, wisdom; from Mohuya and Papiya, the constancy of sisters. And I am never without the unfailing love of Damon and Brian. I live in Canada and the U.S., performing in theatre, film and television. I have three beloved stepchildren, two boys and a girl. And anything I have done that is remotely beautiful, my mother Rubena is the reason.

SUSAN SWAN

I started out as a journalist on a Toronto daily, knowing I was going to write fiction. Having a child was less plotted, something I would one day do, like graduating from high school. I had no idea my daughter would provide me with one of my most treasured relationships. My novels have had wide international publication and my stories have appeared in *Granta* and *Ms.* magazine. My novel *The Wives of Bath* was recently made into a feature film, *Lost and Delirious*, with release in thirty-one countries. I am an associate professor of humanities at York University, Toronto.

JANE URQUHART

Born in Little Long Lac, Ontario, in 1949, I grew up in Toronto and received my B.A. in English (1971) and a second B.A. in visual arts (1975) from the University of Guelph. My works, as a writer of poetry, short fiction and novels, include *The Whirlpool* (1986), *Storm Glass* (1987), *Changing Heaven* (1996), *Away* (1997), *The Underpainter* (1998), *Some Other Garden* (2000) and *The Stone Carvers* (2000). I currently live in Stratford, Ontario.

ALISON WEARING

When I was seven or eight years old, I knew I wanted to write. I remember wandering through the fields behind our house, composing elaborate and (to my mind) extremely elegant titles for the books I planned to pen. I felt proud and confident. Determined. Strong. I offer my story in honour of that little girl, with the hope that it helps even one woman stand tall.

WANDA WUTTUNEE

I am a lifegiver: to Cody, thirteen, and Drew, ten, who are proud of their Cree and Portuguese heritage. I am a student: of life and all things that surround us and have a Ph.D. in Aboriginal economy. I am a teacher: program director for Aboriginal students earning business degrees at the University of Manitoba and professor of Native studies, where students learn about our people. *A day without sunshine is like, well, night.*

Cover Image: *Vinaterta Lady*

Vinaterta: An Icelandic-Canadian layered prune torte, which, when sliced, reveals thin black and white stripes.

Vinaterta Ladies: A collection of sketches of stylized female figures by Toronto artist Katrina Koven. They are united by their signature vinaterta stripes, which appear on some feature in each of the sketches. Whether with a blue face, spiral tail or lopsided eyes, the figures encourage women to celebrate their differences, their infinite beauty and the boundless array of moods specific to the female experience. The figure on the cover of this book, as with all of those in Katrina's collection, proudly flaunts her unique approach to being a woman.

ACKNOWLEDGMENTS

We were guided and supported by others whom we want to acknowledge with beams of appreciation: Catherine Shields for providing warmth, wisdom and keen insight during the selection and editing process; Anne Giardini, for guiding us expertly through contract details; Sylvia Anderson Koshyk for helping to organize the book—and her sister; James and Fred Anderson for their support and writerly instincts; Katrina Koven for the artwork that has been our beacon in the bookstores; Ruth Partridge for her constant loyalty and assistance with the project; Susan Roxborough, Tanya Trafford and Anne Collins for their professional insights and gracious guidance; all the contributors from the original *Dropped Threads* for their enthusiasm and suggestions; and, of course, Gary Martin and Don Shields, whose love and support keep us bolstered.